THE
UNIVERSAL
CRAMMER

NIL · DESPERANDUM

EVERYTHING YOU EVER LEARNED AT SCHOOL
BUT HAVE LONG SINCE FORGOTTEN

First published in Great Britain by Think Books in 2008
This edition published in 2008 by Think Books,
an imprint of Pan Macmillan Ltd
Pan Macmillan, 20 New Wharf Road, London N1 9RR,
Basingstoke and Oxford
Associated companies throughout the world
www.panmacmillan.com
www.think-books.com

ISBN: 978-1-84525-063-8

Text ©: Pan Macmillan Ltd; Design ©: Think Publishing
Author: Susannah Frieze with specialist contributions by Anthony Burt,
Gavin Thomas and Fay Warrilow
Think Books: Tania Adams, James Collins, Jenny Darwent, Camilla Doodson,
Roy Johnstone, Emma Jones, Sally Laver, Lou Millward, Matthew Packer,
Marion Thompson and Alice Whitehead

1 3 5 7 9 8 6 4 2 1

A CIP catalogue record for this book is available from the British Library.

Printed and bound in the UK by CPI Mackays, Chatham

Visit www.panmacmillan.com to read more about all our books and to buy
them. You will also find features, author interviews and news of any author
events, and you can sign up for e-newsletters so that you're always first to hear
about our new releases.

Cover illustration: Georgina Luck

THANKS

For invaluable help on both larks and labour, I have to
thank Tom Parker (the most knowledgeable man I know),
Phil Drinkall, Anthony Frieze, Philippe Sacerdot, Alexandra
Hillier and the staff at both the British Library and
Hammersmith Library.

For stepping in at the last minute, Anthony Burt, Gavin
Thomas and Fay Warrilow, and for assistance at Think, Ben
Ashwell, Aaron Biddles, Elizabeth Mann, Hazel Swain and
Kelly Woodruff.

CONTENTS

INTRODUCTION

In a brain filled with the detritus of a busy 'grown-up' life (bus timetables, children's shoe sizes, all the countries that are part of the Schengen Agreement, that quote from Nietzsche that I would always like to remember), all the stuff we learnt at school seems completely swamped. At the time it seemed irrelevant – learning those Wham! dance moves was much more important – but given the perspective of the intervening years, there's a surprising amount for which we could grudgingly thank those long-suffering beasts, our teachers. But *The Universal Crammer* isn't just about reminding us what we've forgotten, it could even be a tool for telling us what to remember in the future – to arm ourselves, or our children, or our friends (dinner parties don't have to be about just weather, sex and politics, after all) with some tools to understand the world beyond the everyday. And if that's beginning to sound pompous, then don't worry, we're also here to have some larks.

I

HISTORY

History doesn't repeat itself – at best it sometimes rhymes.

Mark Twain, US author

FOR THE LOVE OF THE COMMON MAN:
10 VICTORIAN PHILANTHROPISTS

• **George Peabody:** rich American who came to live in the UK in 1837. In 1869 he set up Peabody Trust with an initial endowment of £500,000. Starting in London's Spitalfields, the Trust has since built hundreds of Peabody Buildings, with flats rented out to the working class.

• **Octavia Hill:** granddaughter of redoubtable reformer Dr Southwood Smith, she bought three cottages in London's Marylebone in 1864, did them up and rented them out at a rent that covered only her costs.

• **Sir Titus Salt:** Yorkshire textile manufacturer who founded a new town, Saltaire, for his employees in 1853. His metropolis boasted decent housing, parks, a social club and libraries – but no pub.

• **WH Lever:** soap manufacturer who, like Salt, built dwellings, a church, a library, schools, a hospital and a meeting place for his workers at Port Sunlight, Merseyside. The project was started in 1887.

• **George Cadbury:** predated *Charlie and the Chocolate Factory* – and in 1879 completed his town Bournville, south of Birmingham.

• **Lord Shaftesbury:** aka Anthony Ashley-Cooper: the champion of children, with 10 of his own. Responsible for several

Acts improving lives of working youngsters. Also known for sanitation campaigns and slum clearance work.

• **John Passmore Edwards:** Cornish publisher, social reformer and life-long champion of working classes. Founded 24 libraries, endowed the London School of Economics and established more than 50 other major buildings. When he died in 1911, *The Times* wrote: 'He did more good in his time than almost any other of his contemporaries.'

• **Thomas Jackson** (1850-1932): practical evangelist who attempted to address the plight of the poor. Noted for his work in Whitechapel area of London's East End.

• **Charles Dickens:** tireless campaigner against poverty and social stratification of Victorian society. Directly and indirectly responsible for highlighting the plight of the underprivileged through his novels and journalism.

• **Joseph Rowntree:** Quaker chocolatier from York, born 1834, who gave half his enormous wealth to four foundations that still flourish today, addressing low-cost housing, poverty and public health – as well as raising funds and carrying out research.

The kings and queens of England, including our current sovereign:
Willy, Willy, Harry, Ste,
Harry, Dick, John, Harry Three,
One, Two, Three Neds, Richard Two,
Henry Four, Five, Six – then who?
Edward Four, Five, Dick the Bad,
Harries twain and Ned the Lad,
Mary, Bessie, James the Vain,
Charlie, Charlie, James again.
William and Mary, Anna Gloria,
Four Georges, William, and Victoria.
Ned Seventh ruled till 1910,
When George the Fifth came in and then
Ned went when Mrs Simpson beckoned,
Leaving George – then Liz the Second.

MORE THAN A HILL OF BEANS

The Agricultural Revolution, which began in 1750, might have been rapidly overshadowed by its younger, bigger, darker older brother, the Industrial Revolution. But at the time its effects were felt far and wide.

Prompted by rising food prices and with demand exceeding supply, the old system of tiny strips of farmed ground and the vast patchwork of common land was radically changed by the Enclosures Acts.

These enabled separate strips to be compacted into bigger holdings provided you were a landowner prepared to pay about £6,000. In addition, local common land was divided up.

Between 1760 and 1793, no fewer than 1,355 Enclosure Acts were passed, plus another 1,934 between 1793 and 1815.

However, the new scheme caused suffering to most villagers, who had depended on the common land to eat. Even those who had a compact holding were hard put to afford the cost of fencing and hedging.

But both the amount and variety of foodstuffs increased and became slightly cheaper.

In Norfolk, the most affected county, a four-field setup replaced the former three-field method, and improved crop rotation. This *modus operandi* became known as the Norfolk system and was widely adopted elsewhere.

Whig *noun historical:* 1) a member of the British reforming party that sought the supremacy of Parliament, succeeded in the 19th century by the Liberal Party. 2) a supporter of the American Revolution. 3) a 17th-century Scottish Presbyterian.

- **Origin:** probably a shortening of Scots whiggamore, the nickname of 17th-century Scottish rebels, from whig to drive.

Tory *noun* (pl Tories): 1) a member or supporter of the British Conservative Party. 2) a member of the English political party that opposed the exclusion of James II from the succession and later gave rise to the Conservative Party. 3) *US hist* a colonist who supported the British side during the American Revolution.

- **Origin:** originally denoting Irish peasants dispossessed by English settlers and living as robbers, and extended to other marauders, especially in the Scottish Highlands: probably from Irish *toraidhe* 'outlaw, highwayman'.

Source: Compact Oxford English Dictionary

HELLFIRE AND BRIMSTONE

Once freedom-of-speech campaigner John Wilkes MP became a thorn in Prime Minister Lord Bute's side, the previously close friends fell out for good. They had forged their friendship getting up to no good in what we now call the Hellfire Club run by Sir Francis Dashwood. In fact, it was never originally known as the Hellfire Club, but by several names, like the Brotherhood of St Francis of Wycombe, and then, when he moved into his friend Francis Duffield's Medmenham Abbey (with its underground caves), the Monks or Friars of Medmenham Abbey on the Thames. Here the members of the club gambled heavily, drank 'into their cups', swapped pornographic pictures and dressed up in fancy costumes to horse around in prostitute-led sex rituals that may or may not have had Satanist elements thrown in for extra spice.

When Bute became Chief Minister, he put one member of the Hellfire – the Earl of Sandwich – in charge of the navy, but did not give Wilkes any post at all, at which point all Hellfire broke out. Makes you wonder what Wilkes got up to in those caves, eh?

The one duty we owe to history is to rewrite it.

Oscar Wilde, Irish playwright

INDUSTRIAL REVOLUTION: WHY US?

In 1750, Britain was far from the richest or most enlightened country in Europe. But by 1830, it was both the wealthiest and strongest thanks to the first stages of the Industrial Revolution. But why did this spasm of know-how and industry combine to such dramatic effect?

First, we had increased our own market for British goods by colonising India, Canada and more islands in the West Indies. And with growing demand for goods at home, it was clear that new, quicker ways of doing things had to be found.

Second, in contrast to the more totalitarian and repressive regimes of mainland Europe, Britain was footloose and fancy-free, encouraging scientists to experiment without fear of contravening some arcane law or other. Thus, the early inventors were able to fiddle away unmolested at their new machines.

Third, the fruits of all this activity notably expanded the ranks of the rich – there were the emerging middle classes, farmers with increased incomes from the improved methods, and the nabobs of the trading routes of the East and West Indies. The upshot: cash aplenty for investment, and freedom of movement of goods and people.

A fourth factor was the rise of the various splinter groups of the Puritan and Calvinist faiths – Quakers, Methodists and other nonconformists – who prized both success in business and lack of personal indulgence. All of which put more gold into the coffers.

Also, British banks were now sophisticated enough to have developed credit and investment channels to finance the plethora of projects. In addition, the raw materials – coal and iron ore, and so on – were to be found in abundance within our shores.

Towns sprang up around the mines, factories and ports – then the advent of steam power, transforming manufacturing, agriculture and transport, made the nation richer and more powerful still.

And with the mushrooming of the middle classes, the byword was change through peaceful political reform rather than the spasmodic revolutions that bedevilled other European countries.

THE AGE OF INVENTION

1698: Thomas Savery's steam pump for extracting water from mines
1701: Jethro Tull's mechanical seed drill
1711: Thomas Newcomen's improved water pump for mining
1731: Tull's horse-drawn hoe
1764: James Hargreaves' cotton-spinning jenny
1769: Richard Arkwright's water wheel-powered cotton-spinning frame
1775: Alexander Cumming's flushing lavatory; and Arkwright's carding machine that produced fibres ready for spinning
1781: James Watt's rotary steam engine
1785: Edward Cartwright's power loom that improved the quality and speed of cloth weaving
1816: Sir Humphry Davy's safety lamp for mining
1835: William Henry Fox Talbot's negative/positive photographic process
1840: James Naysmith's steam hammer and machine tools for the iron industry; and Rowland Hill's self-adhesive postage stamp, the Penny Black
1856: Henry Bessemer's process that converted pig iron into steel
1901: Hubert Cecil Booth's powered vacuum cleaner

I'LL HAVE NO TRUCK WITH THAT

Until the 1870s, it was common for employers to pay their workforce in kind rather than in cash. Some handed over articles made in their factories; others set up 'tommy shops' where coupons or specially fashioned 'coins' could be exchanged for goods in the factory-owned shop – a system known collectively as 'truck'.

While employers argued that this freed up their cash to expand the business, create employment and ultimately benefit their staff, the workers not unnaturally pointed out that this made them virtual slaves. They were also unhappy with the quality of the goods and tommy shops' artificially-inflated rates.

Even when truck was banned – after 1871 it became illegal to pay wages other than in cash – some employers got round this by paying wages that were then spent in public houses which they owned. This ensured that a good proportion of the wages flowed back to them.

CRAFTY CRAM... RAMSAY MACDONALD

Born in 1866, the illegitimate son of a Scottish fisherwoman, Ramsay MacDonald left Scotland, where he was a teacher, to become a journalist in London. He first came to political prominence in 1900 when elected secretary of the LRC (the Labour Party's early acronym) – although, the story goes that some thought they were voting for another MacDonald, a trade union leader. MacDonald entered the Commons in 1906 and became chairman of the International Labour Party, but attacked Britain's entry into World War I and was ousted in 1918. He returned in 1922 as MP for Aberavon and 11 years later became Labour's first prime minister and foreign secretary. His administration, however, failed to cope with the fallout from the Depression and he resigned in 1931. He then formed a national government at the invitation of King George V in a split from Labour, but finally bowed out of Parliament in 1935.

ANYONE FOR A CUPPA?

There was, of course, a significant fly in the ointment of the closing years of the 18th century in Britain – the loss of America. In 1760, there were 13 separate colonies or states along the eastern seaboard of our cousin across the pond, with a total population of about 2½ million, that took about 25% of all Britain's exports: tools, weapons, nails, steel, clothes, dishes and furniture etc. But the mercantilism that informed the relationship between colony and parent country (no industry could be developed in competition with a British counterpart) and the Navigation Acts that insisted that all trade to and from the colonies had to be carried out in British-only ships were the brew for a truly huge storm in a teacup – culminating in the infamous Boston Tea Party of 1773. Of course, the Tea Party was actually a very sedate affair: the damaging Boston moment had already happened – three years before, at the Boston Massacre when resentment at Boston being used as a British garrison flared into open revolt when an American wig-maker's apprentice mistakenly accused a British soldier of playing fast and loose with payment – the final straw for the Bostonians. Ten years after the Tea Party, 13 years after the Massacre, Boston's honour was satisfied when the Treaty of Paris recognised the independence of the 13 United States.

Find the connection between a former US president and
a popular cuddly toy.
Answer on page 312

FLY THE RED FLAG!

The rise of the Labour Party in
the 19th century was inestimably
helped by the failure of older rival
organisations to sort themselves out
and deal with the social problems
of the late Victorian era.

Liberal MP Joseph Chamberlain,
one-time president of the Board
of Trade, wanted his party to deal
with the well-documented poverty,
unemployment, health and housing
issues. But Liberal Prime Minister
William Gladstone would not make
the connection between social
weakness and the need for a strong
government to step in.

Similarly, Randolph Churchill
(father of Winston) wanted the
Conservatives to follow Disraeli's
policies on social reform, but his
boss, Lord Salisbury, would have
nothing of it.

From the ranks of the TUC
came the Lib-Labs, MPs from the
top skim of the working classes,
initially in support of Gladstone,
and without much in common with
the masses who lived in poverty.
Then along came Keir Hardie, who
had left school at eight, worked
in the pits from the age of 10 and
become a self-educated miners'
leader while still in his teens.

Rejected as a Lib-Lab candidate
by the local Lanark Liberal
Association (too red in tooth for
them), he formed the Scottish
Labour Party and eventually won
the London seat of West Ham as an
independent Labour candidate after
inspiring others to form their own
local Labour Parties. His arrival at
the Commons in 1892, with brass
band, red flag and flat cap, caused
a commotion.

A year later in Bradford, the
various local Labour parties
coalesced with some other socialist
societies to form the first official
Independent Labour Party (ILP).
It was poor, small and fragmented
and initially Hardie could not
persuade the TUC that the
working-class movement needed
direct political representation.

However, a disastrous decision
by the law lords in 1901 – they
made the Amalgamated Society
of Railway Servants pay £23,000
to the Taff Railway Company
to compensate for strike action
– pushed even the snottiest craft
unions into Hardie's waiting arms.
Now he had money, organisation
and high-quality leaders. And by
1924 Labour was in power.

The Roman army begain around 753BC and
lasted well over a millennium.

QUOTE UNQUOTE

*History will be kind to me because
I intend to write it.*
Winston Churchill, former British prime minister

GIVING THEM THE RUNAROUND

Among the headlining Mines Act of 1842 and the Factory Act of 1844,
the less contentious Railway Act of 1844 often passes unnoticed. But this
was the instrument, pushed through by Gladstone when he was Sir Robert
Peel's minister at the Board of Trade, that created the 'Parliamentary Mile'.

This ruled that the third-class fare should not exceed one penny for each
mile travelled. It also decreed that every railway company had to send at
least one train every day to carry third-class passengers. Suddenly, ordinary
people had cheap travel – an almost revolutionary concept in its day.

- **Seven Years' War** (1756-1763): a truly global conflict, fought in India, America, Canada, across the world's oceans, and involving all of the major European powers of the period. A million or more died.

- **Anglo-Mysore Wars** (1766-1799) and **Anglo-Maratha Wars** (1775-1818): first of these was a series of wars fought over three decades in India between the kingdom of Mysore and the East India Company. Both conflicts led to South Asia being consolidated into the British Empire in India.

- **American Revolutionary War** (1775-1783): also known as the American War of Independence. It was fought between Britain and its 13 colonies in America. Hostilities became international when foreign powers waded in to support the American colonists. Britain's unbeatable naval supremacy cut no ice on land where it had only a small land army. Surrender at Yorktown in 1781 led to the Treaty of Paris two years later: Britain had lost. The US was up and running.

- **Napoleonic Wars** (1803-1815): what started as a continuation of wars sparked by the French Revolution then involved Napoleon's French Empire (unstoppable until his disastrous 1812 invasion of Russia) and a shifting set of European allies. Hostilities ended when Napoleon met his Waterloo in June 1815.

- **Anglo-Dutch Java War** (1810-1811): fought entirely on the island of Java in colonial Indonesia between Britain and Netherlands. The British won the war but lost the lands; in 1816, they returned Java and other East Indian possessions to the Dutch as part of the agreement ending the Napoleonic Wars.

- **Canadian Rebellions of 1837**: frustrations in political reform and religious/ethnic conflict led to a revolt by French Canadians and English Canadians against the British Colonial Government. Britain won but conceded 'responsible government' to the colony. Also, Upper and Lower Canada were merged – and official assimilation of French-Canadians took place.

- **First Anglo-Afghan War** (1839-1842): one of the first major conflicts of 'The Great Game', the struggle between Britain and Russia in Central Asia. Sometimes called 'Auckland's Folly', the war was an unmitigated disaster for Britain.

- **Second** (1843-1880) and **Third** (1919) **Anglo-Afghan Wars**: eventually ended in ambiguous concession by Britain that Afghanistan had the right to determine its own affairs without any interference (ie from Russia).

- **First Opium War** (1839-1842): fought by Britain, forcing China to import British opium; gained Hong Kong as a result.

- **Second Opium War** (1856-1860): Britain brought in the French and Russians; all three nations eventually won long-lasting trade, diplomatic and religious concessions from the Chinese.

- **Anglo-Sikh Wars** (1845-1846) and (1848-1849): fought by the East India Company; resulted in subjugation of the Punjab which was renamed North-West Frontier province.

- **Crimean War** (1854-1856): this involved Russia and an alliance of Britain, France and Turkey (Ottoman Empire). Mostly fought on the Crimean Peninsula, the hostilities are considered by some to have been the first 'modern' conflict. It featured heavy armaments, trenches, the telegraph, railways – and modern nursing. This turned out to be a largely Pyrrhic victory since Russia pretty much ignored the terms of the subsequent treaty.

- **Anglo-Persian War** (1856-1857): this was fought against Persia but was actually about Afghanistan and the Great Game – this time concerning the disputed city of Herat. Persia finally agreed to surrender its claims.

- **Indian Mutiny** (1857): uprising of sepoys in East India Company army in present-day Uttar Pradesh. The conflict then spread throughout central India, but was doomed by a lack of concerted resistance. However, it spelled the end of the East India Company and the start of direct British Government rule.

- **Anglo-Zulu War** (1879): from complex beginnings, this African war was notable for its uniquely bloody battles, which finally put paid to the Zulu nation's independence.

- **First Boer War** (1880-1881): trade routes, diamonds, gold and the British thirst for Empire collided with the dogged independence of the Boers. Battle defeats led Britain to allow tacit Boer autonomy under the UK umbrella, but the Witwatersrand gold rush and simmering tensions led to the **Second Boer War** (1899-1902): a disastrous mess known as the last British imperial war. It was notable for its cost (£200 million) and the despicable use of concentration camps by us Brits.

- **Anglo-Sudan War** aka Mahdist War (1881-1899): protracted response to the Sudanese revolt against (British-controlled) Egyptians, and resulted in the tragedy of Gordon's death in the siege of Khartoum. Britain though ultimately secured victory against the savagery of Mahdi-led Sudanese dervishes.

- **Anglo-Burmese War** (1885): the last of three wars in the 19th century. Burma lost both its sovereignty and independence.

- **Boxer Rebellion** (1899-1901): began as an anti-foreign, anti-imperialist, peasant-based attack on all foreigners in northern China until a multinational coalition came to the rescue. Spelled the end of the Qing Dynasty and the birth of the Chinese Republic.

- **World War I** (1914-1918).

- **Irish War of Independence** (1919-1921): guerrilla war against the British, fighting for Home Rule; ended in stalemate that tipped into Irish Civil War (1922-1923).

- **World War II** (1939-1945).

COULD DO BETTER

History: 'Margaret has now so sure a grasp of her historical work that she can offer a critical judgement with assurance. Her interest is primarily in the interplay of personalities and she finds the more impersonal aspects of history less absorbing than one might expect from one of her ability.'
School report of Margaret Forster (1938-), novelist, biographer; The Carlisle and County High School for Girls, 1956.
From *Could do Better*, **edited by Catherine Hurley**

CRAFTY CRAM... SIR ROBERT PEEL

Third-generation product of industrialist success, educated at Harrow and Oxford; early opponent of Catholic emancipation. Earned a reputation for being pragmatic and persuadable when in Wellington's ministry. He helped pass an Emancipation Bill in 1829.

Despite early opposition, he passed the (Parliamentary) Reform Act in 1832. As Party leader from 1834, he wrote the 'Tamworth Manifesto' letter to his constituents, explaining his readiness to reform.

Peel is sometimes credited with the 'birth' of the Conservative Party from old Toryism: the spirit of reform guided by the watchwords to 'conserve the interest of the country'.

When in power from 1841, Peel lived up to his word, championing: Mines Act 1842, Factory Act 1844, Railway Act, Repeal of Corn Laws 1846 and Public Health Act 1848.

On trade, Peel was no less bold: the repeated cuts on tariffs in 1842 and 1845 kept the industrialists happy and turned Britain into the 'Workshop of the World'. His Bank Charter Act 1844 regulated the banks and gave the Bank of England special prominence, introducing the 'cheque' and ensuring fewer bank failures.

Equally pragmatic in foreign policy, Peel and Foreign Minister Lord Aberdeen negotiated the 1842 Treaty of Nanking, which ended the first Opium War, and the 1846 Oregon Treaty which set the '49th parallel' frontier between the US and Canada. But Ireland was trickier: a miscalculation by Peel had led to the alienation and arrest of Home Rule advocate and serving MP Daniel O'Connell; Peel's unpopularity in Ireland was exacerbated by 'too little, too late' action on the Irish Famine.

THE AGE OF IRREVERENCE

Great hams of thighs, bosoms tipping out across the page, blowsy profiles with shakily handwritten speech bubbles spilling from the lips – the late 18th-century cartoon (and the unfettered cheek about the language and criticism employed) is easily recognisable.

It's seen at its most irreverent in the 1792 'Vices Overlook'd... Avarice, Drunkenness, Gambling and Debauchery', which captions portraits of the royal family. But it could have been so different – there was a moment when the famously British freedom of the press faltered and nearly fell.

In 1771, a universally derided rule forbidding the reporting of Parliamentary debates in newspapers (hence the popularity of cartoons, which were deemed to get around such strictures) was broken by two publishers, Thompson and Wheble. Their arrest, by order of the Commons, aroused the ire of renegade MP and magistrate John Wilkes and the Lord Mayor of the City who released the publishers and jailed the Commons messenger.

The Commons then imprisoned the Lord Mayor, which led to rioting all over the capital, with the mob crying out in favour of 'Wilkes and Liberty'. Everyone backed down in the end and the rule remained. But it is significant that never again was there any attempt by the powers-that-be to interfere with the freedom of the press.

MARTYRS TO THE CAUSE

The Tolpuddle Martyrs might sound like relics from the medieval period but they were actually the early victims of industrial action. George Loveless, a labourer in the Dorset town of Tolpuddle, asked officials of the nascent trade union body, the GNCTU, to set up a branch for those he represented after their wages were suddenly reduced from 40p a week to 30p. He and five other leaders of the protest were then arrested: the trial at Dorchester showed they had done nothing illegal in forming a Union branch but they were hammered anyway, being charged under the Mutiny Act of 1797 for taking an oath on joining the Union, and sentenced to an eye-watering seven years' transportation and imprisonment in Tasmania. This appalling travesty took two years to unpick: in 1836 the Tolpuddle Martyrs were finally pardoned.

As knee-jerk policies go, the Corn Laws have to take the prize. During the Napoleonic Wars, it had not been possible to import foreign corn, so British farming had risen to the challenge. It hugely expanded wheat production and set high prices for wheat and other grain – this, in turn, led to high incomes for farmers, while landowners pocketed high rents through leasing out tenant farms

The problem was what to do with this artificially buoyed-up situation once the war ended – the importation of foreign corn would upset the apple cart and send prices, incomes, rents and landowner bank balances tumbling.

Since the landowners still controlled the unreformed Parliamentary system, it was easy enough in 1815 to shove through the Corn Laws, which decreed that no grain could be imported until the cost of the home-grown variety reached the wartime price.

What was then extraordinary was that these laws stuck around for the next three decades – even when the 1832 Reform Act gave industrialists a share in the political system. But then the various ministries of the 1820s, 1830s and 1840s didn't quite have the nerve to take the land-owning classes by the scruff of the neck and force them to back down.

Russell and the Whigs, for example, did nothing while in office (1831-1840) but once in opposition were very happy to support the persuasive Richard Cobden MP in his campaign to repeal the Corn Laws' iniquities. The Anti-Corn Law League, an amalgamation of various mini-leagues, was formed in 1839 to fight for the Laws' abolition.

Trade depressions in 1837 and 1839-1841, forced the issue: high bread prices meant high wages; if corn was allowed in, foreigners would have money to buy British goods, so helping the trade doldrums. Peel's cuts in tariffs had opened him up to accusations of unfairness – why was only corn (and farmers) still the cosseted baby of protectionism?

In 1845, with the Irish Famine showing the likes of Peel and Russell what the sharp end of being unable to afford bread was like, Peel introduced a Repeal Bill. What followed was a pitched battle: party lines between Whig and Tory were blurred by the dug-in stances of town versus country. But in June 1846 the Corn Laws were no longer: imported grain was allowed, with the nominal duty of one shilling.

Disraeli, who had violently opposed the Laws' Repeal, notably made no attempt to reinstate them when in office.

Between 1429 and 1431, this child visionary raises an army and helps clear the English out of northern France during the Hundred Years' War. The French king, Charles VII, whom Joan encourages to seize his destiny, reigns with great success for 30 years after her death. She was canonised in 1920.

WORK IT OUT

Who am I?

I married a lawyer, I was arrested on numerous occasions for my role in demonstrations, but I helped change the lives of women in Britain in the 20th century.

Answer on page 312

Being a working-class child in 19th-century Britain was little better than being born into slavery. You were regarded as a cheap resource by industrialists and a cash cow by your harassed parents – as long as you had any. If not, you were an orphan sent by Poor Law authorities to be housed in the very factories you were then enslaved to.

Whether you toiled in urban factories or rural fields depended on which political party appeared to support you. The Whigs, with their country estates, campaigned vigorously for townspeople's working rights while actively suppressing movements which aimed at improving the lot of poor rural communities.

In 1802 Robert Owen, a factory owner better than some, persuaded Parliament to pass an Act limiting the working day of pauper children to 12 hours. Seventeen years later Sir Robert Peel (father of the more famous Sir Robert) got the House to extend that Act to all working children, and prohibit youngsters under nine from working at all.

But these provisions applied only to cotton mills and were seen as largely ineffective – their enforcement was left to local magistrates who, more often than not, were either factory proprietors themselves or hand-in-glove with the local mill owners.

The 1833 Factory Act went a bit further, but the 1834 Poor Law Amendment Act was a shocker – an apparent reform, it thought nothing of the effects of its institutional harshness on those it was seemingly trying to protect.

Meanwhile, a child's life got no better. An 1842 Royal Commission looked at youngsters in the mines, where children as young as four were employed as 'trappers', opening and closing ventilation doors in the pitch dark for 12 hours a day.

The Act that followed banned women and girls from working underground at all (though boys of 10 and over could still be employed) but didn't mention the length of the working day. Such tiny incremental improvements could have gone on *ad infinitum* but when the likes of Anthony Ashley-Cooper (later Lord Shaftesbury) and Charles Dickens became involved, some real improvements both in the working and living conditions of poor families began to come about.

Education was the way out of the darkness. In 1870, the landmark Forster Act led to other Acts which helped to create a national system of education, in which the school-leaving age crept ever upwards (11 in 1893, 12 in 1899, 14 in 1918, 15 in 1947 and 16 in 1966). By 1950, education was free across the board.

GOOD LUDD, M'LUD

Never let it be thought that the Industrial Revolution was one great instant wealth generator without any detractors; eg even though textiles were increasingly in demand, both for uniforms and export, growing mechanisation led to increasing unemployment among the old hand-workers of the domestic system.

In Yorkshire, in 1811, croppers – who were put out of commission by the introduction of the power loom and new shearing machines – attacked the factories. In the Nottingham and Derby areas, similarly disenchanted artisans attacked all factories that used the new stocking-knitting machinery.

What was strange was that both of these attack parties claimed that they were inspired and led by a mythical modern-day Robin Hood character called King Ludd. However, there is no proof that such an individual existed (there may or may not have been an earlier reference to a Ned Ludd in 1779).

Today, the term 'Luddite' is used to refer somewhat disparagingly to someone who resists the advance of modernisation or technology. But there is evidence to suggest that the original Luddites were acting as much out of self-preservation as from fear of change.

NOT VERY CIVIL

Displaying yet again the supreme irony of the English language, the Spanish Civil War was anything but. Started after an attempted *coup d'état* (by rebel parts of the army against the government of the Second Spanish Republic), the conflict devastated Spain from 1936 to 1939. It ended in victory for the rebels (the Nationalists) over the Republicans and the founding of a Fascist dictatorship led by General Franco.

For the rest of the world, it was not only a 'world war by proxy' as we watched the forces of fascism and communism slug it out, but the first media war. Journalists, photographers, artists, poets, rebels hitherto without a cause – everyone was there, some genuinely engaged with the cause and others more fancifully involved. Craig Brown, in *1966 and All That*, puts it suitably irreverently: 'The Spanish Civil War took place between a) General Frankie Vaughan, the Spanish Florist leader and b) a small but prestigious group of English and American authors... including a detachment of the Bloomsbury Grope. They arrived in a tank driven by Vita Shredded-Wheat, directed by Virginia Woof and designed in lovely greens, pinks and mauves by Duncan Grunt, with gunner Dame Edith Spitwell taking it up the rear.'

Coal had been Britain's ace up the sleeve for hundreds of years before the Industrial Revolution (a look at a map shows how muscled with coal fields the flanks of our green and pleasant hills are), but the fact that everybody – the new iron industry, the textile industry with its steam-driven industry and, of course, both the shipping and railway industries – needed coal in vast quantities suddenly catapulted coal into the limelight. Suddenly, men had to go down deeper to get coal, brave new dangers and operate new machinery. From 45 million tonnes in 1846, output increased to 65 million in 1856 and doubled to 100 million in 1863. By 1913, an unimaginable 300 million tonnes of coal were being carved out annually, of which 100 million were exported. But oil was the new kid on the block, especially for shipping; electricity was increasingly used in homes and industries and there was the pinch of greater heat-efficiency and home-economy. Demand for coal declined, exacerbated by the fact that British prices were too high, especially after 1925, by which time other nations – the USA with its seemingly bottomless pit of natural resources, a recovering Germany and new industrial nation Poland – were catching up, with newer mines, more mechanised pits and a cheaper workforce. Industrial action in 1921, only erratically supported by the Triple Alliance, the exhaustion of World War II and the 1947 inclusion in the relentless nationalisation programme meant that, by 1950, the sun was well and truly beginning to set at the pithead of British Coal.

REDS UNDER THE BED

The 1924 general election, the first in which 'the wireless' was used, set the scene for the sort of hysterical 'media skulduggery' that we would see for the rest of the century. The *Daily Mail*, strongly anti-Labour and fearful of Bolshevism, produced 'The Zinoviev' letter, which the Foreign Office accepted as being a communication from a Russian leader to the British Communist Party. The document showed how to gain control of the trade union movement and bring about a workers' revolution.

Despite screaming headlines about the 'red peril' and the dangers of having a Russki-loving Labour government, the episode did Ramsay MacDonald and his party little damage – it gained half a million more votes than in 1923. As for the letter, it later proved a forgery.

He who controls the past controls the future; and he who controls the present, controls the past.

George Orwell, British author

NOT FAIR FOR THE FAIRER SEX

They were ruled by a woman for nearly the entire century but Queen Victoria did little for female emancipation – at least from our smug schoolkid's perspective. It seemed to us girls that to be a woman in the 19th century must have been a thankless burden.

At the beginning, the female gender was trapped by the dilemma familiar to anyone who'd read Jane Austen: women of a certain class couldn't work at anything except being a governess (having probably been educated at home themselves) and had precious few rights. If they were householders (rich widows), they could vote in local and school board elections but otherwise they were disenfranchised. All the assets of a married woman automatically became her husband's – no sharing here – the minute they got married and even if he left.

Women were beginning to shift a little restively in favour of basic emancipation – a path that would later develop into a fight for similar education and jobs as their brothers, the right to own their own property and, only last, to get the vote and so be on an equal footing with their menfolk.

Quite late in the century, in 1870 and 1882, Parliament finally passed the Married Women's Property Acts, allowing married women to retain ownership of their own dowry.

Meanwhile, women were forming suffragette societies, chaining themselves to railings in Downing Street and, in the case of Emily Davison, hurling herself under the hooves of the Derby runners at Epsom in 1910 in a bid to get the great and good's attention.

But the boys in the Commons held out. In 1918 they gave all males the vote – and reluctantly to women over 30. Only from 1928 did the fair sex get the vote on the same terms as men after an epic struggle that rather put our griping about pimples and school uniforms into perspective.

WORK IT OUT

Who am I?

I was born in Dartmouth, I was an ironmonger and I invented the atmospheric steam engine.

Answer on page 312

LET THEM EAT... THEMSELVES

When Marie-Antoinette was heard to say about the shortage of bread for peasants, 'Oh, let them eat cake!' (she actually said 'brioche' – another sort of bread, but we English didn't bother to translate her remarks properly) she neatly put herself in line for the guillotine in the dramatic Revolution that followed. Cut to 50 years later, to the Andover Workhouse where the 'Guardians' had given their poor inmates so little food that they had resorted to eating rotting bone marrow. Outcry followed, but the Guardians defended themselves by saying that they had merely followed the guidance of the government, when they took the bracing view, in the Poor Law Amendment Act of 1834, that making the conditions in workhouses even harsher would 'discourage' families from sending children there (leading critics to nickname workhouses 'Bastilles' in reference to the French Revolution). Did such institutionalised harshness provoke an immediate fall of the government or a revolution? Not even close. While citizens all over Europe were revolting over harsh conditions... the British just seemed to get on with the job in hand.

ROUND THE HOUSES

It may have started its English life as Saxe-Coburg-Gotha, but with the anti-German sentiment surrounding World War I, our royal family then decided to change its name to that of one of its holiday houses.

Balmoral, Sandringham, Buckingham and Osborne could all have been contenders, but the royals plumped for Windsor, their abode in the home counties. But how do we remember all the other ruling houses and the order in which they come? Well, it's time to belt up – No Point Letting Your Trousers Slip Half Way. In other words, Norman, Plantagenet, Lancaster, York, Tudor, Stuart, Hanover, Windsor.

Today we take the universality of the police entirely for granted, but in the early part of the 19th century that was far from the case. Highwaymen held up travellers willy-nilly and mobs rioted – and all because of the absence of any proper constabulary. In London alone, there were 70 different 'police forces', made up of unpaid constables and creaking old watchmen, and supervised by the various parish authorities.

In the 1750s, two magistrate brothers had set up the Bow Street Runners, who frightened most gangs out of London but could go no further. Between 1815 and 1822, the government set up a 'spy system' of *agents provocateurs* who nominally helped impose law and order but by the sneakiest of methods – spying, informing, falsely inciting. But, it wasn't until 1829 that Sir Robert Peel founded the Metropolitan Police, headquartered at Scotland Yard.

Initially it consisted of 3,000 men, who were paid £1.05 per week. The force not only led to a fall in crime in London but also inspired other towns to establish similar organisations. It wasn't long before the constables were called 'Bobby's Boys' and subsequently 'Bobbies'.

GETTING ABOUT

Before the Industrial Revolution, getting about was a trial. You had the choice of a boneshaking rattle in a carriage along rutted lanes and cobbled streets, or a long, tedious and often dangerous boat trip.

In 1894 *The Times* estimated that by 1950, every street in London would be buried nine feet deep in manure because even that late no one saw beyond the horse. But from the moment the first passenger railway opened between Stockton and Darlington in 1825, the train spread rapidly. By 1843, during the 'railways mania', there were nearly 3,219km/2,000 miles of line. This more than doubled in the next two years and by 1855 there were nearly 12,875km/8,000 miles of track. Trams, canals, buses and even the outlandish penny-farthing bicycle provided yet more alternatives to man's four-footed friend.

For example, having been eclipsed by the American clippers, made from tougher more plentiful American timber, British merchants built their own versions, as well as iron sailing ships, and pioneered steam propulsion.

The opening of the Suez Canal worked like a charm, cutting 1,000 miles off the journey to Australia. And by 1880, British shipping dominated the world. Now we just needed to hone our skills on that newly invented roller skate...

THE IRISH PROBLEM:
SIGNIFICANT DATES 1750-1950

1780: worst features of Navigation Acts repealed

1780: uprising in Ulster and Wexford, helped by French. Failed

1800: Act of Union – Irish Parliament abolished, Ireland split into 100 constituencies. Free trade

1780: Roman Catholic Emancipation Act. Irish hero Daniel O'Connell takes seat in Commons

1780: Pitt bans national demonstration, arrests O'Connell, who is later released. A broken man, he dies in 1847

1780: census showed that there were nine million people in Ireland, half of whom lived in 'windowless mud cabins of a single room', dependent on potatoes for both money and subsistence

1845: famine. Fungus attacks Irish potato crop – within six months there is poverty, starvation, homelessness and disease. One million die, two million emigrate

1858: Fenians formed in US to fight for Irish independence

1860s: Fenian activity in US, Ireland and Britain – killings and bombings

1868: British election. 'My mission is to pacify Ireland,' says Gladstone

1869: Irish Church Act – Protestantism no longer official state church

1870: First Irish Land Act – empty attempt to stem landlord abuses and evictions

1875: Charles Stuart Parnell is elected MP for County Meath

1879: Parnell, already 'uncrowned king of Ireland', elected president of Land League

1882: Kilmainham Treaty attempts to stem violence; Cavendish, Secretary of State for Ireland, murdered by Dublin gang called 'Invincibles'

1886: Gladstone's Home Rule Bill rejected by Commons

1890: Parnell broken by scandal of O'Shea divorce

1893: Gladstone's Second Home Rule Bill rejected by Lords

1912: Ulster Covenant – 500,000 Protestants pledged to defend their part of the Union

1914: Home Rule Bill finally shoved through

1916: Easter Rising

1917: Sinn Fein created: Eamonn de Valera becomes its president

1919-1921: guerrilla war

1920: Government of Ireland Act – separate Parliaments in Dublin (Dáil) and Belfast

1921: treaty – Dáil voted to accept but de Valera seceded. Civil War until 1923

1932: de Valera's Fianna Fáil party wins election

1939-1945: Ireland remains neutral in World War II – froideur between the republic and UK

1949: British government formally accepts that Eire is independent and no longer part of the British Commonwealth

The moment that Harold is killed by an arrow in his eye.
The Latin words translate 'Here King Harold has been killed'.

WIDOW OF WINDSOR OR MERRY WIDOW?

Queen Victoria: child queen who then became our longest-reigning monarch (an awesome 63 years and seven months); devoted wife who spent nearly her whole marriage pregnant (nine surviving children in 17 years), only to lose husband Albert to typhoid in 1861, when their youngest was only four years old; ever-after black-clad national treasure inextricably entwined with our view of the Empire at its zenith; collector of holiday residences (Balmoral, Sandringham, Osborne House); almost total enigma.

Who was Victoria? And what is the John Brown story? At school, we hadn't yet seen *Mrs Brown*, the wonderful film with Judi Dench and Billy Connolly, but we already had that pupil's nose for possible gossip... So, great was the joy when we found out that at her request, next to Victoria in her coffin were laid two mementoes: one of Albert's dressing gowns draped beside her, while, in her left hand, was placed a piece of John Brown's hair, along with a picture of him. More intriguing still came the recent news, in 2008, that Victoria's hand wore the wedding ring of John Brown's mother, placed there after her death. So, RIP Mrs Brown or Gloriana Victoriana?

10 HISTORIC LIFESAVERS

Sir Humphry Davy (1778-1829): discovered that nitrous oxide, 'laughing gas', removed pain and suggested it be used during surgical operations.

Michael Faraday (1791-1867): Davy's assistant, who discovered (1838) that ether had the same effects as nitrous oxide.

James Simpson (1811-1870): professor of midwifery at Edinburgh University who used chloroform as a painkiller during childbirth; the anaesthetic became very fashionable once it was revealed that Queen Victoria had used it during the birth of her seventh child, Prince Leopold.

Louis Pasteur (1822-1895) discovered that disease was caused by germs. This led him to experiment until he produced a cholera vaccine (1879), thus carrying on from Englishman Edward Jenner, who had discovered the cure for smallpox. Pasteur went on to produce vaccines against typhoid, the plague, yellow fever and typhus; the two of them were pioneers of vaccination.

Joseph Lister (1827-1912): guru of antiseptics, he was also professor of surgery at Glasgow University. He studied Pasteur's work and worked out that it was germs that infected the open wounds of patients in hospitals.

Elizabeth Garrett Anderson (1836-1917): first Englishwoman doctor, against considerable opposition. A pioneering physician and political campaigner, she founded the New Hospital for Women in London and paved the way for Acts that allowed women to enter the medical professions.

Francis Galton (1822-1911): half-cousin of Charles Darwin and all-round genius, described as 'an anthropologist, eugenicist, tropical explorer, geographer, inventor, meteorologist, proto-geneticist, psychometrician, and statistician'. Among much ground-breaking, he also coined the phrase 'nature versus nurture'.

Florence Nightingale (1820-1910): trailblazed way for female nursing and introduced concepts of hygiene, compassion and systematic excellence into hospital care.

Mary Seacole (1805-1881): not nearly famous enough Jamaican-born pioneering nurse and Crimean War heroine, who overcame double prejudice, being a female and of mixed race.

John Snow (1813-1858): one of the fathers of epidemiology and waterborne disease, he traced the source of a cholera outbreak in London's Soho in 1854; also, leader in the adoption of anaesthesia and medical hygiene.

Who is the odd one out?

- Winston Churchill
- David Lloyd George
- Arthur James Balfour
- Margaret Thatcher

Answer on page 312

LABOURING A POINT

It was a weary Britain that picked itself up after VE Day in 1945 – only to pitch straight into a general election. The result was totally unexpected, given the near mythical status of war leader Winston Churchill; Labour won a runaway victory, with a majority of 145 seats. It was the first election in which the party gained a clear majority of seats and the first time it chalked up the most votes. Indeed, Labour came close to winning more than 50% of all the votes cast.

The reasons for the landslide were varied. Though Churchill was a hero, voters distrusted the Tories' domestic and foreign policy record before the war; also, the Labour contingent in the cross-party wartime government acquitted themselves well, especially Clement Attlee whose mild-mannered, quiet competence suddenly seemed preferable to Winston's bluster.

The victors promised to create full employment (both for demobbed servicemen and the women whose labours had helped to maintain full factory production), a tax-funded, universal health service and a 'cradle-to-grave' welfare state. Labour's campaign slogan was 'Let us face the future' – and for six years the party did just that, restoring the lost markets and overseas investments as well as the British infrastructure. Also, it made a start on making good the overseas debt and the losses inflicted on British shipping.

It was a poisoned chalice, made more difficult by the depressing need to continue with rationing. Yet between 1945 and 1950, Labour did not lose a single by-election. And their vote actually went up in the 1950 general election. But the second Attlee administration proved a husk of its former self and it was obliged to go to the country again in 1951. This time the Conservatives scored a narrow 26-seat majority – Winston was back in town.

II

GEOGRAPHY

Geography is just physics slowed down,
with a couple of trees stuck in it.

Terry Pratchett, from *The Last Continent*

Up the ladder or the long way home? We all know that the lines of longitude and latitude are imaginary lines used to locate position on the globe, but how do we remember which are which?

Lines of latitude are drawn parallel to the equator (the zero degrees point of the scale), and up and down to the poles (at 90 degrees) like the rungs of a ladder, while lines of longitude trace the 'long' north-south route between the two poles.

Longitude is measured in degrees from the Greenwich meridian, leading us to remember the origin of the time setting GMT and the close relationship between time, latitude and longitude. Before longitude was developed in the 1750s, sailors mapped their position by putting themselves east or west of any old meridian, but since the Brits then ruled the seas and their Astronomer Royal always referred all his lunar-stellar distance tables to 'his' meridian back home in Greenwich, this is what gradually became the prime meridian.

When fellow Brit John Harrison invented a chronometer (clock, in modern parlance) that was accurate and portable enough to take to sea and calculate the longitude position properly as the 'time' away from the Greenwich 'zero' hour, the relationship between mapping, Greenwich and time was complete. Now latitude and longitude are expressed, first in the old degrees, then minutes, then in seconds for 1/60th pinpoint positioning. And which comes first? Think alphabetically and put latitude before longitude – so, for example, the Statue of Liberty is located at 40 degrees 41' 22" north, 74 degrees, 2' 40" west. Easy, eh?

QUOTE UNQUOTE

For the execution of the voyage to the Indies, I did not make use of intelligence, mathematics or maps.
Christopher Columbus, explorer

WHISTLE DOWN THE WIND

Winds are caused by the movement of air from areas of higher pressure to areas of lower pressure (caused by hot air rising and cooling) – the greater the difference in pressure, the faster the wind blows. Although the behaviour of the wind is affected by features such as land and water, there is a basic worldwide system of trade winds, westerlies and polar easterlies that have a discernible pattern of behaviour. Down at the seaside, local winds result from landmasses heating and cooling faster than the adjacent sea, producing onshore winds in the daytime and offshore winds at night. Winds are not always the gentle, puff-cheeked entities we see illustrated in Renaissance paintings; the fastest wind speed (as opposed to jetstream speeds above) that was ever measured on Earth was in May 1999, when a tornado struck the suburbs of Oklahoma City at 318mph.

EARTHQUAKES

We all think that earthquakes are measured on the Richter scale (they're not, they're measured on the MMS scale, but the media, and therefore everyone else, ignores that), but do any of us remember what that actually means? Charles Richter was a Californian seismologist who in 1935 came up with the system of 'ranking' earthquakes (when two parallel tectonic plates jam up against each other, then break free with an abrupt and violent movement) according to the energy released by their shock waves. The crucial thing to remember about the Richter scale is that with each integer increase, there is an increase of 30 times the energy released. For example, a 4.0 earthquake has 30 times the power of a 3.0 tremor, and a 5.0 quake is a massive 900 times as powerful as the 3.0, hence the ability to measure a small rumble, in which the window frames might rattle, to a Kobe-sized disaster, which destroys buildings, roads and changes the landscape – all on the same scale. The shock waves given off by a hand grenade will score 0.5 on the Richter scale; the famous 1906 San Francisco earthquake was 8.3. Despite our attempts to classify earthquakes, scientists remain baffled as to how to predict them... Meanwhile, Britain has up to 300 earthquakes a year, but they are so small that the public notices only about one in 10 of them.

Interestingly, hurricanes/cyclones cannot form on the equator, because there the Coriolis effect is too small. At school we all learned about the fact that the Earth tilts on its axis but in most cases promptly forgot about the Coriolis effect because that's where Geography suddenly started to get complicated. When the Coriolis force was first identified in the fields of physics research, the clever chaps soon realised that the most commonly encountered rotating frame of reference was the Earth itself. Movements of air in the atmosphere, water in the ocean – and weather patterns, like storms, in between – should flow directly from areas of high pressure to low pressure, but because of the Coriolis effect they actually tend to veer to the right in the northern hemisphere and to the left in the southern. This veering kicks off the revolving aspect of hurricanes and turns them from an area of low pressure, with a bit of angry cold air being sucked in from the top, into a moving force: clockwise in the southern hemisphere and the opposite in the northern hemisphere because of the 'mirroring' aspect of rotational dynamics. But one popular schoolday myth can be exploded – the old bathwater chestnut. Contrary to the avowals from our more exotic friends that one had only to cross a few miles across the equator to witness the phenomenon of the change in direction of bathwater whirling down the plughole, there is no change in the direction the bathwater runs out. This is not only because the Coriolis parameter is simply too small at the equator but because it only works for rather larger water-movement systems than a leaky old bath...

WHAT'S IN A NAME?

Did you know how hurricanes are named? For every year since 1953, there has been a pre-approved list of names for tropical storms and hurricanes in the North American region – they started off as female only, but switched to alternating genders in 1979. Hurricanes are named alphabetically from the list in chronological order (with the first one in the year starting with 'A') – which is a clue to how bad 2005 had already been when Hurricane Wilma blew through the Caribbean. Usually the six lists of names are recycled every six years, but if there is an especially damaging hurricane, the name is retired for at least 10 years for reasons of sensitivity; in 2005 alone, the names Dennis, Katrina, Rita, Stan and Wilma were all retired.

When we were at school, life was a little simpler. The existence of the ozone layer hadn't yet fully filtered down to us kids; chlorofluorocarbons (CFCs) were for A Level chemistry students and their negative effects could be laid easily at the door of heavy industry rather than wasteful consumers. All we had to learn was the following table:

Pollutant	Cause and effect	Knock-on effect
Sulphur dioxide	Created when oil and coal are burned – with power stations the major source.	Sulphur dioxide in the atmosphere dissolves in water droplets to form sulphuric acid, increasing the acidity of rain, leading to serious blight among the forests and rivers of northern Europe.
Carbon monoxide	Comes from vehicle exhausts; fatal in high concentrations.	Carbon monoxide, if inhaled, inhibits the bloodstream from being properly oxygenated and in high doses can very quickly be deadly (which is why it is so popular for suicides). Long term, it causes chronic breathing conditions.
Carbon dioxide	Produced by burning fuels; screens radiation (including sunlight).	Effects are manifold – high take-up of CO_2 in the oceans, for example, is producing marked changes in several species.
Hydrocarbons and nitrogen oxide	Produced by vehicle exhausts.	Responsible for urban smogs found in cities like Beijing and Los Angeles, where summers are hot and sunny.
Smoke	The Clean Air Act of 1956 cleared up the UK but, overseas, loggers in Brazil and Indonesia were already beginning to choke their neighbours.	It's not just the smoke but the destruction of several endangered species – most famously, the orang-utan.

WORK IT OUT

What can run but never walks, has a mouth but never talks, has a head but never weeps and has a bed but never sleeps?

Answer on page 312

WHICH WAY IS EAST?

Some of the best responses from GCSE Geography exams in 2006:

Q: Name the four seasons.
A: Salt, pepper, mustard and vinegar.

Q: How is dew formed?
A: The sun shines down on the leaves and makes them perspire.

Q: What is a planet?
A: A body of earth surrounded by sky.

Q: What causes the tides in the oceans?
A: The tides are a fight between the Earth and the moon. All water tends to flow towards the moon, because there is no water on the moon, and nature abhors a vacuum. I forget where the sun joins in this fight.

GEE UP, HORSEY

Horse latitudes are regions of high pressure centred around 30 degrees latitude either side of the equator (more formally known as subtropic highs), which are warm and don't have much wind. The story has it that it was this lack of wind that drove sailors of the 16th and 17th centuries to desperate measures: if they were stuck in these conditions, utterly becalmed and going nowhere fast, they sometimes threw their horses overboard or otherwise disposed of them in an effort to conserve water on board. Perhaps this is not the time and place to examine the origins of the phrase 'I could eat a horse'.

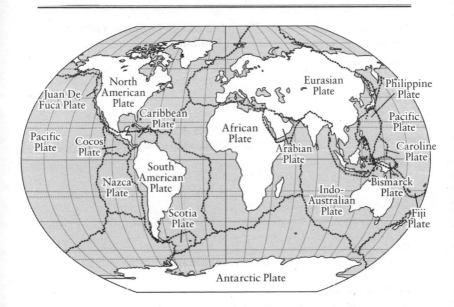

Of the four layers that make up the Earth, the outermost crust is made mainly of granite and basalt at a varying thickness of 8-40km/5-25 miles. It was formed originally by molten rock (magma) welling up from the liquid core of the Earth along lines of weakness in the layer of rocks, a staggering 2,900km/ 1,802 miles thick, known as the mantle. There are two types of crust – oceanic and continental. Oceanic crust can be forced down into the mantle, continental can only shift around and out. It is the movements of these split pieces that together cause changes in the Earth's surface. Slightly absurdly, the split sections of the crust are called tectonic plates and the resultant activity is known as plate tectonics. Tectonic plates, of which the biggest seven roughly equate to our continents, are still moved by the convection currents of the hot magma forcing its way through the mantle. Some move away from each other (divergence) and some move towards each other (convergence), and it is along these plate boundaries and collisions that earthquakes rumble, volcanoes erupt, deep sea trenches gape and fold mountains are wrenched up. When Mercury Rising sang about 'faults in the system', the parallels were obvious: faults form along lines of preexisting weakness, causing earthquakes and massive movements of land – a primeval sort of rock 'n' roll.

LARGEST SAND DESERTS OF THE WORLD

Desert	Location	Area sq km*	Area sq miles*	Average annual rainfall
Sahara	North Africa	9,065,000	3,500,000	Less than 25mm in some areas
Gobi	Mongolia/North east China	1,295,000	500,000	Under 50mm in some areas
Patagonian	Argentina	673,000	260,000	Less than 30mm
Rub' al Khali	South Arabia	647,500	250,000	Less than 80mm
Kalahari	West Africa	582,800	225,000	Up to 500mm in rainy season
Chihuahuan	Mexico/South west US	362,600	140,000	Around 240mm
Taklamakan	Northern China	362,600	140,000	Below 100mm
Great Sandy	West Australia	338,500	130,000	Between 300-400mm
Great Victoria	West Australia	338,500	130,000	From 200mm
Kyzyl Kum	Uzbekistan/Kazakhstan	259,000	100,000	Less than 300mm
Thar	India/Pakistan	259,000	100,000	About 350mm

* allowing for difficulty in measuring due to lack of clear physical boundaries

WEEKEND MINI BREAKS

In the 19th and 20th centuries, urban factory workers reported an increased likelihood of rain during the working week. Intense activity from both factories and cars from Monday to Friday was producing particles that prompted moisture in the atmosphere to form raindrops, as well as creating the right conditions for precipitation by producing the necessary rising warm air from chimneys and smoke stacks. With the modern world's increasingly 24/7 timetable, this weekend wonder has slackened and no study has yet discovered why bank holidays conversely seem to invite more precipitation than any other weekend.

ONE BIG SINK ESTATE?

The London Basin (incorporating not just the capital, but an area taking in most of the home counties) is one of our more obvious artesian basins – and one in which millions upon millions wash their hands every day. Its two 'rims' are the North Chilterns and the North Downs, and rainfall from these collects in the layer of chalk that underpins the more famous London clay. When wells are bored through the clay to the saturated chalk, the water rises up to the level of the water table outside the rims. Other sources of water are escaping springs at the boundary where the chalk meets impervious rocks: some emerge on the bed of the River Thames. Although the basin is drained mainly by the Thames, it does not coincide with the Thames drainage basin; its main headstream is actually the lesser-known Kennet, which flows from the Marlborough area, joining the Thames at Reading.

THOSE WERE THE DAYS

Looking back through the long sections on British industry in our Geography notes, there is something touchingly nostalgic and olde worlde about the key assumptions and premises therein. Woe betide the student who wasn't able to site a wool mill on a map, taking into account the parroted factors of raw materials, power source, markets, water supply, transport networks, labour and government policy that affected the location of industry.

The diagram of the factory system was learnt off by heart and regurgitated with confident strokes of the pen in O Level classes up and down the country. Examinees were expected to know the different requirements of the various heavy industries or 'secondary industries' (primary being farming, forestry,

mining and such activities where basic materials were extracted from the land) and those of the derisively relegated 'tertiary industries' – which casually lumped together retail, finance, administration, transport and tourism. These days, of course, primary industries teeter, shored up by subsidies; secondary industries are all but out of the picture and it is the power of the third that keeps Britain great. The colourful ties and snappy suits of the retail and financial services; the vast panoply of the state administration that has mushroomed so abundantly in the first years of this century; the earning power of tourism · – all straddle the GDP of this once industrial nation, putting the subject of British industry meekly back into the 'forgotten' file once more...

HOW TO MAKE A VOLCANO

You will need

For the volcano: Small drinks bottle, 600g/1lb 5oz of flour, 300g/10½oz of salt, 3tbsp of cooking oil, 370ml of water, brown or green food colouring and mixing bowl. *For the eruption:* 60ml/2fl oz water, 1tbsp baking soda, 60ml/2fl oz vinegar, orange food colouring, few drops of washing-up liquid, funnel, jug and a square of tissue.

Making the volcano

Mix the flour, salt, cooking oil, food colouring and water in a large bowl until smooth and firm. Build up the mixture around the plastic bottle to create the volcano, leaving the neck of the bottle open and clear.

Making the eruption

Once the volcano is ready, place it in a tray to catch the overflow from the eruption. In the jug, mix together the water, vinegar, a few drops of washing-up liquid and the orange food colouring. Using the funnel, carefully pour the liquid into the bottle. Put the baking soda into the small piece of tissue and fold, drop it into the top of the bottle and wait...

The chemical reaction

$$NaHCO_3 + CH_3COOH \rightarrow Na+ + H_2O + CO_2 + CH_3COO-$$

Carbon dioxide is released creating the fizz.

(Source: The National Space Centre)

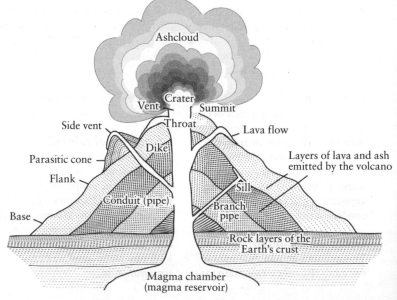

HURRICANES: THEY'RE A FORCE OF NATURE

Did you ever wonder what the difference was between hurricanes in the Atlantic and north Pacific, typhoons in the west Pacific and cyclones in the Bay of Bengal and the Indian Ocean? Of course you didn't, because you were a good student who learned at school that all these wrecking blowers were the same wind... Hurricanes (or whichever name you prefer to call them) come about when a cocktail of warm air rising from the ocean surface is thrown in with revolving trade winds that start to wind the storm up – add a dash of cooler air being sucked downwards into the lower-pressure centre and you get a spinning top of a storm, shaken and stirred. With its 'eye' of calm winds and low pressure, surrounded by a whirling vortex of high 241kmph/150mph winds, water-laden with heavy thunderstorms, hurricanes can have a devastating effect on buildings and coastal land forms – not least because the sea can surge up to 5m/16ft more than usual.

THE RAIN IN SPAIN...

We may complain about it endlessly but the world depends on rain. Put simply, it is a form of precipitation in which separate drops of water fall to Earth from clouds: the result of cooling air condensing into water vapour. Once the dew point has been reached, it turns into fine droplets and then into raindrops. There are three types:

Frontal rainfall
Not nudity, but the rain that occurs in the clash between the front of a mass of warm moist air from the tropics and the front of a mass of cold air from the poles – where the warm air loses out and the water vapour it is carrying chills and condenses to form clouds and rain.

Orographic rainfall
This occurs when an airstream is forced to rise over a mountain range – further away from the land, the air cools, condenses and rain falls.

Convectional rainfall
A more dramatic version of rain, associated with hot climates and usually accompanied by a thunderstorm. It occurs when the extreme heat of the ground surface causes the air to rise rapidly, cool abruptly and, with a heavy load of water vapour, fall as torrential rain.

Weather 'fronts' occur when two air masses of different temperature or humidity bump into each other. In the weather of the mid-latitudes (ie our weather), this happens frequently, as warm tropical air is bumped into by cold air from the poles. The warm air, being lighter, tends to rise above the cold, condense, then fall as rain and snow, hence the changeable weather conditions at fronts and in this country.

A cold front is where the cold air wins out in the collision between a cold air mass from below, displacing a warm air mass.

A warm front is when the warm air wins the 'battle' and marches on.

An occluded front is where a cold front catches up with a warm front from behind and then merges with it, lifting the warm air into a narrow wedge above the surface.

Isobars are the way we see all weather on weather maps – they are the lines that link all places with the same atmospheric pressure, usually measured in millibars. A depression, or area of low pressure, is shown by the isobars being close together; when they are far apart, that's a sign of high pressure and good weather. A good way to remember this is to think of a furrowed brow of anxiety about bad weather (ie the furrowed lines of isobars); a clear forehead means a clear day. Troughs are areas of low pressure between two high-pressure areas, causing lines of vaguely organised precipitation that seem to occur independently of fronts.

Depressions (or, at their peak, cyclones) are areas of low pressure, that often start when a front bulges disproportionately. What usually happens in British depressions is that warm tropical air advances northward, pushing a wedge into the cold polar air. This causes the pressure to fall and a depression to develop. Once formed, the depression moves eastward and a closed, circular system of isobars develops around it. Strangely, winds blow anticlockwise around depressions in the northern hemisphere and clockwise around anticyclones – but blow in opposite directions in the southern.

Anticyclones are areas of high pressure, far larger than depressions and moving more slowly. They are formed from sinking air that warms and dries as it descends. We like anticyclones – they bring that fine, clear-skied weather in summer and icy, calm, sunny days in winter.

Ridges (the opposite of troughs) is an elongated area of high pressure between two low-pressure areas. The weather is similar to anticyclonic weather, but lasts for less time.

THE DEVELOPMENT GAP

Contrasts between developed and developing nations

	Developed World	Developing World	Reasons
Birth rate per 1,000	Less than 20	Over 30	1. Lack of modern industry
Life expectancy	Over 70 years	Less than 50 years	2. Lack of capital
Population growth	Less than 2%	Over 2%	3. Lack of technology and industrial base
Literacy	Over 80%	Mainly less than 40%	4. Traditional farming methods 5. Overpopulation
Food consumption	Over 3,000 calories	Less than 2,000 calories	6. Cultural and religious conservatism or taboos
Agriculture	Commercial	Subsistence	
Education: Primary	Less than 5%	Over 50%	7. Low standards of education
Secondary	30-45%	15-40%	8. Crippled by debt and/or corruption
Tertiary	50-65%	10-20%	
GNP	High	Low	

WEATHER ACCORDING TO THE ANCIENT GREEKS

Frigid, temperate and torrid aren't just descriptive terms from a Readers' Wives column, these were definitions used by Aristotle to divide the world into climatic zones. He, like all the Ancient Greeks, believed that civilised people could only live in the temperate zone (into which fell Greece). Most of Europe and the north was part of the harsh 'frigid' zone, while most of Africa and points south and east were considered torrid. Nowadays, the world is still mapped out by climate, but based on a more detailed system laid out by German climatologist Wladimir Köppen and illustrated by his student Rudolph Geiger in 1928. Köppen divided the world into six basic zones: A (tropical humid), B (dry), C (mild mid-latitude), D (severe mid-latitude, continental), E (polar) and, added later, H (highland). All five classifications can be found in the continent of North America: eg A, Florida; B, Arizona; C, LA; D, Chicago; E, Nunavut, Canada.

12 EXAMPLES OF BRITISH COASTAL FEATURES CAUSED BY EROSION AND DEPOSITION

1.	The coast of South Devon	Headlands and bays	Bands of resistant and less resistant rock alternate; the softer bands are worn away to form bays separated by headlands of the harder rock.
2.	The 'White Cliffs' of Dover	Cliffs	Wave action at the base of the land causes a notch to be cut. The overhang is weathered away, leaving a sharp face.
3.	Paviland Caves	Caves	The sea attacks weaknesses in the cliffs and widens them to form caves.
4.	Monk's Cave, Aberystwyth	Blowholes	Air pressure trapped in caves by wave action weakens the roof, causing holes to be blown through. Waves can be pushed up through the holes at high velocity, resulting in spectacular blasts of water.
5.	Nash Point, Glamorgan	Wave-cut platforms	As erosion continues, the cliff face retreats, leaving a fairly level area of rock exposed at low tide.
6.	Durdle Door, Dorset	Sea arches	When two caves back into each other from each side of a headland.
7.	The Needles, Isle of Wight	Sea stacks	When sea arches collapse in the middle.
8.	North Cornwall, Aldeburgh, Blackpool	Beaches	The main feature of coastal deposition, varying from tiny beaches in inlets and pebbly beaches to long sweeps of sand exposed at low tide.
9.	Shapinsay, Orkneys	Storm beaches	Heavy seas, a long fetch and heavy tides pile up boulders, rocks and pebbles. The resultant ridge is often a very steep beach (up to 45 degrees).
10.	Orford Ness, Suffolk	Spits	Strips of sand or pebbles extending from one side of a bay, deposited where tides meet with calmer waters.
11.	St Agnes, Isles of Scilly	Bars or shoals	A spit extends out across a bay, closing it off and leaving the water behind as a shallow lagoon or sea marsh.
12.	Chesil Beach	Tombolos	When ridges of deposited material join islands to the mainland.

Since our default topic of conversation is nearly always the weather, it makes sense to try to understand what 'makes' the weather. The hydrological cycle may not sound very exciting, but armed with its revolutions, we can look out of the window and begin to understand why it always seems to be raining, sunny or cloudy.

Weather is all about the relationship between water and temperature and refers to the day-to-day variation of atmospheric and climatic conditions at any one place over a short period of time. Climate is the term that describes the general weather conditions over a 30-year period – temperature, wind and amount of rainfall. The hydrological cycle is the continuous merry-go-round whereby fresh water is circulated between the Earth's surface and its atmosphere. It evaporates from the oceans and it is carried by winds until eventually it falls back to the Earth as precipitation (the geographer's umbrella term for rain, snow, sleet, mist and fog). For the rain that goes into the ocean (about 77%) the cycle is therefore completed; if it falls on land, it filters through the Earth's surface back into rivers or down to stores of groundwater; from here it will eventually evaporate back into the atmosphere. If this sounds like a gentle, low-key process, consider the figures: during this cycle, about 380,000 cubic kilometres of water are evaporated every year.

Given that 97% of the world's water is stored in the oceans (which cover 70% of the world's surface), it would take a million years for every drop to pass through the hydrological cycle. Along the way, clouds, wind and other weather features are involved in the party.

WORK IT OUT

Identify the odd one out:
- Stratocumulus
- Stratus
- Cirrostratus
- Cumulus
- Cumulonimbus

Answer on page 312

PLACING THE STORM

There's nothing more satisfying than when an old wives' mantra just happens to be true. Counting the number of seconds between the flash of lightning and the sound of thunder and coming up with how far away the lightning (and therefore the heart of the storm) was at that moment, turns out to have reasonable rationale behind it. The only trouble is the unit used...

We equated seconds with miles but, in fact, a gap of three seconds represents about a kilometre, while five seconds has to pass before we could say the lightning was a mile away. The reason, of course, lies in the speed of sound.

Thunderstorms are usually caused by an intense heating-up of the ground surface during summer: the warm air rises rapidly to form vertical cumulonimbus clouds, in which electrical charges (negative ions) accumulate. When the cloud can take no more, the electricity is discharged back to the ground in the form of lightning, with or without the characteristic crack. The air it passes through heats up so intensely that it expands rapidly, creating shock waves that are heard by observers as a crash or a rumble of thunder: obviously, the closer the observers, the quicker the sound waves reverberate through them.

CARBON FUELS CRISIS?

Back in the days of O Level Geography, we learned that by 2020, 80% of the world's energy resources would have been exhausted, leaving us perilously close to a fuel-free age where we had nothing to call upon but the power of the wind, the waves and the sun. Since then, energy consumption in both the developed and undeveloped world has risen above all expectations and we hover ever closer to that 2020 tipping point. Yet the predictions all those years ago were before the discoveries of the Russian oil and gas reserves, and only recently we were told that the North Sea probably harbours many times as much oil again as had previously been thought.

Not that this discovery does us much good: with the global demand for 87 million barrels a day being met by the supply of only five million barrels, we lurch from one oil barrel price crisis to another. So, what does all this teach us post-O Level geographers? When it comes to what's under the surface of the Earth, we still don't know the scale of the reserves down there, we still don't have a failsafe, affordable way of extracting it and we are still fighting wars and peddling misery because of it.

GET OUT THE STICKY-BACKED PLASTIC

A crucial part of studying the weather at school involved knowledge of, construction and analysis surrounding a Stevenson screen – that integral component of a school weather station. Put simply: it was a white-painted wooden cabinet or box with louvred sides and floor, a hinged door facing north (to reduce the number of solar rays entering when readings were being taken) and an insulated roof that was mounted so that the thermometers inside were about 1.5m above the ground. Inside there were maximum and minimum thermometers to measure air temperature, and wet and dry bulb thermometers for measuring humidity. All of which enabled it to record the weather as accurately as possible: the white paint reflected away radiation, the roof insulated the interior and the louvres ensured ventilation. We owed its existence to British engineer and meteorologist Sir Thomas Stevenson, father of Robert Louis Stevenson, author of *Treasure Island*.

AIN'T NO MOUNTAIN HIGH ENOUGH

The highest mountain ranges in the world were formed during the relatively recent Alpine orogeny, (mountain-building period), between five and 20 million years ago. Counter-intuitively, the taller a mountain is, the younger it is – putting the Himalayas (along with 12 of the world's 13 highest mountains) firmly in kindergarten.

No less pipsqueak are the other Alpine ranges, the eponymous European Alps, the Andes of South America and the Western Cordillera off the west coast of North America. Older mountain ranges tend to be further inland and, having formed tens of millions of years before, are more worn down. To be a mountain range, a landmass has to be at least 330m/1,000ft above the surrounding topography,

but because we now measure topography as being above sea level, the crown of once-tallest mountain (Everest) was awarded wrongly. The world's tallest mountain is actually Mauna Kea, the highest point on the island of Hawaii. Although it measures only a puny 4,206m/13,799ft above sea level, this dormant volcano is a stratospheric 10,200m/33,465ft high when measured from the seabed to its peak – nearly three quarters of a mile taller than Everest. Hence the emerging convention of 'tall' (from bottom to top) versus 'high' (from sea level to summit). Now described as the highest mountain, Everest is nearly as high again as Mauna Kea, and growing at the rate of an exciting 4mm a year.

TYPES OF WIND

Bise	Dry, cold, northerly wind from Switzerland.
Chinook	Famous North American warm wind.
Doldrums	Trick entry... doldrums are the complete absence of winds that occurs when the trade winds converge.
Dust devil	Columns of brown, dust-filled air caused by warm air rising dozens of feet on dry, clear days, and travelling over the ground at up to 60mph. The gentler, junior sibling of a tornado.
Fohn	Notorious European Alpine warm wind.
Jetstream	High-altitude winds (also westerlies).
Mistral	Unpleasant cold wind in Mediterranean France – the maddening effect of which can be mounted as a legal defence in a murder trial.
Monsoon	Winds in South Asia that flow from ocean to continent during the summer (from southwest, April-Oct) and from continent to ocean in the winter (from northeast, Oct-April). It is the summer monsoons that grab the headlines, carrying huge amounts of water and causing deadly floods in low-lying river valleys and deltas. However, crops depend on the rain it brings.
Polar easterlies	Dry, cold prevailing winds blowing in from high-pressure areas of the polar highs at north and south poles, from east to west – unlike the westerlies, they are often weak and irregular.
Sirocco	Infamous warm wind from the Sahara that blows red dust across the Mediterranean and is associated with storms and heavy rains that reach their peak in autumn and spring.
Tornado	Extremely violent revolving storm with swirling, funnel-shaped clouds, caused by a rising column of warm air propelled by a strong wind, which can rise to a great height while having a diameter of only a few hundred metres or less. They move with wind speeds of 100-300mph, with devastating consequences.
Trade winds	Winds that blow towards the equator from the northeast and southeast (caused when hot air rises at the equator and air from north and south moves to take its place). Because of the Earth's west-to-east rotation, the winds are deflected towards the west and move north and south about five degrees with the seasons.
Westerlies	Winds flowing at mid-latitudes (30-60 degrees north and south of the Equator), west to east around the Earth. Unlike trade winds, they are very variable and produce stormy weather.

Before Mount Everest was discovered, what was the highest mountain on Earth?

Answer on page 312

AIN'T NO RIVER DEEP ENOUGH?

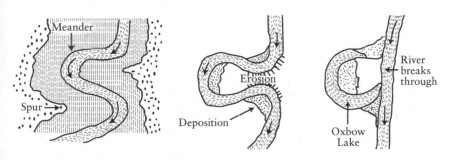

Oxbow Lakes

There is something beautifully logical about the actions of a river – we always know its direction: from higher ground to lower, but its speed depends on the volume of water and the gradient of the slope. Throughout its course, a river is weighing up its energy input with its energy output, gaining energy from the volume and force of the water and losing it through friction with the land surface, picking up eroded matter as it goes.

When the river, by dint of lessening downhill pitch or volume, goes into deficit energy, it reduces its burden with deposition (when movement slows down, allowing the sediment to settle) in an attempt to regain its previous equilibrium between energy input and output. Everything about a river's long profile – from the dramatic interlocking spurs of its upper reaches to the flood plains and oxbow lakes of its lower meanderings – can be explained by this constant hunt for balance.

A quick glance at the features of the river can also position it approximately in relation to its source: fast, furious and steep puts it close, makes it young and impetuous; meandering gently across a less dramatic landscape, softly laying down the baggage it has collected throughout its life. Now that's what you call deep.

CLOUD CLASSIFICATION

It is nigh on impossible to recollect what the different cloud-types are called – they are classified according to the height at which they occur and their shape, but their names are confusing at best, insanely irritating at worst. Our only hope is to come up with an equally irritating mnemonic, starting at the top: 'Cirrus sings Alto then puts on his Stratus aftershave to Cum back upstairs'.

High clouds	• Formed of ice crystals • Have a base between 18,000 and 45,000 feet	*Cirrus* – white filaments – 'mares' tails'.
		Cirrocumulus – small rippled elements – 'mackerel sky'.
		Cirrostratus – transparent sheet, often with a suggestion of halo; sometimes interpreted as harbinger of storm.
Medium clouds	• Formed of water droplets and ice crystals • Have a base between 6,500 and 23,000 feet	*Altocumulus* – layered, rippled elements, generally white with some shading.
		Altostratus – thin layer, drab, grey, allows sun to appear as if through opaque glass; potential to produce rain and snow.
Low clouds	• Usually formed of water droplets • Have a base below 6,500 feet	*Stratus* – wispy cloud of fog with uniform base that hangs a few hundred feet above ground and often brings drizzle.
		Stratocumulus – the 'classic' cloud: layered, series of rounded rolls, generally white with some shading, don't usually bring rain.
		Nimbostratus – thick layer, low base, dark; rain, sleet or snow may be continuous.
Vertical clouds	• Start low, but form vertically	*Cumulus* – large, billowy 'cotton puff' clouds with dark bottoms and bright tops that can reach up to 10,000 feet; may produce brief showers.
		Cumulonimbus – towering thunderheads, dark on the bottom with white 'anvil-tops' than can extend to 50,000 feet. Often produce lightning and heavy precipitation, including hail.

War. God's way of teaching Americans geography.

Ambrose Bierce, US journalist

UNDERSTANDING ORDNANCE SURVEY MAPS

It was a major part of Geography study at school, and crucial to those mud-soaked Duke of Edinburgh's Award trips, but ever since then most of us have been put off map-reading by the sheer nerdiness of the pursuit. By now, most of us wouldn't have much of a clue how to orientate with a proper map (sat nav or sad nav? You decide) but it doesn't take much to unlock the secret of the OS map and, as soon as you do, your inner nerd emerges – because these maps are fascinating if you know how to use them.

For grid references, a crucial mnemonic is that you must go along the corridor before you go up the stairs – ie to establish a grid reference look at the bottom left-hand corner of the grid square… note down the horizontal grid reference first, then the vertical one. That gives you a four-figure reference number to the grid square – say, 6253. For a six-figure reference, go along the corridor within the square, remembering that there are 10 subdivisions, and then up the stairs

again – if your destination is bang in the middle of the square, your grid reference would now read 625335.

To calculate distance, a trusty piece of string is your ally – hold it to one end of your route, wiggle it along the path of your route and pinch it where the route ends. Then measure your length – say it's 10cm. On a 1:12.5 000 map, where 4cm equates to 1km. Your route would therefore be 2.5km. As for contour lines, they couldn't be simpler: the lines join points of equal height above sea level. The difference between one line and the next is usually 5m (10m in mountainous areas) so the closer together the lines, the steeper the hill – they're numbered too with, surprise, surprise, the bigger the number, the higher the topography.

Then, when you've sorted out what all the symbols and markings mean (which tends to vary from map to map) and found out that this is no treasure map (X does not mark the spot, it marks a Roofed Structure Seed, whatever that may be), it's away we go!

Longest in the UK	The Severn, Wales and England	220 miles long
Shortest in the UK	The Morar, Scotland	Quarter of a mile, from Loch Morar to the Atlantic, an area famous for being the location of *Local Hero*
Longest in the world	The Nile, Egypt	4,100 miles long
Shortest in the world	D River, Oregon, US	120ft – links Devil's Lake with the Pacific Ocean
Largest in the world (by volume)	The Amazon, Brazil	Accounts for 20% of the world's total river flow: discharge at mouth is approximately seven million cubic feet per second
Touches more countries than any other	The Danube	Begins in Germany, emerges into the Black Sea, passing through 10 countries en route: Austria, Slovakia, Hungary, Croatia, Serbia, Montenegro, Romania, Bulgaria, Moldova and Ukraine
Deepest in the UK	River Usk, Wales	The deepest at its mouth than any other, even the Thames, rising by up to 30ft between high and low tides
Widest in the world	The Amazon, Brazil	During the dry season, it is a mere seven miles across but sometimes, during the rainy season, it reaches widths of 28 miles – wider than the English Channel between Dover and Calais. It is also an entirely unbridged river...
Greatest drop	Yarlung-Zangbo River, China	Cutting along the northern foothills of the Himalayas, this previously undocumented newcomer to the league tables then drops an awesome 5,000m from the high Tibetan plateau, falling from 5,070m in the west to 155m in the east

URBAN MORPHOLOGY

Urban morphology does not describe the habit of townspeople to morph into depressed versions of their earlier selves, but the pattern of a city's regions. These, we learned from our textbooks, tended to fall into the following regions: the central business district or CBD, also known as 'downtown', which was the commercial centre that contained the main shopping centres, offices and government departments, with high rateable values decreasing outwards from the peak-value intersection. Next up were residential regions, industrial areas and 'twilight zones' (looks like we're back to those depressed townspeople again) which were 'regions of decaying industry and housing, usually fairly close to the city centre, with high crime rates, racial conflict, vandalism, more disease, higher mortality and lower levels of literacy'. Nowadays, of course, life isn't that simple – our business parks, light industrial estates and brownfield housing developments are turning twilight zones into areas of high yuppiedom, where the only conflict is between shared Wi-Fi zones and poop-scooping wars.

MILLION CITIES

'Million cities' were conurbations with over a million residents, suffering from that rather more dramatically named geographical term, 'population explosion'; cities like Bombay, Calcutta, Mexico City or São Paolo. It was a phrase to strike fear into every Geography reviser, as we were meant to write knowledgeably about one in our exams. Despite many Western cities having their own population explosion, the term 'million cities' was applied more often to those cities in less developed countries which we then foolishly called Third World countries – a term that no longer exists, as it was part of the classification of countries during the Cold War. 'First World' countries were those aligned with the US, 'Second World' were those countries siding with the Soviet Union and 'Third World' were originally the nations historically non-aligned, though the term soon came to mean a poorer or less developed country.

Once the USSR was dissolved, such lines of alliance were lost, leading to the less evocative (though admittedly less judgemental) acronyms LEDC (Less Economically Developed Countries) and MEDC (you guessed it, More Economically Developed Countries). Second World is now a virtual reality world created for online users – somewhere a lot more exciting than a creaking Communist curtain.

Climate is what we expect,
weather is what we get.
Mark Twain, US author

A GAME OF CONSEQUENCES:
WHAT MEANS WHAT IN PLATE TECTONICS?

Volcano
Where: Destructive margin or boundary, involving oceanic crust.
Action: Plates move towards each other, creating a subduction zone where the denser plate is pushed down by the other. The friction produced will melt the descending plate, forcing heat to rise and magma to force its way to the surface through cracks.
Result: Water tries its best to cool down the expelling magma from the outside in, sculpting the rock into a smooth and recognisable inverted funnel of rock.

Fold mountains
Where: Destructive margin between lighter continental crust.
Action: Plates meet and push together.
Result: Pressure causes crust to crumple upwards.

Sea-floor spreading or continental drift
Where: Constructive margin.
Action: Plates move apart, exposing the mantle and allowing the hot magma within to bubble up.
Result: Where magma hardens, new crust forms, usually as mid-ocean ridges, often in the form of a chain of volcanoes, or rift valleys when on dry land.

Earthquake
Where: Conservative margin.
Action: Plates move side by side – called a conservative margin.
Result: A build-up of pressure causes an earthquake.

Faults
Action: Strains and stresses within mantle cause plates to crack or fracture along lines of weakness.
Result: Rocks on either side of the fracture move, creating a normal fault, where one side of land slides down more than the other, a horst block, where land between parallel faults rises, or a rift valley, where the land sinks between parallel faults.

TIS THE SEASON TO BE JOLLY

The relationship between the change in the position of the Earth's axis in relation to the sun lies at the root of our seasons. As the Earth orbits the sun, its axis always points in the same direction – so if you stood in the same place at the summer solstice and at the winter solstice, the sun would be higher in the sky for the summer and much lower for the latter. Since the Earth is tilted (23.5 degrees) the sun's rays hit the southern and northern hemispheres unequally, so when its rays hit one half directly (summer), the other hemisphere receives diffused rays (winter). When it is summer in the northern temperate latitudes, it is winter in the southern temperate latitudes, and vice versa. Tropical regions only have two seasons: the wet and the dry, while monsoon areas around the Indian Ocean complicate matters by having three: the cold, the hot and the rainy. A season itself is merely defined as a period of the year that has a characteristic climate. Differences between the seasons are more marked inland than near the coast, where the sea has a moderating effect on temperatures – so, deeply inland places like Chicago suffer great extremes between scorching hot summers and icy winters.

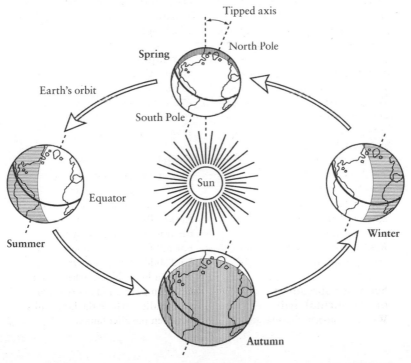

III

ENGLISH LITERATURE

Literature is where I go to explore the highest and lowest places in human society and in the human spirit, where I hope to find not absolute truth, but the truth of the tale, of the imagination and of the heart.

Salman Rushdie, author

BLANKET EXAM QUESTIONS FOR... PROSE

- .... is an important character in this book. What are his/her main features? How do you react to him/her?
- .... is a hero/villain. How is he/she presented in the novel?
- ....'s character changes throughout the novel. Is this for better or for worse?
- Why does .... behave as he/she does?
- Imagine that you are .... at an important point in the novel (or at the end). How would you explain what is happening and your reactions?

Just slot in your literary character of choice and away you go. It's possibly not worth doing this for that Jilly Cooper blockbuster hiding on your bedside table.

SIGN OF THE TIMES

We were probably blissfully unaware of it at the time but, even in the hallowed cloisters of our classrooms, we weren't just being crammed with apparently useless knowledge, we were educational lab rats, often made to run the treadwheels of current educational or political thinking. Some remember endless discussions, framed as composition or comprehension or an introduction to philosophy, about nuclear proliferation and living under the Shadow of the Bomb. Others remember being asked to compare and contrast the 'absurd' social mores of Jane Austen and Oscar Wilde with modern-day relaxations, never suspecting that the outside world was actually just as hidebound by social convention and delineation.

Racial prejudice was another hot topic for literature: where the racism shown in *Of Mice and Men* by John Steinbeck was compared with that shown in *Passage to India* by EM Forster, both of which seemed as far away from reality as each other. Meanwhile, up in Toxteth, houses burned and blows were exchanged between black and white. The final theme, so prevalent in the late 70s, throughout the 80s and into the 90s, was paranoia about the future, expressed in the choice of set texts like *Animal Farm* or *1984* by George Orwell and *Brave New World* by Aldous Huxley. With the benefit of hindsight, this book choice had to have been motivated more by the bleakly dystopian vision shared by most of the educational establishment than by their literary merits alone. Meanwhile, us schoolchildren carried on, twitching our tails and performing our occasional tricks, like any good caged animal.

HOW TO READ A BOOK

In our school days, we were taught that our reading would be more rewarding if we took stock of the following elements:

• Plot
What are the main points of the story? Where do significant changes occur? When are new characters introduced? How many different plotlines are there? How are they connected?

• Characters
What are your first impressions? Do these change as you read on? Which characters are not the main protagonists but are important to the story in other ways? Who do you like and dislike?

• Themes
What are the important themes (broad ideas or types of experience) running through the novel? Are they the usual – love, hatred, conflict, relationships – or something very specific to this book? How do they develop? Do you think the writer is trying to make a point? Has it worked?

• Setting
Is there relevance to the historical time/era in which the novel is set? Is that setting contemporaneous to the author? Is the novel set in particular place(s)? How does the writer help you to imagine this? Is the setting convincing?

• Style, form and structure
For some books, this can be difficult to nail, but for others this is glaringly idiosyncratic: does the way it is written have an impact on you? Dialogue – is it used effectively? Are there ways in which individual characters speak that you think are memorable?

• Personal response
How do you respond to the book? Do you want to hurl it across the room or go back to the beginning and read it all over again? To what sort of person, if at all, would you now recommend the book?

WORK IT OUT

Unscramble these well-known writers:
- Do nasty harm
- My noble rite
- Toilets
- No legal parade

Answer on page 312

No easier to understand, even after all these years...

WHEN that Aprilis, with his showers swoot*,   *sweet
The drought of March hath pierced to the root,
And bathed every vein in such licour,
Of which virtue engender'd is the flower;
When Zephyrus eke with his swoote breath
Inspired hath in every holt* and heath   *grove, forest
The tender croppes* and the younge sun   *twigs, boughs
Hath in the Ram his halfe course y-run,
And smalle fowles make melody,
That sleepen all the night with open eye,
(So pricketh them nature in their corages*);   *hearts, inclinations
Then longe folk to go on pilgrimages,
And palmers for to seeke strange strands,
To *ferne hallows couth* in sundry lands;   *distant saints known*
And specially, from every shire's end
Of Engleland, to Canterbury they wend,
The holy blissful Martyr for to seek,
That them hath holpen*, when that they were sick.   *helped

Befell that, in that season on a day,
In Southwark at the Tabard as I lay,
Ready to wenden on my pilgrimage
To Canterbury with devout corage,
At night was come into that hostelry
Well nine and twenty in a company
Of sundry folk, *by aventure y-fall   *who had by chance fallen
In fellowship*, and pilgrims were they all,   *into company
That toward Canterbury woulde ride.
The chamber, and the stables were wide,
And *well we weren eased at the best.*   *we were well provided
And shortly, when the sunne was to rest,   *with the best
So had I spoken with them every one,
That I was of their fellowship anon,
And made forword* early for to rise,   *promise
To take our way there as I you devise*.   *describe, relate

Chaucer, *The Prologue, The Canterbury Tales*

As schoolchildren, comparing prose often ended up being less about understanding the different texts and more about realising that literature has universal themes. Take a popular exam question for those who studied both *The Merchant of Venice* and Harper Lee's *To Kill A Mockingbird*: 'Compare the various types of prejudice found in both and say how you react to them'.

Here's how you should have responded. First, look at *The Merchant of Venice*, with its racial and religious prejudice. Shylock is Jewish, despised by his fellow Venetian merchants, who are Christian, but suddenly needed by them when he can lend them money. Shylock 'helps' them, but for his own ends and revenge; not a sympathetic character, his own daughter runs off and marries a Christian; he is left alone.

Then let's shift to the racial and able/disabled prejudice in *Mockingbird*, where Atticus Finch is trying to stem the prejudice shown to Tom Robinson, while his children Jem and Scout battle their own prejudices concerning Boo Radley. While tragedy stalks the grown-ups, the children resolve their issues: Jem and Scout discard their prejudices and end up having their lives saved by Boo Radley. The difference between the two texts is that *Mockingbird* characters are redeemed by their transcending of prejudice; Merchant characters give in to prejudice on all sides – even our 'heroes' Bassanio and Antonio never repent their anti-Semitism, while Shylock, their victim, is not ennobled by his suffering but is a mean old buzzard who (almost) deserves everything he gets.

At the end of answering the question, even the most sheltered of schoolkids would now have been aware that it wasn't just in the playground that people were horrible to each other, and that it was far better – and morally more rewarding – to challenge prejudice than to play along with it. *Et voilà* – life lesson learned.

QUOTE UNQUOTE

A book is a fragile creature. It suffers the wear of time, it fears rodents, the elements, clumsy hands.

Umberto Eco, Italian novelist

Macbeth

- **In one line:** a furious film-noir drama of ambition, success, treachery and the disintegration of a once-brave but fatally flawed man.
- Superstition dictates that those involved in *Macbeth* refer to it only as 'The Scottish Play' because of the ill-luck that surrounds it. In its first staging, the boy who played Lady Macbeth died backstage; in 1849, more than 30 people were killed in a riot started by a fight between two actors and in one week in 1934, four actors playing Macbeth fell ill.
- It was written as a blatant suck-up to James I, after the shock of the Gunpowder Plot, as a morality tale against trying to topple a king.
- Macbeth's rank as Thane (of Cawdor) is a real title, awarded for military service. It is still a live title, and the present (25th) Thane of Cawdor and his wife were named as one of *Vogue*'s Best Dressed Couples in 2007...
- **The quote:** 'Out, damned spot! Out, I say!'

JANE AUSTEN: SPINSTER OR SIREN?

Neither, though she died single. Jane Austen's own life mirrored the harsh economic realities faced by so many of her heroines: whereby true love is a weak and feeble force if it does not come hand-in-hand with money and prospects. Neither she nor her sister Cassandra married – Cassandra, because her fiancé died in the West Indies, mere months before they were to have married, and Jane because she had been frustrated in love at the tender age of 20.

When her family was settled and still reasonably prosperous under the aegis of her beloved father's living from the church, Jane met Tom Lefroy, the quietly intelligent and charming cousin of some neighbours. Even on scanty evidence, there seems little doubt that they formed an attachment, but his family, knowing how penniless he was and how few prospects Jane had, soon removed him from any further entanglement and sent him back to Ireland (where he later became Lord Chief Justice).

It was a theme that recurs in her novels – between Edward and Elinor in *Sense and Sensibility*, for example – but unlike those fictional situations, Jane never saw Tom Lefroy again, and so never got the second chance that she bestows on her heroines.

THE GLOBE

The Globe Theatre as it would have appeared in Shakespeare's time.
The theatre was built c.1598 on the South Bank of the Thames. After a
painstaking reconstruction, the modern day Globe opened its doors to
the public in 1997, just yards from the site of the original building.

HOUSTON, WE HAVE A PROBLEM

All's Well That Ends Well, Measure for Measure and *Troilus and Cressida*
are seldom studied pre-A level – possibly because there is an element
of moral ambiguity about them that would sit uneasily with a teacher
attempting to guide young minds onto the straight and narrow. They're not
all comedy, they're not tragedies and there's no outright moral resolution
at the end: our heroes and heroines are sometimes equivocal in their
heroism; the sinners don't necessarily repent. For this reason, scholars of
Shakespeare have often got around the issue by calling them the 'Problem
Plays' – which certainly calls a spade a spade. Nowadays, we would
probably label them black comedies or satires, where any moralising is
suspended in favour of some tongue-in-cheek treatment of the darker sides
of human nature: corruption, greed, stupidity and cupidity.

HOW TO WRITE A LITERATURE ESSAY

- **Read the question** and answer relevantly.
- **Start with an introduction** that shows you have read the question, and you know which titles or texts you are going to use. Indicate that you are now setting the scene in which to answer that question.
- **Make your point**, develop the point by making clear what you mean; back up your point with apposite quotations or references.
- **Order your ideas** into a seamless flow, not a mismatched jumble of random thoughts.
- **Be original** – do not be afraid of your own opinion but back it up with textual evidence.
- **Show off with other source material**, background knowledge and your own masterful use of language – your subjects aren't the only writers on trial.
- **Hang on to the basics** of punctuation, with spelling, grammar, a confident style, sentences of varying lengths and an understanding of pace.
- **Know the medium being discussed** – place it within the context of its time.
- **Finish with a conclusion** that harks back to the introduction.

TWEEDLE-DI AND TWEEDLE-DUM

When you go to a concert and see a conductor marking time with his baton, you think nothing of it. Rhythm in poetry is simply marking time. The baton equivalent is the meter – the series of / and x above the word, or, put simply 'di' and 'dum'. So the phrase: 'The ball it bounces down the stairs' would be marked like this:

x	/	x	/	x	/	x	/
The	ball	it	boun-	ces	down	the	stairs
Di	dum	di	dum	di	dum	di	dum

And all the technical stuff is simply different manifestations of di and dum. The labels for meter combine the name of a kind of foot (such as iambic or trochaic, ie x / is an iamb and / x is a trochee) with the number of feet in each line: dimeter for two feet, trimeter for three, tetrameter, pentameter, hexameter, heptameter, etc. So the rhythm above is iambic tetrameter – di dum di dum di dum. Not so dumb, but not rocket science either.

I was working on the proofs of one of my poems all morning, and I took out a comma. In the afternoon I put it back again.

Oscar Wilde, British playwright

WORK IT OUT

Name the poet and poem from these famous lines:
1. A snake came to my water trough
2. Bent double, like old beggars under sacks
3. Do not go gentle into that good night
4. Earth hath not anything to show more fair
5. How do I love thee? Let me count the ways
6. I met a traveller from an antique land
7. Macavity's mystery cat: he's called the hidden paw
8. O my love's like a red, red rose
9. Quinquireme of Ninevah from distant Ophir
10. Season of mists and mellow fruitfulness
11. The curfew tolls the knell of parting day
12. Tyger! Tyger! burning bright
13. What is this life if, full of care

Answers on page 312

IT DOES WHAT IT SAYS ON THE TIN

A colourful passage in *Measure for Measure* provides the perfect example of Shakespeare's brilliant skill at choosing character names:

'First, here's young Master Rash, he's in for a commodity of brown paper and old ginger... Then there is here one Master Caper, at the suit of Master Threepile the mercer... Then have we here young Dizzy, and young Master Deepvow, and Master Copperspur, and Master Starvelackey the rapier-and-dagger man, and young Dropheir that killed lusty Pudding, and Master Forthright the tilter, and brave Master Shoetie the great traveller, and wild Halfcan that stabbed Pots, and I think forty more...'

OFF BY HEART

A metrical feet mnemonic

Trochee trips from long to short
From long to long in solemn sort
Slow Spondee stalks; strong foot! Yet ill able
Ever to come up with Dactyle trisyllable.
Iambics march from short to long; -
With a leap and a bound the swift Anapaests throng;
One syllable long, with one short at each side,
Amphibrachy's haste's with a stately stride;
First and last being long, middle short, Amphimacer
Strikes his thundering hoofs like a proud high-bred Racer.

Samuel Taylor Coleridge, 1806

WRITE ABOUT WHAT YOU KNOW

We were always told to write about what we knew in our English Lang lessons, but how did this translate to the writers we studied in English Lit? George Orwell's *1984* was obviously a bleak futuristic fantasy, given that he wrote it in 1948. But it was also clearly rooted in Orwell's World War II experiences. Not only was Room 101 (the most feared room at the Ministry of Love and the scene of Smith's ultimate downfall) named after an actual conference room at BBC Broadcasting House, but there are also parallels throughout with the rhetoric and politics surrounding the end of the war and the first encroachments of the Cold War. The poverty and exhaustion of post-war Britain is the model for the grind and deprivation of permanently-at-war Oceania; and the Senate House, where the Ministry of Information was housed during the war, was clearly the model for Smith's place of employment, Minitrue, the Ministry of Truth.

Luckily, although a recent article said that in 1894 it was predicted London's streets would be buried under nine feet of manure within 50 years, living through 1984 ourselves reassured us that though authors wrote about what they knew at the time, they didn't have a clue about what would be the true horrors of the 80s.

(Or, how to make yourself sound as if you know what you're talking about)

Alliteration	Repetition of same consonant sounds for effect – 'the great, grey-green, greasy Limpopo river' (Kipling)
Antithesis	Construction in which words are opposed but balanced – 'For many are called, but few are chosen' – (Bible, Matthew 22:14)
Assonance	When vowel sounds rhyme – 'Tyger! Tyger! burning bright' (William Blake)
Caesura	Pause in the... middle of the line
Couplet	Self-contained pair of rhyming lines
Diction	In poetry, the specific choice of words by the poet
Dramatic irony	Something said without the character realising its full importance
Foot	In poetry, a group of syllables in a fixed pattern (like a bar, in music)
Free verse	To particular rhyme or rhythm and no fixed structure
Hyperbole	Extreme exaggeration, for effect – 'he was as old as the hills'
Iamb	Iambic foot in meter – annotated x / or di dum
Image	One or more words, which conjure(s) an immediate impression to the senses of sight, hearing, touch, taste or scent
Litote	Positive and emphatic statement made by denying something negative – 'no mean feat'
Lyric	Poetry which is musical, with songlike qualities (originally a song accompanied by a lyre)
Metaphor	Where two things are concisely compared by saying that one is the other – 'he was a raging bull in the ring'
Meter	Rhythm or beat that comes from the number of syllables in a line
Onomatopoeia	Where the sound of a word conveys its meaning – 'crash! slithering, buzz'
Oxymoron	Contradictory or incongruous ideas placed together for effect – 'cruel to be kind'
Quatrain	Verse of four lines
Rhetoric	Declamatory language used to persuade or influence
Simile	Where a sometimes fanciful or unrealistic comparison is made, using words like or as – 'The Assyrian came down like the wolf on the fold' (Byron)
Verse	Group of lines – also known as a stanza

It was during the run-up to O Levels that we began to get a glimmer of understanding about the plurality of mankind – that there weren't just goodies and baddies but shades of grey in between. These shafts of illumination probably came to us in other areas of our studies as well, but it was in English literature that we were trained to analyse character and, in doing so, to appreciate the many and sometimes contradictory facets of personality.

So, in *Great Expectations*, we see Pip develop from pipsqueak to snob, to redeemed and devoted adopted son of Magwitch. Or, in *The Mayor of Casterbridge*, we see Michael Henchard's basic weakness of character and the consequences thereof – suffering, both deserved and undeserved. Minor characters were trickier but often more rewarding to work out. The Aged P, in *Great Expectations*, was not just memorably adorable but, we soon realised, was there both to throw Pip's own failings of character into sharp relief and to make us realise that Pip was never beyond salvation.

In *1984*, it is the initial friendliness and attractiveness of the shopkeeper Charrington and then his brutal betrayal and revelation that he is a member of the Thought Police, which is more shocking than the outright badness of Citizen Smith's interrogator O'Brien.

Luckily, the key to character analysis was simple: look at the events in which the character is involved; work out their qualities or faults; see how they affect or are affected by the plot; consider their impact on the development of other characters around them and identify key episodes or watershed moments. One inspirational teacher went further – when you think you understand a character, he declaimed, start to put them into an imaginary situation and see how they would react... so, put Sir Toby Belch into an AA meeting, or Silas Marner into the queue at the Bradford & Bingley, or *Great Expectations'* Estella into a speed-dating dinner party. When you think you know how they'd react, then you've handled the character analysis.

WORK IT OUT

In the DH Lawrence novel of the same name, who was Lady Chatterley's lover?

Answer on page 312

A CURSE UPON YOU

Cursing Shakespeare-style was one of those 'hilarious' activities we passed off as legal entertainment during our English lessons. Calling each other fat-kidneyed cankerblossoms was surely all part of our education, we reasoned. Pity the poor teacher. There's no denying, however, that our Will had a good ear for colourful language, used even by the king in *Henry IV* – 'Sblood, you starveling, you eel-skin' being one of his milder rebukes. Nowadays, Shakespearian cussin' is big business – you can buy packs of cards, log on to an 'Elizabethan Curse Generator', or just assemble customised insults from pre-packaged lists. So, next time you get a parking ticket, say this to your traffic warden, 'A pox on you, you churlish, distempered, reeky, purpled, queasy, yeasty, bunch-backed, dog-hearted rabbit-sucker!' and feel smug all day (if still £40 poorer). But always bear in mind that Shakespeare himself took the act of cursing seriously enough that he ordered one to put on his own gravestone: 'Blest by the man that spares these stones, curst be he that moves my bones.'

The Mighty Iambic Pentameter

Being able to drop into conversation the fact that if Shakespeare used a meter it was nearly always iambic pentameter is, actually, a life skill. Honest. Better still if you know what it means. Essentially the iamb is the foot of meter marked x / or di dum – with the name coming from the Latin *iambus* from the Greek word iambos meaning lame – that is, a weak step before a strong step (geddit?). It is also the most frequently used 'foot' in English verse, in lines of various lengths, and is widely believed to fit the natural rhythm of our tongue. The pentameter bit refers to the number of feet in each line – penta in this case indicating five – and was far and away Shakespeare's preferred meter in both his plays and his sonnets. Have a glance at one of Macbeth's famous speeches:

x	/	x	/	x	/	x	/	x	/	
To-	mo-	row	and	to-	mo-	row	and	to-	mo-	row

x	/	x	/	x	/	x	/	x	/	
Creeps	in	this	pet-	-ty	pace	from	day	to	day	

And hands up if you spotted the stray syllable at the end of the first line? Gold star for you: Shakespeare paid only lip service to the rules of meter and as long as he had the five basic feet, was happy to tag on extra bits and pieces at the end if he felt like it. Similarly he sometimes reversed the first foot to be a trochee (dum di or / x) – this was done for effect, to make the beginning of the line more important, as in a greeting – as in, Father! Hello! (trochee then iamb).

A CRAFTY CRAM: FIVE KEY FACTS ABOUT...

Twelfth Night

- **In one line:** Love can transform ordinary people; no disguise can hide that.
- *Twelfth Night or What You Will* is the only Shakespeare play to have a subtitle.
- **The comic characters:** Sir Toby, Sir Andrew, Maria, Malvolio and Feste – represent Elizabethan (universal) personality types in caricature: jolly knight, daffy knave, clever servant, pompous social-climber and wag.
- It is Shakespeare's most musical play – every act has one or more songs.
- **The quote:** 'If music be the food of love, play on, give me excess of it...'

WHO WAS YORICK?

Known to Hamlet, but not as well as some would have it (the actual quote is 'Alas, poor Yorick! I knew him, Horatio'). Yorick was talked about in the play as being the long-deceased court jester of Hamlet's father, who used to carry the boy Hamlet on his back in play – 'a fellow of infinite jest, of most excellent fancy'. At the time of staging, however, it was popularly supposed that Shakespeare was using poor Yorick as a way of paying homage to star Elizabethan comedian Richard Tarleton, who had been dead for the same length of time as Yorick. This tradition of paying homage to once-great comedians was repeated, slightly bizarrely, by Kenneth Branagh in his 1996 film of *Hamlet*. In a flashback during Mel Gibson's Yorick speech, equally venerated funnyman Ken Dodd is shown as Yorick, capering on all fours with a young Hamlet on his back.

FROM HACK TO HOUSEHOLD NAME

Charles Dickens, a life

Charles Dickens lies at the heart of English Literature. We may have dreaded studying him at school – well, his novels were just so much *longer* than anything by George Orwell or Harper Lee – but no pupil's life would be complete without *Great Expectations*, *David Copperfield* or *A Christmas Carol*. Dickensian names alone are worth the price of purchase: if only to imagine the fun the great man had, while writing his weekly instalments of thrilling episodes, in coming up with character names such as Chuzzlewit, Podsnap, Turveydrop and Wackford Squeers.

His own story was a Dickensian one of rags to riches. As the son of an imprisoned debtor, Charles was sent to work in a blacking factory, where he endured appalling conditions for three years, before being rescued by his released father. Such personal experiences gave him the hard edge of detail that is so celebrated in his novels – those, and his training as a journalist. After a few years as a straight journalist, Dickens began publishing sketches under the pseudonym of Boz, which then grew into *The Pickwick Papers*. They were an instant hit and Dickens never looked back. His energy was legendary – he travelled the world, lecturing against slavery in America, sired 10 children by his long-suffering wife *and* had a mistress, Ellen Tiernan, for whom he left his wife. He died of a stroke in 1870 and is buried at Westminster Abbey.

BLANKET EXAM QUESTIONS FOR POETRY

- Compare the way .... is presented in two different poems.
- What different views about .... are to be found in two of the poems you have been studying?
- How does the treatment of .... differ in these poems?
- What do you notice about the approach and the ways of expression in two poems on the subject of ....?
- Compare the ways in which Writer A and Writer B present their poems on the subject of ....

Unspoken was the command that we enter a theme other than 'love' into the blanks – there are other things in poetry besides love ....

LIFE IS JUST A BOX OF CHOCOLATES

... you never know what you're going to get (*Forrest Gump*, 1994). The same is true of Shakespeare's minor characters. The main protagonists are usually depicted in a broad dramatic sweep and you get a feel for them early on. Othello is heroic but flawed by both his arrogance and his paranoia; Lady Macbeth is a scheming monster; and Hamlet is a sensitive ditherer. But it's the minor characters that provide the surprises, not just because of their colourful names, elements of comic relief and occasionally knockabout scenes, but because it is often through them, deliberately or inadvertently, that the action plunges a certain way. Take Rosencrantz and Guildenstern in *Hamlet* – two rascals set to spy on Hamlet by Claudius and take him to England, secretly to his death. But Hamlet turns the tables and instead sends them unwittingly to their deaths. He has acted decisively, has saved his own life in a sudden change of pace from the previous soliloquising and from here on in the play has a dramatic urgency – all because of two minor, unmissed characters. Such minor players also, when originally staged, provided some low-concept catching-of-breath entertainment for the 'groundlings' (those in Elizabethan theatre who had to stand for the whole play) before a big scene requiring replenished concentration. This was Shakespeare's own little 'interval', just without the ice-cream and queues for the women's loos...

Places of literary pilgrimage

Dickens World Theme Park
Built on the site of a former
navalyard in Chatham, Kent,
where Dickens played as a boy.
Attractions include The Haunted
House of Ebenezer Scrooge and
Fagin's Den: not a workshop in
pickpocketry but a soft play area.

Shakespearience
Part of the Stratford homage, this
is aimed squarely at children with
its visually stunning 'holographic'
renditions of key scenes.
Surprisingly atmospheric and all
done in the best possible taste.

Wordsworth's Dove Cottage
Romantic poet Wordsworth
lived here, in the picturesque
village of Grasmere, from
1799 to 1808 and now the tiny
whitewashed house is a (slightly
cramped) museum. Nearby, Rydal
Mount (his family home that's

still owned by his descendants)
is also open to the public.

Jane Austen's Chawton House
After years of peripatetic living
enforced by the poverty-inducing
death of her father, Jane, her
mother and sister Cassandra were
eventually given this modest house
on her brother's estate, leaving Jane
free to get back into the swing of
her writing until she died, probably
of cancer, in 1817. It is where she
revised *Pride and Prejudice* and
Sense and Sensibility and is now
a museum and library.

Brontë sisters' Haworth Parsonage
Set in the dramatic moorland
that inspired all the Brontës, this
house was their lifelong home and
is extraordinarily well-preserved.
Opened as a museum back in
1928, it is filled with the Brontës'
possessions and notes.

COULD DO BETTER

When in his dogmatic moods he writes appalling essays, devoid of all
argument, of a sort that will catch the examiner's eye all right but will
certainly antagonise him.
**Sir Max Hastings, former editor of *The Daily Telegraph* and *Evening
Standard* and military historian
From *Could do Better*, edited by Catherine Hurley**

Sonnet: 16th century, from Italian *sonnetto*, a little sound. A lyric poem in 14 lines, usually of iambic pentameter. The Italian or Petrarchan sonnet has two parts: an octet (rhyming abbaabba) and the sestet (rhyming variously but usually cdecde). Henry Howard, Earl of Surrey, devised the form that Shakespeare then adopted and wrote 154 of, now called the Shakespearian sonnet (rhyming ababcdcd efefgg).

Limerick: 19th century, from the Irish town of Limerick. A five-lined piece of light verse, rhyming aabba and generally varying in meter between anapaestic trimeter and anapaestic dimeter. (ie di-dum-di-di-dum-di-di-dum and di-dum-dum-dum-di). Popularised by Edward Lear, who used it for nonsense verse, its simple form and swinging rhythm make it suitable for both children and humorous use.

Haiku: 9th century from Japan. A non-rhyming, non-metered poem in 17 syllables, arranged in three lines with a rigid 5-7-5 syllable distribution.

Ode: 16th century, from Latin *oda* and Greek *aiode*, a song. A long lyric poem that addresses a person, thing or place, or celebrates a notable event. Has three main forms: Pindaric (ancient Greek form with three stanzas, the last of which is unrestricted); Horatian (imitating Roman poet Horace, constant stanza form throughout, often a quatrain rhyming aabb with the first two lines longer than the third and fourth); and irregular, the most popular English form, popularised by Wordsworth.

Ballad: 14th century, through old French *balade* from Provençal *balada*, a dance or dancing song. Traditionally and primarily an oral narrative poem, often sung to a simple instrumental accompaniment and often without an acknowledged author. Developed in various ways: literary ballad with stanzas usually of four iambic lines rhyming abcb, but there is no set form; popular ballad, mainly in US and Australia, whereby famous deeds and lives were versified (harking back to original oral history tradition); and, in popular culture, the love ballad – that famous excuse for soppiness and slow-dancing.

Monologue: a poem in the form of a soliloquy, in which one person utters his or her thoughts 'aloud'.

Narrative or Epic: 16th century, from Latin *narrativus*, suitable for telling. Poetry that tells a story, from epics like Milton's *Paradise Lost* to Elizabeth Barrett

Browning's 11,000-line story *Aurora Leigh* (1857) that her husband Robert Browning called a 'novel in verse'.

Blank verse: 16th century. Unrhymed verse, almost always in iambic pentameters, introduced into England by Henry Howard, Earl of Surrey, in his translation of Virgil's *Aeneid*, and established by Milton's *Paradise Lost*. Generally divided into blocks of lines known as 'verse paragraphs'. Thought to have been booted out by free verse, but was revived by the likes of Robert Frost and TS Eliot.

Free verse: 20th century, a loan translation of French *vers libre*. Verse written without a regular metrical pattern, but regarded as verse not prose because of its rhythm and the use of such devices as imagery and concentrated language. Was developed by late-19th century poets like Rimbaud and became the dominant form of 20th century poetry. A few poets, like Walt Whitman, have combined free verse with rhyme, alliteration and lines of equal length to powerful effect: when done well, like Whitman, free verse is blindingly good; when done badly, it just looks like lazy prose.

Elegy: 16th century, from Latin *elegia* and Greek *elegeia oide*, a song of mourning. Originally applied to a poem in elegiac metre (alternating hexameter and pentameter lines) and traditionally a lamentation for the dead, often ending in a mood of calm and consolation, as if comforted by the poem itself.

Nonsense verse: late 18th century. Light verse on fantastical and improbable subjects where the humour is often emphasised by rare words and unexpected juxtapositions. Often intended for children, but often appeals to an adult sense of the ridiculous or of possibility.

WORK IT OUT

To which poet does this refer?
   My first is in poetry, but never in song
   My second's in Ireland, where I do come from
   My third is in heat, but never in cold
   My fourth is in centre, that which cannot hold
   My fifth is in second, and also in still
   My whole is a poet whose first name is Bill

Answer on page 312

- .... is an important force in this play. In what ways is it presented?
- Is the ending of the play appropriate? Have we been prepared for it in what has gone before?
- The author uses .... in this play. Consider the effect of these on your reactions to what is happening.
- Can the actions of .... be justified in this play?

Feeling like a theatre critic now? Mission accomplished.

THE ART OF THE OPENING

There are no hard and fast rules about what constitutes a good opening line – but what is undeniable is the importance of having one. 'Twas ever thus, but even more so in these days of limited attention span, intense competition and the need to make writing pay. One new author was told by her editor that he only ever read the first three lines of each submission, reasoning that if he wasn't grabbed after three lines, then he wasn't ever going to be.

Some writers go for the short, sharp shocker, like Dickens's classic opening to *A Christmas Carol*: 'Marley was dead, to begin with'. Others are more ruminative but no less shocking, such as George Orwell, another of our schoolday favourites, who started his essay *England, Your England* (written during World War II) with the words: 'As I write, highly civilised human beings are flying overhead, trying to kill me'. This idea of paradox is one that is often explored in the opening line, such as Clive James's opening to his *Unreliable Memoirs*: 'Most first novels are disguised autobiographies; this autobiography is a disguised novel'.

Then there are those writers who forsake the short and grabby opener rule of thumb for long sweeping invitations to join them on their journey through the book. Take this one: 'By all accounts, the working class is busy creating a hell on earth for itself: rubbish lies uncollected in the street, old-age pensioners are mercilessly raped whenever they venture out after dark, dying like flies in any case and their corpses left unburied, everybody in work is on strike and the rest are unemployed.' It's long, it's hyperbolic and it sounds like some bleak dystopian sci-fi novel, but it was actually written in our lifetime, being the first line of one of Auberon Waugh's columns, giving a flavour of life in Britain in 1979.

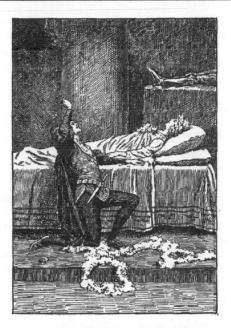

Romeo and Juliet, Act V, Scene III

A CRAFTY CRAM: FIVE KEY FACTS ABOUT...

Hamlet

- **In one line:** Insane Dane or posturing prince? Hamlet dithers but finally avenges his father's murder – everyone dies except Horatio.
- Hamlet has been performed more than any other play in the world – and translated more than any other play in the world.
- It is the longest of Shakespeare's plays.
- Did Hamlet sleep with his mother, Gertrude? The best answer was given by John Barrymore (who played Hamlet on Broadway): 'Yes, but only in the New York company'.
- **The quote:** 'To be or not to be, that is the question: Whether 'tis nobler in the mind to suffer the slings and arrows of outrageous fortune...'

THINGS THAT GO BUMP IN THE NIGHT

Ghosts in Shakespeare are nothing like their modern Halloween equivalents – no white sheets or misty wraiths, they tend to return looking just as they did at the moment of death. Banquo's ghost, in *Macbeth*, appears at the banquet with a bloody face, wounds still pouring blood. Hamlet's father, though visible only to him, has the white face and pained look of someone who has been poisoned. In common with other ghosts in Elizabethan and Jacobean literature, Shakespeare's ghosts appeared on earth with a mission in mind, either serving as a warning or an exhortation to seek revenge.

START WITH A BANG, NOT A WHIMPER

Ten opening lines from texts from our schooldays

1. 'When he was nearly 13, my brother Jem got his arm badly broken at the elbow' *To Kill a Mockingbird* by Harper Lee.
2. 'When a day that you happen to know is Wednesday starts off by sounding like Sunday, there is something seriously wrong somewhere' *The Day of the Triffids* by John Wyndham.
3. 'To the red country and part of the gray country of Oklahoma, the last rains came gently, and they did not cut the scarred earth' *The Grapes of Wrath* by John Steinbeck.
4. 'In my younger and more vulnerable years my father gave me some advice I've been turning over in my mind ever since' *The Great Gatsby* by F Scott Fitzgerald.
5. 'Now what I want is, Facts' *Hard Times* by Charles Dickens.
6. 'For a long time, I went to bed early' *In Search of Lost Time* by Marcel Proust.
7. 'There was no possibility of taking a walk that day' *Jane Eyre* by Charlotte Brontë.
8. 'It was a bright cold day in April, and the clocks were striking thirteen' *1984* by George Orwell.
9. 'It is a truth universally acknowledged, that a single man in possession of a good fortune must be in want of a wife' *Pride and Prejudice* by Jane Austen.
10. 'It was the best of times, it was the worst of times, it was the age of wisdom, it was the age of foolishness, it was the epoch of belief, it was the epoch of incredulity, it was the season of Light, it was the season of Darkness, it was the spring of hope, it was the winter of despair...' *A Tale of Two Cities* by Charles Dickens.

Despite its constant presence in classrooms across the globe, *To Kill a Mockingbird* has courted controversy since its release. Even though the moral stance is unimpeachable, the book's racial slurs, profanity and the use of rape as a plot device have ruffled small-town parents' feathers for decades. As late as the late 1990s, school districts in the Canadian provinces of New Brunswick and Nova Scotia attempted to have the book removed from school curricula, saying: 'The terminology in this novel subjects students to humiliating experiences that rob them of their self-respect and the respect of their peers... The word "nigger" is used 48 times in the novel.'

Luckily, such small-minded protests were rarely successful: Harper Lee's own response to the first sign of trouble from a school board in Virginia, in 1966, was to send a cheque for $10 to the board as a contribution towards enrolling them 'in any first grade of their choice'. But by the end of the 1960s, Lee was fed-up with defending *To Kill a Mockingbird*: she stopped writing articles or giving interviews and essentially retired from public life and, largely, from writing altogether. It hasn't stopped *Mockingbird*, however, or Ms Lee's own reputation: she has been showered with honours, including an honorary doctorate from the University of Notre Dame, during which the entire graduating class gave her a standing ovation with the book in hand. In 2007, she was awarded the Presidential Medal of Freedom by President George W Bush, who almost managed to make sense when he concluded: 'One reason *To Kill a Mockingbird* succeeded is the wise and kind heart of the author, which comes through on every page... it has influenced the character of our country for the better; it has been a gift to the entire world'.

QUOTE UNQUOTE

Books have to be read (worse luck it takes so long a time). It is the only way of discovering what they contain. A few savage tribes eat them, but reading is the only method of assimilation revealed to the West.

EM Forster, novelist

The comparison of different poems was a recurring feature in our English Lit exams and one which reached its zenith or nadir, depending on your point of view, in a recent exam where candidates were asked to compare the 'poetry' of Amy Winehouse with that of Sir Walter Raleigh. What those sly dogs of examiners realised was that, if you concentrated on comparing two or three poems, you inadvertently honed your powers of poetry observation. Just being asked to 'appreciate' one poem is daunting – comparing two seems much easier and, oh, whoopsadaisy, in doing so, you're 'appreciating' both. These were the key signposts of difference along the way: in setting (not just place but time: one may be modern, one classical), in voice, in mood, and in the use of poetical devices – meter, rhyme, choice of language, imagery and 'effects'.

That exam question in full – *as taken from Cambridge University English Literature paper, May 2008*

The Oxford English Dictionary defines 'lyric' as 'Of or pertaining to the lyre; adapted to the lyre, meant to be sung'. It also quotes Ruskin's maxim 'lyric poetry is the expression by the poet of his own feelings'.

Compare poem (a) a lyric by Sir Walter Raleigh, written 1592, with Amy Winehouse's lyrics in (b)

a) SIR WALTER RALEIGH
As you came from the holy land
Of Walsinghame,
Met you not with my true love
By the way as you came?
How shall I know your true love,
That have met many one,
As I went to the holy land,
That have come, that have gone?
She is neither white nor brown,
But as the heavens fair;
There is none hath a form so
divine In the earth or the air...
Taken from *As You Came from the Holy Land*, 1592

b) AMY WINEHOUSE
For you I was a flame
Love is a losing game
Five storey fire as you came
Love is a losing game
Why do I wish I never played
Oh, what a mess we made
And now the final frame
Love is a losing game
Played out by the band
Love is a losing hand...
Taken from *Love is a Losing Game*, 2007

Acording to a 2008 book by Gary Dexter, the legend of *Hamlet* dates back to at least 400 years before Shakespeare, to the canon of Danish historian Saxo Grammaticus, in which he expounded on the tale of Amleth, a prince of Jutland. Unlike Hamlet, Amleth doesn't hang about, but spectacularly revenges himself for his uncle's calumnies – tying down drunken courtiers as they sleep, setting fire to their palace and running his uncle through with a sword. Looking at publication dates, the English translation of Amleth's gory tale was only released in 1608 (*Hamlet* was written in 1600) so Shakespeare must have heard the tale orally or read it in French. So far, so simple. But then there's *Ur-Hamlet*, the term given to an earlier, non-Shakespeare version performed in 1594 and popularly supposed to have been written by Thomas Kyd. Recent evidence, however, has pointed to the *Ur-Hamlet* as being just an early draft written in the mid 1580s by Will himself, as a christening present for his son, born in 1585 and named, appositely enough (the spellings were interchangeable then) Hamnet. What adds poignancy is the fact that this early version had a 'happy' ending where Hamlet triumphs in his revenge. So why did the later version see Hamlet (and every other significant character, save Horatio) die a grisly death? Sadly, young Hamnet himself died, aged 11, in 1596. Was *Hamlet* then the howl of pain and rage by a bereaved father?

TOP OF THE POPS: 2006 WORLD BOOK DAY POLL

From a poll in which all British librarians voted when asked the question, 'Which book should every adult read before they die?'

1. *To Kill a Mockingbird* by Harper Lee
2. The Bible
3. *The Lord of the Rings* trilogy by JRR Tolkien
4. *1984* by George Orwell
5. *A Christmas Carol* by Charles Dickens
6. *Jane Eyre* by Charlotte Brontë
7. *Pride and Prejudice* by Jane Austen
8. *All Quiet on the Western Front* by EM Remarque
9. *Birdsong* by Sebastian Faulks
10. *The Grapes of Wrath* by John Steinbeck

IV

ENGLISH LANGUAGE

*The English language is rather like a monster
accordion, stretchable at the whim of the
editor, compressible ad lib.*

Robert Burchfield, scholar, writer and lexicographer

OUR MOTHER TONGUE

In the opener to his book *Mother Tongue,* Bill Bryson writes: 'More than 300 million people in the world speak English and the rest, it sometimes seems, try to.' The *Oxford English Dictionary* lists about 615,000 words but that is only part of the picture: slang, curses, technical and scientific language would add thousands more. Of these, Mr Bryson estimates that about 200,000 words are in common use – double those used by the French – giving us a vocabulary and nuancing of words that other languages simply don't have. No other language, for example, seems to need books of synonyms like *Roget's Thesaurus.* The trouble is that even within that richness lies complexity and double meaning: it takes the *Oxford English Dictionary* five pages and almost 15,000 words to explain all the different meanings and uses of the word 'what'. Now imagine being a teacher, trying to communicate these sorts of complexities to a classroom of sullen teenagers.

APPROPRIATE BEHAVIOUR

It's one of the great soundbites of recent years, but do you remember being tested for appropriate 'tone' in your English Language exam? Witness the advice given to revisers of English Language in the early 1980s: 'In conversation we may use the expression, "dead nice" to express approval, but it would add less than nothing to a description of a dress, a book or a person in a written essay. "Moan" is a popular alternative to "complain" – but no examiner would like to read that Juliet "moaned" when Romeo was banished, or Heathcliff (from *Wuthering Heights*) was "a bit of a moaner".' The point was to make us match the tone of our writing to the appropriate level of the question or essay we were writing – avoiding

not just slang but the wrong register (one candidate was upbraided for describing Macbeth as 'upset' after the murder of King Duncan, when 'appalled' would have been less feeble). This idea of appropriacy in language goes back hundreds of years: in the 16th century, Roger Ascham used the term 'decorum' when talking about writing style; 200 years later, Jonathan Swift put it beautifully simply: 'Proper words in proper places'. One exception was in direct speech. The sentence: 'Blimey but that was a long slow-dance for Peter and Jane', would not have worked but '"Blimey!" exclaimed Peter as he and Jane finally pulled apart, "that was a long slow-dance!"' might just have passed muster.

WORK IT OUT

Which word in the English language is most often spelled incorrectly?

Answer on page 312

THE PARTS OF SPEECH

Every name is called a **noun**
As *field* and *fountain*, *street* and *town*.
In place of noun the **pronoun** stands,
As *he* and *she* can clap their hands.
The **adjective** describes a thing
As *magic* wand and *bridal* ring.
The **verb** means action, something done.
To *read*, to *write*, to *jump*, to *run*.
How things are done, the **adverbs** tell,
As *quickly, slowly, badly, well*.
The **preposition** shows relation,
As *in* the street or *at* the station.
Conjunctions join, in many ways,
Sentences, words, *or* phrase *and* phrase.
The **interjection** cries out, 'Hark!
I need an exclamation mark!'
Through poetry, we learn how each
Of these make up the **parts of speech**.

MY WORD, MRS MALAPROP

Malapropism describes the substitution of a word in error with one that resembles it, often to comic effect, and always for a nonsensical result. The actual term takes its name from Mrs Malaprop (from the French *mal à propos* or inappropriate), a character in Sheridan's 1775 play, *The Rivals,* who boasts about her lover: 'He is the very pine-apple of politeness'. George 'Dubya' Bush is the unwitting Mr Malaprop of our era, with such classics as: 'We cannot let terrorists and rogue nations hold this nation hostile or hold our allies hostile,' or, the short but sweet: 'It will take time to restore chaos and order.'

CHECKLIST OF GOOD WRITTEN ENGLISH

- Change your style to suit both your audience and the task given to you.
- Vary your vocabulary.
- Spell your words correctly – especially those which appear in the exam material.
- Punctuate your work appropriately.
- Structure complex sentences in a variety of ways.
- Write work which demonstrates all these qualities at the appropriate length.
- Organise ideas into a logical sentence of well-formed paragraphs, also known as tell a story.
- Be sensitive to the tone and atmosphere you want to create.

THE SHORT, SHORT STORY

The short story has been around for millennia but the short, short story is a more modern twist. At school, we might have called it The Best Homework Ever but Dave Eggers, the precocious writer of *A Heartbreaking Work of Staggering Genius*, has a more profound perspective. He explained to *The Guardian* that one of his favourite writers was Lydia Davis, who often wrote stories as short as one paragraph, frequently as brief as one sentence. One of his favourites was *Samuel Johnson is Indignant*. The whole story was this: 'That Scotland has so few trees'.

The point that Lydia Davis made to Eggers was that, often when she wrote, she was seeking to answer a question so that if the explanation was as short as a line, then so be it. 'This,' said Eggers, 'freed me from the assumption that stories had to have a familiar arc and equally familiar length. So about two years ago I started jotting down notes for short, short stories, most of them taking their cue from some small moment that I watched or thought about – usually something that wouldn't or couldn't find its way into a novel, and which didn't warrant a longer story. The results are very different from Davis's – hers are brilliant acts of philosophical origami, while mine are little moments in the lives of abnormal people.' Eggers then went on to write short, short stories for *The Guardian*, which prompted them to run a short, short story competition. Meanwhile, an unbeatable über-short story has to be Ernest Hemingway's: 'For sale: baby shoes, never worn'.

First defined in the 16th century, from the Latin *comma* and Greek *komma*, meaning a piece cut off, the humble comma is flexible, useful and has many uses – and abuses. It is used, essentially, to clarify the meaning of sentences, especially those composed of many clauses, in the following ways:

● To mark off elements in a sequence or list of words where there is no conjunction (connecting word) or there is only a final conjunction: *Hair gel, sugar solution, Brylcreem and even humble soap were all ways in which the Mohican hairstyle was maintained.*
● In pairs, to indicate an aside or parenthesis – more elegant than the use of brackets: *She is, you know, a terrible tease.*
● To separate clauses of sentences: *If you want a boy to call you, you must never call him first.*
● In some cases, to introduce direct speech: *She said, 'I'd rather die than wear that ra-ra skirt,' and promptly threw it away.*
● To clarify meaning and prevent ambiguity: *Father's cooking was limited to baked beans, bubble and squeak, and bacon and eggs, boiled until they were as hard as rocks.* Or the phrase, which will forever be associated with Ms Lynne Truss in her book on punctuation: *'Eats shoots and leaves, rather than a badly behaved man who: Eats, shoots and leaves.'*

Being a coat of many colours, the comma is also used in ways not directly associated with punctuation, indicating thousands in numerals, so that a confusingly large 50405060730 becomes 50,405,060,730. Then there are the traditional, but now usually discarded, applications to addresses and salutations in letter writing so that an address is written: 20, Luxembourg Gardens and a letter is started: 'Dear Ian, I hope you enjoyed your 41st birthday party.'

QUOTE UNQUOTE

The English have no respect for their language, and will not teach their children to speak it.
George Bernard Shaw, Irish playwright

FROM ALE TO ZEITGEIST: THE DEVELOPMENT OF THE ENGLISH LANGUAGE

The boast that we have the world's richest, most eccentric, most varied and most descriptive language is an easy one to remember, but what most of us may have forgotten is how and why. Both seem simple enough to answer: we've had such a multiplicity of sources over the millennia and, unlike other nations who may have had languages in parallel (ie an invader's language beside their own native dialect) we have always been the magpies of the language sphere, borrowing and stealing words from other languages until we have ended up with a glorious pot-pourri which is neither English, in the strictest sense of the word, but nor is it anything else: it's our own unique amalgam. Here is a short and basic history lesson on its roots:

Celtic: the first language spoken in the British Isles: from bard, bog and bunny to whisky and trousers.

Latin: though the Romans ruled over us for 400 years from 55BC, their influence on our language then was slight; but later, in the 15th and 16th centuries, both Latin and Greek adaptations began to lace their way through our everyday vocabulary.

Anglo-Saxon: first came the Angles, then the Saxons, then the Danes and the Vikings, and out of this melting pot came Old English. Their contribution to our language was famously earthy and basic, too basic for one textbook writer who merely commented that 'some Anglo-Saxon words are frowned upon in polite conversation and are certainly not appropriate for examination papers'. More homely examples include father, mother, son, daughter, head, arm and bread.

Norman-French: 1066 and all that meant that Norman-French was the language of the nobles, the administration and of business; Latin was for education and religion; Old English was for the peasants. What emerged was Middle English, a class-conscious language where peasants looked after sheep, pigs, deer and cattle (from Old English words) which then became mutton, pork, venison and beef (from Norman-French words) when served up at their lords' tables.

Middle to Modern English: by the time Chaucer wrote his *Canterbury Tales*, English had become respectable. Then there was the great Vowel Shift of the 15th and 16th centuries, after which pronunciation became a little more standardised. Ever since then we have been 'borrowing' words from every language around us (schadenfreude, ad nauseam, fait accompli, debut, gymkhana, boomerang, wigwam, orange, etc) and becoming the richer for it...

PHONETIC ALPHABET

I:	I	ʊ	u:	Iə	eɪ	John & Sarah Free Materials 1996
READ	SIT	BOOK	TOO	HERE	DAY	
e	ə	ɜ:	ɔ:	ʊə	ɔɪ	əʊ
MEN	AMERICA	WORD	SORT	TOUR	BOY	GO
æ	ʌ	ɑ:	ɒ	eə	aɪ	aʊ
CAT	BUT	PART	NOT	WEAR	MY	HOW
p	b	t	d	tʃ	dʒ	k	g
PIG	BED	TIME	DO	CHURCH	JUDGE	KILO	GO
f	v	θ	ð	s	z	ʃ	ʒ
FIVE	VERY	THINK	THE	SIX	ZOO	SHORT	CASUAL
m	n	ŋ	h	l	r	w	j
MILK	NO	SING	HELLO	LIVE	READ	WINDOW	YES

The Phonetic alphabet: The smallest unit of sound that can change the meaning of a word is called a phoneme. There are 26 letters in the English alphabet and around 44 phonemes in the dialect called Standard English. This means that letters cannot represent phonemes and so other symbols are used. Each phoneme is given a symbol so that the pronunciation of any English word can be represented in writing.

WELL, I NEVER...

For most people, exams were a time of unalloyed misery – hours of being crammed into a sweaty hall when we could have been watching Wimbledon or sunbathing risquély in the park. But if only we'd read the: 'General advice for candidates taking English examinations', we might have realised what fun and exhilaration could be had from our O Levels.

'An examination has something in common with other contests – swimming, orienteering, badminton. In these, people pit themselves against the elements, or their environment, or other human beings. Examinations share with other strenuous contests the possibility that you will actually enjoy the battle. If you can manage to face it with zest this will show in the improved quality of your answers. Smoking is not allowed in the examination room, and eating is discouraged. A few boiled sweets are the most you will want in any case.'

WORK IT OUT

What do these words have in common when it comes to their spelling?

- Guarantee
- Guy
- Pirogue
- Guess
- Rogue

Answer on page 312

SWEET NOTHINGS, SWEETER EVERYTHINGS

It seemed amusing that we were expected to learn how to compose different sorts of letters at school, and gigglingly hilarious that this skill included the art of the business letter (see list of preferred business speak over old-fashioned jargon, right), but this was another of those skills that unknowingly equipped us for life. Covering letters for job applications, letters to a school to persuade them to take our children, even billets-doux for our loved ones; there is a joyful universality about the art of letter-writing, be it via email or old-fashioned snail mail.

First off, the boring stuff: date and place; yours truly or yours faithfully if you don't know the addressee's name (eg 'Dear Sir/Madam'); yours sincerely if you do know them, but you're being formal – these are little details that contextualise the letter and make everything clear. Before starting the letter, you need to think about what you want to get out of

it in the end: are you asking for something, just sharing something or declaring something? The best rule of thumb is to state clearly in the opening paragraph why the letter has been written.

Use a fresh paragraph more often than in straight prose, for the sake of clarity. Pitch the 'tone of your voice' appropriately – writing: 'Yo, babycakes!' to a potential employer will only work if you want to work for Hugh Hefner. If it's a business letter, avoid chattiness – time is precious and a professional's attention span is a delicate flower. However, the most charming personal letters are often those that are chatty and discursive, almost as if the person writing the letter were standing with you in the room.

Above all, remember that there's a reason why we like getting written letters above texts or even emails – they are rare beasts indeed, but oh so worth preserving.

BUSINESS JARGON WE WERE TOLD TO AVOID

JARGON*	Recommended in 1983*	2008 SPEAK**
In connection with your inquiry, we have to acquaint you that our practice is to prefer payment by cheque	We prefer to be paid by cheque	It's Maestro time or the bailiffs
Such employment does not involve the necessity of obtaining a certificate of fitness	A fitness certificate is not needed	We won't believe your forged documents anyway
Be good enough to advise us	Tell us	Share with us
The attention of your good selves	Your attention	Oi!
Have delivered same	Have delivered it	Have emailed it
Acquaint with	Tell	Share with you
Alternative	Other	Alternative
Anticipate	Expect	Reckon
Commence	Begin	Get underway
Consider	Think	Brainstorm
Inform	Tell	Share with you
Proceed	Go	Advance
A proportion of	Some	Whatever
Purchase	Buy	Take a loan out on
Residence	Home	Unit
To state	To say	To verbalise
Terminate	End	Let go
Utilise	Use	Utilise

* as provided by *Letts Complete Revision Study Guide 1983*
** as suggested frivolously by *The Universal Crammer*

NICE AND PRECISE

The discovery that 'nice' did not mean nice, but meant 'precise' brought a strange joy to this student of the English language; a sort of pedantic exhilaration that the need to summarise – the art of the précis – also provoked. At last, here was a required skill that we actually used every day, from infancy to senility – the human instinct to listen to something, read something or observe something and then to pick out its salient points when telling someone else about it. As we know from dinner party bores, some people are better than others at summarising pithily or re-telling a story entertainingly. To save you from becoming one such bore, here are our tips for the art of the précis.

Look at the passage – be it a work report, a long article or a dinner party anecdote and read through it fairly fast; don't stop at tricky words or concepts, at this stage, the aim is to catch the basic sense and shape of the piece. Then re-read painstakingly, ticking or underlining the points that still seem important. If there's time, jot down the points in your own words, trying to boil down the flesh of the descriptions to their bare essentials. Count up your scribblings. Remind yourself of your original aim – how do you want to angle your précis? – and then write your summary. If there's a particularly beautiful or attention-grabbing word in the original, then keep it in your summary to liven it up – but draw the line at one: the aim here is for ascetic purity not florid waxings. Got all that? Now we'll précis those tips into 25 words: Speed read, slow down. Boil down, tot up. Aim for a single pearl not a flashy choker, polish prose. Sit back. Nicely done. Precisely.

MANNERS MAKETH, MAN

As well-mannered children, we ended every meal asking: 'Please can I leave the table?' to which the baffling response came: 'I don't know – can you? You certainly may.' It was an early introduction to the can and may dilemma – the former implies a physical ability to do something, the latter implies that, having taken the physical ability to do something for granted, that the necessary permission has been given, as in: 'You may go out tonight if you can afford the time'. There is also a hint of future uncertainty, as in: 'He may play a good game of hockey, but his ankle is giving him gyp'. Can and may are also defective verbs, meaning that they lack the full range of tenses and forms – eg there is not an infinitive 'to may' nor a future tense: 'I shall can!' – so they are truly tricky little beggars. Approach with caution.

STYLE QUEENS AND FASHION MAVENS

In 1749, Lord Chesterfield wrote, in a letter to his son: 'Style is the dress of thought'. He was writing about language not clothes, but the analogy to fashion is still relevant. The concept of good versus bad writing style does change – and will go on changing. Eighteenth century 'prescriptivists' decried the habit of the ancients of repeating themselves – and vaunted 'elegant variation' instead (so that 'Shakespeare' in one line became the 'Swan of Avon' in the next); a century later, Albert Camus' 'degree zero writing' was praised for its plainness, unmarked by any flourishes of grammar or vocabulary. The encouraged view of style, when we were at school, had clear do's and don'ts (below), but in the 21st century, such dogma is dated: expression is all, elegance trails far behind, and do's and don'ts are dead.

DO'S AND DON'TS OF WRITING STYLE c.1983

DO
- Try to be simple, brief and sincere.
- Take trouble always to choose the right word.
- Keep your sentences clear in construction and use active verbs where there is a choice.
- Aim for variety of construction between one sentence and the next.

DON'T
- Be longwinded and include affectation.
- Use commonplace words, phrases or clichés.
- Include clumsy or confused sentence structure; or excessive use of passive verbal constructions.
- Be dull – don't make your writing monotonous, and beware of repeated sentence patterns.

From *Letts Complete Revision Guide (1983)*

QUOTE UNQUOTE

Morals and manners will rise or decline with our attention to grammar.
Jason Chamberlain, US Clergyman

SPELLING: AN INTRODUKSHUN

Left to their own devices, a child will write their stories entirely phonetically and with only the scantest attention paid to vowels – like the four-year-old who started her own fairy tale, 'Wnsupnatm...' instead of 'Once upon a time' she came by it honestly: wnsupna-tmallwordswerewrittenwithnogap-sandwithveryerratikspeleng.

First, a bright spark thought of putting gaps in between words, then Dr Johnson became the first universally-read-and-obeyed man of letters to standardise English spelling. In so doing, he left us with at least two legacies beyond the obvious 21lb labour of love that was nine years in the making. One is that by attempting to set spelling rules, out of the 615,000 or so words that make up the English language, there are still thousands of exceptions to any of the good Doctor's rules. The second is that, in standardising spelling, he has bequeathed an intolerance upon his descendants: it is universally acknowledged among all but the most iconoclastic of statesmen and tycoons that spelling mistakes in written work can prejudice an impression more than any brilliance of expression or inspiration. Spelling mistakes jar and distract, throwing the reader off the scent of the narrative drive of the writing. Leaving aside the texting excrescences of 'gr8' and 'c ya l8er' for a moment, this is why we bother getting spelling right.

BLACK IS WHITE. DISCUSS

'TV broadens the mind, stifles conversation, makes people lazy, befriends the lonely, is politically biased and encourages violence', was the quote that invited a discussion essay in the Joint Matriculation Board's June 1975 paper (whereas by 1993, students were being actively encouraged to watch TV to persuade them that Shakespeare was relevant to everyday life).

The crucial thing about these 'Discuss...' questions that some of us forgot was that this wasn't the law as laid down by the examiner but a topic inviting debate, disagreement, even disrespect... and there were other rules of thumb: First off, state the case being made or the nature of the problem. Second, list the points to be discussed. Third, if you can, comment on a recent event or media report that has to do with the topic being discussed. And, finally, state your own attitude to the issue with a clear, positively worded sentence such as: 'My own view is that television – when busied by the colourful lives of *Charlie's Angels*, *Hart to Hart* and *Beverly Hills 90210* – serves a useful function as a pressure valve, allowing the mind and body to unwind.'

WELL, I NEVER...

In an anecdote that shows how quickly language changes, at the beginning of the 17th century, when Shakespeare's plays were first printed, possessive apostrophes were largely reserved for 'loanwords' (words taken from one language into another, like garage from the French or foreign names like Romeo) ending in vowels (as few English nouns did). But, by the Fourth Folio of Shakespeare's plays, printed in 1685, his words were suddenly adorned with apostrophes being used in the modern sense.

SPELLING PITFALLS
AND A SPELLABLE SYNONYM

Accommodation	*House*
Accurate	*Exact*
Agreeable	*Nice*
Appearance	*Look*
Argument	*Fight*
Awful	*Terrible*
Beginning	*Start*
Changeable	*Varied*
Committee	*Working party*
Councillor	*Official*
Courage	*Bravery*
Desperately	*Urgently*
Disappointed	*Sad*
Drawers	*Shelves*
Embarrassing	*Shaming*
Everyone	*All*
Exaggerate	*Overstate*
Except	*Save*
Foreign	*Alien*
Gauge	*Level*
Glimpse	*Glance*
Government	*Bastards*
Humorous	*Funny*
Hurriedly	*Rapidly*
Immediate	*Instant*
Independent	*Free*
Interrupt	*Interject*
Knowledge	*Learning*
Lamppost	*Streetlight*
Leisurely	*Easy*
Lose	*Mislay*
Machine	*Device*
Medicine	*Drug*
Muscles	*Sinews*
Mystery	*Puzzle*
Necessary	*Required*
Nuisance	*Bother*
Occurred	*Took place*
Possess	*Have*
Possession	*Item*
Procession	*March past*
Psalm	*Chant*
Quarrelling	*Arguing*
Receive	*Get*
Seize	*Grab*
Separate	*Split*
Sincerely	*Truly*
Solemn	*Grave*
Stomach	*Belly*
Succeed	*Win*
Supersede	*Beat*
Temperature	*Heat*
Usually	*Often*
Vegetables	*Greens*
Weather	*Climate*
Wholly	*Entirely*

CROSSING THE BAR

Transitive and intransitive verbs were simple beasts in our day, up to the day when our language was once and for all invaded by American. Some say we should just acknowledge that the English language is an organic entity that has always profited from its flexibility and brazen attitude to poaching from other languages, and forget about words having an English impact in favour of the American terminologies impacting vibrantly upon our stultified syntax. Others insist that the whole point of the English language being organic is so that we aim, always, for the most beautiful solution to syntax, that Americanisms are more often than not brutally ugly bastardisations of hitherto elegant expressions – and it is to this camp that we now pay homage, with our transitive/intransitive rules.

- **A transitive verb** is a verb that requires both a subject and one or more objects, as in: *Debbie kisses Adam* (Adam is the direct lucky object of kisses) and *Adam gave Debbie a friendship bracelet* (friendship bracelet is the direct object of gave and Debbie is the non-prepositional indirect object of gave).

- **An intransitive verb** is a verb that doesn't require an object, as in: *I am a teenager, therefore I sleep.* Since one cannot actually sleep anything, the verb acts intransitively.

- **An ambitransitive verb** is not something that gender-confused people try to do but is a verb that can be used transitively or intransitively, as in: *Look, I am eating, Mum!* and *Look, I am eating an apple, Mum!* both of which are grammatically correct.

COULD DO BETTER

English: B+ Very good indeed. A sensible writer – producing good work of a high standard consistently throughout the year. Compositions have been particularly well planned and Lynne has made good sense of a lively imagination.
Conduct: Very shy. Inclined to fussiness.

School report of Lynne Truss (1955-), novelist, journalist and author of *Eats, Shoots and Leaves.*
From *Could do Better*, edited by Catherine Hurley

A *bevy* of quails
A *building* of rooks
A *cast* of hawks
A *covert* of coots
A *covey* of grouse
A *gaggle* of geese
A *fall* of woodcocks
A *flight* of doves
A *flight* of swallows
A *herd* of cranes
A *host* of sparrows
A *muster* of peacocks
A *nide* of pheasants
A *paddling* of ducks
A *siege* of herons
A *watch* of nightingales
A *wisp* of snipe

ANSWER THE QUESTION

Not since the midwife slapped us on the bum and provoked our first indignant breath, have we needed to be told to breathe. Yet it was a theme of our entire education and will continue to be for our children, that an instruction as obvious as 'answer the question' is a habit that still eludes us. The battlefields of O Levels, A Levels, GCSEs and even university finals are littered with the bones of past students who skim-read and then Didn't Answer The Question. They have postured heroically, fighting to win their arguments, to vanquish those maths problems and break through the ranks of linguistic declensions, but they did so on the wrong premise, providing the wrong information, solving the wrong equation – and in doing so shot themselves resolutely in the foot.

And, as we later discovered, life is one big exam paper; if you are being asked to say why you would be good for a company's workforce, don't waste time boasting about irrelevant achievements on your CV: answer the question. Similarly, if your doctor asks how much you drink each week, don't deflect the question with your own carefully-worded 'but I exercise' defence. It didn't work then, and it won't work now, unless you are a politician...

THE APOSTROPHE

Well before Lynne Truss rightly got a bee in her bonnet about the 'umble apostrophe, one of our textbooks told us sternly that '99% of English language candidates lose marks for the omission of the apostrophe. This could, and often does, mean the difference between success and failure.' Everywhere we look, the apostrophe is misused, added unnecessarily or omitted completely: signmakers seem to have given up the ghost entirely and those that mourn its absence are mocked for being old-fashioned. Well, our old-fashioned education showed us that the apostrophe need not be a catastrophe, but a useful and illuminating tool. So, let us return to the good old days when an apostrophe meant:

- Mark of **omission** in an abbreviated word – as in *haven't, couldn't, can't, doesn't* – with the apostrophe showing clearly where the missing letter has been omitted.
- Mark of **possession** – as in *Kim Wilde's hit record, Thatcher's Poll Tax, the demonstrators' shouts and yells, that year's victories.*
- Indicated a **plural form, especially in abbreviations**, as in *VIP's* or *MCP's* or in pluralising single letters, as in *minding your p's and q's.*

With some oft-forgotten rules:
- A simple plural needs no apostrophe – as in *'Lettuces 15p each'* instead of *'Lettuce's 15p each'.*
- Names obey the same rules even if they end in 's'; the secret is to think whether they are singular or plural – as in *Charles's hat, the Joneses' neighbours* – though the exception to this is in nouns that are already pluralised without an 's' – as in *women's issues, people's princess.*
- For *do's* and *don'ts*, the rule of thumb is to avoid having two differently used apostrophes in the same word, hence you stick at the 'o' emission apostrophe and drop the plural apostrophe.
- Only nouns use apostrophes to show possession. Pronouns (words that stand in place of nouns) do not – as in *hers, theirs, ours* – with the exception of one's, as in, *one's new mohican was deemed to be common and not in keeping with one's station in life.*
- *Its* and *it's* represent the most common punctuation mistakes of the entire English language, but one that is easily avoided by putting it in context... *It's* is short for 'It is', needing an apostrophe to show the missing 'i', while *its* is the possessive pronoun. The sentence: *'It's easy to avoid if you think of its proper meaning'* would clearly make no sense, written as: *'Its easy to avoid if you think of it is proper meaning.'*

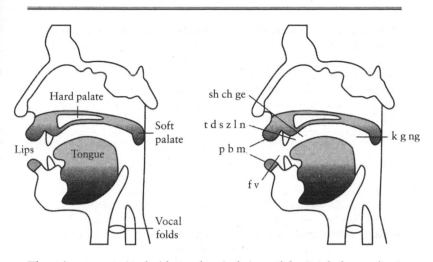

The main areas associated with speech articulation and the sounds they produce.

OHMIGOD!!! DON'T OVERUSE THE EXCLAMATION MARK!!!!!!!

As F Scott Fitzgerald said: 'Cut out all these exclamation points. An exclamation point is like laughing at your own joke.' The pointed, dotty invasion by the exclamation mark into the world of texting, blogging and other 'less disciplined' areas of the English language is, we feel, an abomination and must be halted, undramatically and without excitement (ie without exclamation marks...). Our teachers would be spinning (calmly) in their graves. For them, the exclamation mark was a simple and limited feature of punctuation, used to mark the end of an exclamation, interjection or sharp command in place of a full stop, as in: 'Stand and deliver!' as sung by Adam Ant. Use one exclamation mark at a time – no more than two to a page, as a rule of thumb – and you won't excite the wrath of the punctuation gods. Any more than that and you're heading for trouble. As Terry Pratchett concluded: 'Five exclamation marks, the sure sign of an insane mind.'

WORK IT OUT

In the group of words knew, knitted, knight and khaki, the first three have a silent k, with khaki the odd one out. Pick out the odd ones out in the following groups:

- Average wastage engage courage
- Weaker wealthy jealous treasure
- Access occult exceed success

Answer on page 312

EASING INTO ESSAYS

Many of us are fond of saying that we have 'a book' inside us, but when, in our youth, we were stuck inside an exam hall and told we had 40 minutes to write a composition, that literary wellspring of creativity was a little harder to tap. Some found it fiendish that they were expected to spin gold from straw within a few minutes of sitting down; others found relief in a section of schooling for which they didn't have to cram... but through it all ran a spine of sense that was useful to all essay composers. Jotting down the themes of Opening, Observation, Description, Dialogue and Narrative before you wrote a word was like saddling up a horse before galloping off into the sunset: you could do it bareback and probably get thrown off, or you could depend on the machinery of saddle, stirrups, bridle and reins to keep you safely on track. Even simpler was the advice once given by a sage old English teacher: 'B,

M, E,' he quoted mysteriously one day. 'Beginning, Middle, End. Hook them right in at the beginning, make it exciting. Reel them in with a muscular middle. Cast the ending back to the start in some way – gives it a satisfying sense of completeness, cycle of life, that sort of thing.'

The last great mantra – which is a little more controversial – is Write About What You Know. Tempting as it might have been, given an exam command to write about 'Fighting for Life', to write about a fantastical conflict between Zutons and Futons on Planet Zog 49, doesn't it make more sense to write about something a little closer to home – like, for example, the fight for the right to a social life from our parents! Experience may have been a little thinner on the ground back then but all these tips are useful for life skills now. So come out, all you would-be novel writers, let that book out of you. Just remember to saddle up first.

MY WORD'S LONGER THAN YOURS

Not that it would have helped any sufferer to have known this at school, but even then the irony of the word *hipomonsteresquipedalophobia* meaning 'the phobia of long words' could not have escaped us. Other absurd linguistic phobias include *graphophobia*, the fear of looking at writing (presumably suffered by pharmacists up and down the country), *sophophobia*, the fear of learning ('I'm sorry I haven't done my homework, miss, but I'm sophophobic') and *verbophobia*, the fear of words. Cat got your tongue, Little Miss Verbophobic?

WRITERS ON WORDS

We are little airy creatures,
All of different voice and features:
One of us in glass is set,
One of us you'll find in jet,
T'other you may find in tin
And the fourth a box within
If the fifth you should pursue,
It can never fly from you.
On the Vowels – a Riddle,
by Jonathan Swift,
(1667-1745)

QUOTE UNQUOTE

We don't just borrow words; on occasion, English has pursued other languages down alleyways to beat them unconscious and rifle their pockets for new vocabulary.
Booker T Washington, US educator and reformer

'DIRECT SPEECH,' SHE REQUESTED BUT HE ASKED HER TO BE MORE INDIRECT

The need to record speech in various ways was one of the building blocks of the English language. Direct speech was when we dropped the actual words into vivid, allowably colloquial speech or thought; indirect, or reported, speech was more formal, less lively, but could be usefully succinct:

'Damn you!' Sarah raged at her mother. 'I knew this perm would be a disaster. Why did you make me go through with it? Now what am I going to do about tomorrow's disco? Put a bag over my head?'
or
Sarah cursed her mother for making her go through with the disastrous perm, asking her whether she should just put a bag over her head for the disco the next day.

It's not just the speech marks that show the difference, but also a change of verb tense, pronouns, time reference and tone.

BEING HOMOPHONIC

The trouble with the richness of the English language is that it is possible for its student to get lost in a surfeit of words and phrases, often muddying up their clarity along the way.

• **Synonyms** are words having the same (or very nearly the same) meaning, as in blend/mix, change/alteration, start/begin.
• **Antonyms** are words of opposite meaning, as in difficult/easy, strong/weak, light/dark (or light/heavy).
• **Homophones** are words that sound the same or nearly the same but are spelled differently and have different meanings, as in compliment/complement, principle/principal, gait/gate, whale/wail.

The key to taking the right turn on all of these is to stop and consider the true meaning and context of the word – for very rarely do words carry exactly the same shade of meaning. For example, end and finish are synonyms, but are both appropriate to their context. Compare: 'There was a dead heat at the finish of the egg-and-spoon race' with: 'The constant cheating by 10-year-olds meant the end of the egg-and-spoon race'.

REAL LIFE EXAMPLES OF 'FLAWED' WRITING IN EXAMS OF THE 1980s

Confused sentence structure: I was to be one of the noisy gossips in the opera, a character that did not cause me great difficulty in putting forward, according to my father!

Use of commonplace words and phrases: June 4th dawned bright with not a cloud in the sky but just after midday, when preparations were in full swing, dark clouds raced across the sky and the wind picked up tremendously.

Monotonous sentence patterns: Local factories usually prepare floats on which their employees can enter the carnival, schools prepare floats, Brownies prepare floats, Guides prepare floats, and so the list goes on...

Affectation: A fleecy cloud, a rich ploughed field. We have been moved by the beauty of spinning, dancing toes, we have touched St Paul's with reverence, and laughed at the audacity of the wind.

Choosing the right word: The air was damp with spray from the firemen's hoses, which lay across the road like cooked pasta [spaghetti?].

Passive verbal constructions: Saturday is when most people do things they would be too idle to do on a Sunday. Lawns are mowed and gardens are dug; most of the shopping is done.

Pomposity: In the course of my duty as a policeman, I was proceeding in the direction of Northgate Street.

Attempting to be funny: When Amy tried to tell one of her jokes about the nun falling down the stairs, we all laughed so much that we fell over!!!! It was hilarious!!!

Language is the only instrument of science, and words are but the signs of ideas.
From the preface to the *English Dictionary*, Samuel Johnson, essayist, poet, biographer, lexicographer

All language starts as sounds rather than signs. For the early years of our life, much emphasis is put on speaking clearly to be understood; a beginner reader mouths the words that he or she reads, converting them back into their original form to make them easier to understand. Yet the link between the spoken word and the written word is often thereafter lost.

What some of us learned at school – and were even tested on by examination boards – was an attempt by our educators to re-establish that link – Oral and Aural English. For some it was the easiest way to get credits; for others it was sheer torture: the self-consciousness of reading aloud, the temptation to dip heads and mumble, the agony with which poetry was rendered meaningless and prose was strangled at birth. The tips that were given to us were brisk and no-nonsense, yet they work as well today as they did then: speak up, speak slowly, speak articulately, making a clear distinction between words like 'rabid' and 'rabbit'. Speak fluently, putting the right emphasis on the right words; judge your tone appropriately; avoid pitfalls by practising difficult words out loud as many times as it takes to whittle down the unfamiliarity. Give more than a nod to punctuation – the pauses, stops and inflections of punctuation are your friend not your enemy: they make sense of the densest passages. Above all, let the novelty value of reading aloud be eroded by constant practise, mouthing silently if you will but declaiming, 'Friends, Romans, countrymen, lend me your ears,' if you possibly can. What was possibly not pointed out then, but could be pointed out now, was that the confident orator of yesterday could be the prime minister of tomorrow.

SPELLING CHEATS

There are hundreds of mnemonics for attempting to remember how to spell difficult words but we shall leave you with just one:

Dash In A Real Rush, Hurry Or Else Accident!

V

FRENCH

*Boy, those French – they have a
different word for everything.*

Steve Martin, US actor

WHY FRENCH?

It may be down the list from world languages like English and Spanish, it may be boxed into a linguistic corner by the likes of the Chinese, but French – with its 78 million native speakers, a further 30 million who have adopted French and speak it every day, and up to 600 million French conversationalists – is still the lexicon of love to hundreds of millions.

It's an official language of 29 countries (most of which form La Francophonie, the community of French-speaking countries) and is cited as the 'useless' language that most people would nevertheless like to learn (coming second only to Italian). From our point of view, it was the language most of us had no choice but to learn and therefore, as often as not, we were a little blinded to the romance of it. Still, the French exchanges could be fun…

PLAYING HUNT THE BEAN

Part of learning French was learning about French life – including its folklore and festivals. Beside the usual panoply of religious holidays, there are various saints day festivals.

In Brittany, for instance, there are *Pardons* (processions to the local church to ask forgiveness for sins), and a national holiday *le Toussaint* on All Saints' Day (1 November).

Christmas (*Noël*) usually begins a little earlier than for their sluggard cousins across the Channel, with midnight Mass followed, even later, by the *réveillon*, the festive meal of regional delicacies (goose in Alsace, buckwheat pancakes in Brittany, etc).

Traditionally, the French send cards for New Year – *Le Nouvel An* – rather than for Christmas; also in January is the *6 janvier* holiday, linked with the Epiphany and the

visit of the Magi. A special flat cake called *la Galette des Rois* conceals a hidden bean – he or she who finds it is king or queen for the day (cue total indulgence of under-age despots).

Not all high days are holy days, however: *La Fête Nationale*, more usually called 'Bastille Day', is the national holiday that celebrates the beginning of the French Revolution (this was the day when the Bastille prison was stormed and political prisoners were released).

However, history doesn't dare record whether there were any red faces among the rampaging mob when it was discovered that all this storming effort had freed a grand total of just seven prisoners – two lunatics, four forgers and an aristocrat who, it transpired, had been held there for sexual misdemeanours.

USEFUL WORDS – ORDERING IN FRENCH

Le petit déjeuner, le déjeuner, le diner ... *Breakfast, lunch, dinner*
Commander .... *To order*
Je prendrai* .... *I'll take...*
Et comme dessert? .... *And for pudding?*
Bleu, saignant, à point, médium, bien cuit...................
.... *Bloody, rare, medium rare, medium, well-done*
Le potage ....*Soup*
Le bifteck ....*Old-fashioned word for steak*
Le gigot d'agneau .... *Leg of lamb*
Les frites .... *Chips*
La pomme de terre .... *Potato*
Le poisson.. *Fish*
Les légumes .... *Vegetables*
Le fromage .... *Cheese*
Le lait .... *Milk*
L'eau .... *Water*
Le verre .... *Glass*
Le couteau .... *Knife*
La fourchette .... *Fork*
La cuillère .... *Spoon*
L'assiette .... *Plate*
L'addition ....*The bill*
Service compris .... *Service charge included*

*When ordering, never translate 'I'll have...' – always use *prendre*

DIVIDED BY LANGUAGE

There are endless stories of brands that work well in some countries but not so well in others. Our favourite example at school was a famous babyfood one. A successful manufacturer could not understand why one of its products was hardly shifting in French supermarkets until some bright spark pointed out that the company name was 'Gerber' and that the verb *gerber* meant something rather offputting... Cue 'vomit' babyfood.

Mind you, this was better than when Gerber tried to sell its babyfood in Africa. It kept its popular labels, featuring the cute Gerber baby smiling and dimpling – not realising that in that continent, manufacturers tended to put the contents of their jars on them.

While the English jury is still out on the split infinitive, the fact remains that we often can (as we just did) place the adverb before the verb. But in French, the adverb never comes between the subject and verb of a sentence – invariably coming just after. For example, *Je vais souvent à Paris* (I often go to Paris) must be used rather than *Je souvent vais* (which would draw breaths of horror from your French listeners).

Just to knit it in more securely; for the past tense, the adverb is nearly always placed between the auxiliary and the past participle which looks better than it sounds – *J'ai trop mangé* (I have eaten too much).

CHEAT'S GUIDE TO SIGNIFICANT FRENCH DATES SINCE THE FRENCH REVOLUTION

1789   Storming of the Bastille on 14 July marked beginning of the Revolution (now a national day) until 1799. 'Reign of Terror' period of violence lasted from September 1793 to July 1794.

1793   Execution of Louis XVI. First Republic proclaimed.

1804   Corsican-born Napoleon Bonaparte proclaimed himself Emperor.

1815   Bourbon monarchy restored when Napoleon was defeated at Waterloo.

1830   Revolution. Louis-Philippe hung on as king.

1848   Revolution and dawn of Second Republic. Napoleon's nephew Louis Napoleon (LN) became head of state (crowned Emperor 1852).

1870   Franco-Prussian war ended in defeat of French. LN brought down.

1871   Dawn of Third Republic.

1914   Germany declared war on France.

1918   Germany defeated on French soil.

1919   Treaty of Versailles between Allies and Germany.

1940   France invaded by Germany. Collapse of Third Republic. Government of unoccupied France moved to Vichy.

1944   France liberated by Allies. Resistance war hero General de Gaulle (later French president) becomes prime minister.

1958   Algerian Crisis. Collapse of Fourth Republic. Dawn of Fifth Republic.

1968   Anti-government riots by students in Paris and throughout France.

LET US BEGIN... AN INTRO TO VERBS

It just had to be that the most important part of any sentence – the not-so-humble verb – turned out to be the trickiest part of learning French. Not only were there several forms of regular verbs but also the irregulars run into the dozens. The short illustration of the magnitude of the problem lies in a quick analysis, so don your lab specs and keep up – this *is* interesting.

English verbs usually have no more than two or three different forms in each tense:

I go (1)
you go (1)
he/she goes (2)
we go (1)
you go (1)
they go (1)

But French verbs wipe them off the scoreboard with as many as six different forms:

Je vais (1)
Tu vas (2)
Il/Elle va (3)
Nous allons (4)
Vous allez (5)
Ils/elles vont (6)

In other words, any French student is in for a long slog.

SCHOOL'S OUT FOR SUMMER

No more Latin, no more French,
No more sitting on a hard board bench.
No more Latin, no more Greek,
No more cares to make me squeak.
No more beetles in my tea,
Making googly eyes at me;
No more spiders in my bath,
Trying hard to make me laugh.

Children's rhyme for the end of the school term, taken from Iona and Peter Opie's *Lore and Language of Schoolchildren* (1959)

French is the language that turns dirt into romance.

Stephen King, US author

'OK, OK, JE NE SUIS PAS DEAF!'

Franglais was that deliberate blend of French and English words that kept us amused through French lessons and which we then resorted to when in France itself. Although we think of Franglais as a post-WW2 phenomenon, culminating in the combined efforts of the late, great columnist and wit Miles Kington and the TV series *'Allo 'Allo* that was so popular during our schooldays, the fine art of mangling French to fit in with English actually goes back a lot further than that.

Not content with coining around a third of the English language, we also have Shakespeare to thank for its first recorded instance when, during a scene from *Henry V*, we hear his French princess Catherine trying to learn English from her chaperone Alice, who is trying to teach her parts of the body. The scene is partly in English, mostly in French, with enough pointing for English audiences to get the joke.

Catherine is at first unaware that her off-beam English pronunciations are producing hilarious *doubles entendres* and the scene reaches a climax with the words for gown and foot. 'Foot' from Catherine becomes 'Foutre' or 'f**k', while 'gown' becomes something even more unmentionable – and Franglais is born.

Nineteenth-century American writer Mark Twain later joined in on the act with a letter to his Parisian landlord which included such examples as, 'Pourquoi don't you mettez some savon in your bedchambers? Est-ce que vous pensez I will steal it? ...Tous les jours you are coming some fresh game or other on me, mais vous ne pouvez pas play this savon dodge on me twice. Savon is a necessary de la vie to anybody but a Frenchman...'

However, the medium reached its zenith in Kington's columns and books. One of his best was surely his insistence that the motto of the French Navy was, '*A l'eau, c'est l'heure*!' which translated to a perfectly reasonable, 'To the water, it is the hour!'. That is, until you said it out loud in a deliberately Franglais-ish way...

The result: 'Allo, sailor!'

ROLE MODELS

Celebrities who paid attention in class and who now claim to be fluent in French

Eddie Izzard
Imogen Stubbs
Kate Beckinsale
Jodie Foster
Davina McCall
Helena Bonham-Carter
Kristin Scott-Thomas
Rupert Everett
Prunella Scales
Joan Collins
Nathalie Portman
Jennifer Connelly

IT'S A QUESTION OF GENDER

THE GENDERS. Here we come to that which forms one of the great differences in the two languages. In our language, the nouns, or names, of males are masculine; those of females are feminine; and those of inanimate things, or of creatures the sex of which we do not know, are neuter. Thus, in speaking of a man, we say 'he'; of a woman 'she'; of a house 'it'.

How different the French language as to this matter! In French every noun is of the masculine or of the feminine, whether it be the name of a living creature or not. The names of living creatures that are males are, indeed, of the masculine gender, and those that are the names of females are of the feminine gender: but the names of all other things are either masculine or feminine. *Panier* (basket), for instance, is masculine; and *table* (table) feminine. This would be nothing, if it were merely calling them masculine and feminine. But the articles, the adjectives and the pronouns must vary their form, or spelling, to *agree* with the genders of the nouns. We say *the* basket, *the* table; but the French say, *le* panier and *la* table. We say the *round* basket, the *round* table; but they must say le panier *rond*, and la table *ronde*. We say, speaking of a basket, *it* is round, and we say the same of a table; but they say, speaking of a basket, *il* est rond, and speaking of a table, *elle* est ronde.

William Cobbett, A French Grammar: or, plain instructions for the learning of French (1829)

WORDS ON O LEVEL VOCAB LISTS THAT WE NEEDN'T HAVE BOTHERED WITH, FRANKLY

Faire naufrage	*To be shipwrecked*
La piste d'atterrissage	*Runway*
La perruche inséparable	*Budgie*
L'aubergiste	*Innkeeper*
La pare-boue	*Mudguard*
Les bleus de travail	*Dungarees/overalls*
La meule de foin	*Hayrick*
La moissonneuse-batteuse	*Combine harvester*
Le trefle d'Irlande	*Shamrock*
La balançoire	*Seesaw/swing*
Le cadran solaire	*Sundial*
La surdité	*Deafness*
Les oreillons	*Mumps*
Habitation à loyer modéré	*Council flat*
D'acier inoxydable	*Stainless steel*
Le Tourne-disque	*Record player*
Le/la mécanographe	*'Computer operator'**
L'éclaireuse	*Girl Guide*
Le fourgon à bagages	*Luggage van*

*whatever that might be

THIS TIME IT'S PERSONAL

For most of French syntax, the adjective goes after the noun – *la maison verte*, etc – but there is a clutch of adjectives that always precedes the noun – *beau, bon, excellent, gentil, grand, gras, gros, jeune, joli, long, mauvais, même, meilleur, nouveau, petit, vieux* and *villain*. Numbering 17, it was a tough task to try to remember them all, but a rule of thumb was to think of them as being very personal adjectives, whether towards physical appearance (*gros, jeune, grand*) or towards character (*mauvais, gentil, excellent*).

Then there were the tricky buggers that swapped about according to their meaning, *un cher ami* (a dear friend) but *un vin cher* (an expensive wine) or *de mes propres mains* (my own hands – personal again) or *les mains propres* (my clean hands). And all this was before we'd got into the irregular feminine forms of adjectives....

What is 'le téléphone arabe'?
- Morse code
- Rumours
- Smoke signals
- Phone box

What is 'un trou normand'?
- An aversion to cheese
- Sweet confectionery
- A little glass of alcohol in between courses of meals
- A chunk of puff pastry fried up in a mix of apple brandy and molten butter

Answers on page 312

LE WEEKEND!

True to its roots as an equal injustice to both languages, Franglais is also a major part of the French modern culture, much to the fury of the purist Académie Française.

English words – or at least English roots of words – have crept into the bosom of the French language and nestled there cosily, so the French might go for *le weekend* after they have done *le parking*. Also, they might check *les emails*, give their hair *un shampooing*, then put on *le smoking* (tuxedo) and go for *les cocktails* and *un steak*.

Sometimes, the words adopted don't actually exist in English – like *un relooking* (a makeover), *le footing* (jogging) or *le talkie-walkie* instead of the walkie-talkie.

In 1994, the Académie Française and other French cultural bodies decided that the purity of the French language was being threatened and passed the Toubon Law, making pure French compulsory in government publications, most workplaces, advertisements, parts of the media and within state-funded schools. So it was goodbye 'email', hello *courriel*, although an attempt to root out *le weekend* and replace it with *la fin de semaine* failed at the starting gates.

The fact that this law was quickly nicknamed the Loi Allgood (Tou-bon – geddit?) was a pretty fair indicator of its lasting success in this age of globalisation and the World Wide Web.

Famous French names for every profession (well, the interesting ones!)

Actor/actress Jacques Tati, Brigitte Bardot, Juliette Binoche, Catherine Deneuve, Gerard Depardieu.

Balloonist Montgolfier brothers invented the hot-air balloon.

Cinema Lumière brothers were pioneers.

Composer (if anyone were to hum a few bars of these musicians' top tunes, you would be bound to recognise them): Berlioz, Bizet, Chopin, Debussy, Ravel, Fauré, Messaien, Poulenc, Saint-Saëns.

Dress designer Coco Chanel, Yves St Laurent, Christian Dior, Givenchy, Jean-Paul Gaultier... The list goes on.

Film director Cocteau, Chabrol, Godard, Truffaut.

Flier Blériot was the first man to cross the English Channel by plane, in 1909.

Guide Braille invented the alphabet for the blind which bears his name.

Historical figure Joan of Arc (1412-1431; scourge of the English, burnt at stake); Louis XIV (1643-1715; 'Sun King' built Versailles, absolute monarch); Louis XVI (1754-1793; married to infamous Marie Antoinette, executed during French Revolution); Napoleon (1769-1821; brilliant soldier, made himself Emperor, instituted Code Napoleon new legal system, defeated Poles, Austrians and [nearly] Russians before being defeated at Waterloo).

Mathematician Descartes.

Painter *C17th* Boucher, Poussin; *C18th* Fragonard, Watteau; *C19th* Degas, Manet, Monet, Renoir, Rodin; *C20th* Chagalle, Gauguin, Matisse.

Philosopher (very French to think of this as a profession!): *C17th* Pascal; *C18th* Rousseau (man is happiest in his natural state); *C19th* Valéry; *C20th* Sartre.

Photographer Daguerre was a pioneer of photography – hence early name of photo as daguerrotype.

Saviour Louis Pasteur discovered that micro-organisms are destroyed by heat and discovered a serum to combat rabies. Pierre and Marie Curie discovered radium – leading to the X-ray.

Writers (mentioning any of these in a tone of reverence would be your passport to any smoky, black-clad boîte in Paris): *C17th* Molière, Racine; *C18th* Voltaire; *C19th* Balzac, Dumas, Flaubert, Stendhal, Zola, Victor Hugo; *C20th* Camus, Proust, Mauriac, Gide.

REGIONS OF FRANCE

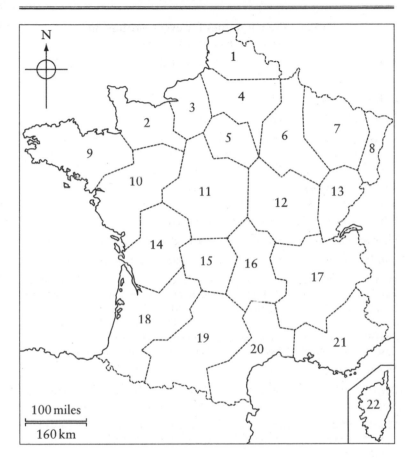

Check that you know how to spell these regions as well as where they are located:

1 Nord	9 Bretagne	17 Rhône-Alpes
2 Basse-Normandie	10 Pays de la Loire	18 Aquitaine
3 Haute-Normandie	11 Centre	19 Midi-Pyrénées
4 Picardie	12 Bourgogne	20 Languedoc-Roussillon
5 Région Parisienne	13 Franche-Comté	
6 Champagne-Ardenne	14 Poitou-Charentes	21 Provence-Côte d'Azur
7 Lorraine	15 Limousin	
8 Alsace	16 Auvergne	22 Corsica

TO BE OR NOT TO BE – THAT IS THE QUESTION

There is a power struggle in French between two irregular verbs, **to be** and **to have**. One is the verb of choice for most verbs when in the perfect tense – *J'ai donné, tu as fini, il/elle a travaillé*, while the other is the bad boy chosen by the wild cards of the French language: that Gang of Sixteen that takes *être* when in the perfect tense, and then fall into line with *être*, agreeing to agree with the subject of the verb (see right).

Être is the most irregular of the -re verbs: from the present (*je suis, tu es, il/elle est, nous sommes, vous êtes, ils/elles sont*) to the future (an unrelated *je serai, tu seras, il sera etc*) and sticking its neck out to be the only verb whose imperfect tense does not start with the stem of the present first person plural, *'somm-'*. Instead, it prefers: *j'étais, tu étais, il/elle était, nous étions, vous étiez, ils/elle étaient*. If we want to get back into bed with French, we must embrace *être* in all its guises. Then, we can really lick those tenses into shape.

FEAR NOT, EARTHLINGS, WE COME IN PEACE

We may be a bit rubbish at learning French, but at least most of us try. Over the pond, it's a different matter. Consider the following:

John Kerry is part of the march past of forgotten presidential contenders, but when he was standing against George W Bush for the presidency of America, there was one interestingly little-known fact about him. Kerry could speak French. Not just 'French-fries' French but fluent French, leading him to chat easily and at length with the various French bigwigs in Washington. Yet when asked a question in French at an open conference, Kerry pretended not to be able to understand it.

It was clear that in a country where around three quarters of people don't even have a passport,

the ability to speak French isn't just rare, it's inadmissible – somehow un-American. In Nebraska in 1918, a law was passed, making it illegal to teach 'alien tongues' in schools; so learning French was clearly close to Martian in the Midwest. These days it is at least legal, but from the Kerry point of view it is still seen as a vote loser.

Meanwhile Bush was on safer populist ground – removing the 'French' from Fries to form 'Freedom Fries' (during a freeze-out with France over Iraq). For good measure he impressed all with his grasp of world etymology when he reportedly said to Tony Blair about the French: 'Their problem is that they don't even have a word for entrepreneur.'

Bien fait, George.

THE 16 VERBS THAT TAKE ÊTRE

Aller – *To go*
Arriver – *To arrive*
Descendre – *To go down*
Devenir – *To become*
Entrer – *To enter*
Monter – *To go up/climb*
Mourir – *To die*
Naître – *To be born*
Partir – *To leave*
Rentrer – *To go back*
Rester – *To stay*
Retourner – *To return*
Revenir – *To come back*
Sortir – *To go out*
Tomber – *To fall*
Venir – *To come*

• Don't forget that past participles must agree with the subject, as in *Elle est montée – She has gone up, she went up*
• All reflexive verbs take *être*, eg *se laver: Je me suis lavé(e) – I washed myself*

WORK IT OUT

Which of these do the French describe as either 'les Bataves' or 'les Nouvelle-Lunes'?
- New Zealanders
- North-African immigrants
- Australians
- Dutch

What do the French refer to when they speak of 'un petit Suisse'?
- Toblerone
- A kind of cheesy yoghurt
- A small cup of coffee with more milk than coffee
- A very dry pork sausage in a pepper crust

Answers on page 312

There exists a vibrant language exchange between the British and the French, the basic idea being that one blames the other for something that they find distasteful. So we call the condom 'the French letter', while the French call it 'la capote anglaise'. We also refer to 'French leave' (an abrupt or unannounced departure), but they call it 'filer à l'anglaise'.

Interestingly, when it comes to 'syphilis', everyone seems to share the blame. The Spanish, who were originally accused of bringing it back from the New World (according to folklore, though since questioned by historians), were the first to call it the 'French disease'; we English joined in with alacrity on this, whereupon the French naturally started calling it the 'English disease'. The Russians, looking across the border at their traditional enemies, called syphilis the 'Polish disease'; equally predictably (though probably more fairly), it was called the 'Christian disease' by Arabian tribes.

When it comes to 'le vice anglais', we don't bother trying to pass the buck to the French. Is that because the truth hurts? In this case, it probably does – since the phrase refers to the flagellation that the English supposedly learned to enjoy through being subjected to the cane at school.

Terence Rattigan, the outspoken playwright, had a view on this in his play *In Praise of Love* (1973): 'Do you know what "le vice anglais" – the English vice – really is? Not flagellation, not pederasty – whatever the French believe it to be. It's our refusal to admit our emotions. We think they demean us, I suppose.'

QUOTE UNQUOTE

When a French book becomes an international hit, it is because of the author and not because of the language. The same goes for movies.
Jean-Jacques Annaud, French film director

L'arrivée/le départ . . . . *Arrival/departure*
Le guichet . . . . *Booking office*
Le trajet . . . . *Short journey*
Le voyage . . . . *Longer journey*
Le quai/la voie . . . . *Platform*
Le wagon-lit . . . . *Sleeping carriage*
Le billet . . . . *Ticket*
L'horaire . . . . *Timetable*
Le train direct . . . . *Non-stop train*
Le chariot . . . . *Trolley*
S'embarquer/débarquer . . . . *Embark/disembark*
Le passager . . . . *Passenger*

COME BACK, WESTMINSTER, ALL IS FORGIVEN

The gloss and celebrity of Sarkosy and Carla Bruni aside, French politics and institutions look hellishly complicated at first glance. Since France is a republic (currently on its fifth version), the head of state is the president (elected by universal suffrage, every five years), with the rules of governance, unlike Britain, all laid down in a written constitution that is remotely linked to that of the First (revolutionary) Republic.

The president then chooses his prime minister from one of the two houses of parliament: L'Assemblée Nationale (the National Assembly) and Le Sénat (the Senate). Members of L'Assemblée Nationale are called 'Députés' and are elected by the people to serve for five years, while the Senators are elected for nine years by delegates from local councils and National Assembly deputies. There are two types of local council: Conseil Général and Conseil Municipal, the equivalents of our county council and town council respectively.

A Président du Conseil Général, elected by the relevant council(s), administers the 'département' (formerly it was the government-appointed préfect that did this).

GRAVE AND ACUTE – WHAT'S THE DEAL?

The grave accent was first used in Ancient Greek where it occurred only on the last syllable of the word in cases where the normal high pitch (indicated by an acute accent) was lowered. In French, phonetically, the grave accent originally marked a heavier, more deliberate tone, while the acute marked a sharp, quick, high pitch. One way of remembering the difference was to say that the grave was more laid back than the sharply forward-pointing acute.

The circumflex (or hat) was not necessarily a pronunciation mark but an indication that there had once been a following letter – so hospital became *hôpital* and hostel became *hôtel*. The reasonably rare diacresis (*le tréma*) appears most famously in *Noël* and indicates that the vowels are pronounced separately – as in 'no-ell', rather than 'nole'. Finally, the cedilla is the little five numeral that hangs off the bottom of a 'c', denoting that it is pronounced 's' in front of the hard vowels 'a', 'o' and 'u'. Without it *garçon*, for instance, would be pronounced 'gar-kon'.

SUBJUNCTIVE CONVULSIVE

Using the subjunctive in French was where the wheels started to fall off *l'autobus*. Luckily, no one except top-level language students had to do anything with the subjunctive other than recognise it and be able to translate it. That is, apart from shoehorning it into sentences in the form of a couple of easily memorable phrases – like the all-time favourite, *il faut que* (it is necessary that). Here then is where it was used:

Quoique (although)
Bien que (although), as in *Bien que le temps fasse mauvais, nous allons sortir*
Afin que (in order that), as in *Mon frére m'a enseigné à fumer afin que j'eusse beaucoup d'amis*
Avant que (before), as in *Je veux vous parler avant que vous sortiez*
Jusqu'à ce que (until) as in *Je pelotait avec Jean-Paul jusqu'à ce que nos parents nous séparassent*

The subjunctive is formed as follows – from the stem of the third person plural, present indicative, adding the endings 'e', 'es', 'e', 'ions', 'iez', 'ent'.

Irregulars include the following:
Aller – J'aille, nous allions, ils aillent
Avoir – J'aie, il ait, nous ayons, ils/elles aient
Être – Je sois, nous soyons, ils/elles soient
Faire – Je fasse, etc

FRENCH HUMAN BODY DIAGRAM

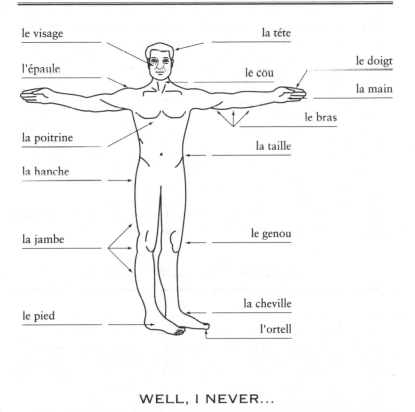

le visage

la tête

l'épaule

le cou

le doigt

la main

le bras

la poitrine

la taille

la hanche

la jambe

le genou

le pied

la cheville

l'ortell

WELL, I NEVER...

How to say the letter 'u' in French

As anyone taught by someone, who sounded as if they were being slowly
pulled down a plughole when they spoke French, will attest – there were
certain no-go zones of French pronunciation because we just knew that
we would never get them right.

But follow these directions and you'll be well away with the most
difficult sound in the French language, that pinched, startled little 'u'.
(Take a tip: practise in a private place at first, otherwise you might attract
some funny stares. Or flies.) Open your mouth. Say 'o'. Draw out the 'o'
until your lips are where they would be to make a 'w' sound. Purse your
lips as tightly as you can. Keeping them pursed, say 'e'. Voilà the French 'u'!

When the adjective precedes the noun, the comparative and superlative forms are simple enough: *moins fort, plus fort, aussi fort que..., le plus fort* – respectively 'less strong', 'stronger', 'as strong as...' 'the strongest'. In all these cases, the word *que* is simply deployed to complete the comparison, ie *Pierre est plus fort que Jean*.

But when an adjective follows the noun – which it does in the majority of cases – the relevant qualifiers tuck in between – eg *la fille la plus amusante* (the most amusing girl) or *l'élève le plus intelligent de la classe* (the cleverest pupil in the class).

Beware of 'better' and 'best' which are differentiated only by their use of the indefinite/definite article – *un meilleur disco* (a better disco), *le meilleur disco* (the very best groove-tastic disco).

WORK IT OUT

What are you ordering?
- Je voudrais deux oeufs à la coque et trois saucisses.
- Je voudrais des escargots et des cuisses de grenouille.

Answers on page 312

ON SPEAKING FRENCH FLUENTLY, RATHER THAN CORRECTLY...

We didn't necessarily believe our teachers – because after all they were the ones who sounded like a character from *'Allo 'Allo*. But they always insisted that it was better just to plunge in and give the whole speaking-French thing a jolly good go than worry unduly about how correct or well-pronounced the end result is.

One of England's better ambassadors to France (with a small 'a' because it was her husband Duff who had the actual job) was Lady Diana Cooper, celebrated throughout Paris for her wit, beauty and sophistication in the wake of World War II. On French speaking, she insisted: 'It's nerve and brass. Audace and disrespect, and leaping before you look and what-the-hellism – that must be developed.'

WHERE THE BLANKETY-BLANK AM I? USEFUL WORDS – PLACE, DIRECTION, DISTANCE

In the direction of . . . . *Du côté de*
North, east, south, west . . . . *Nord, est, sud, ouest*
Far, not far, here . . . . *Loin, pas loin, ici*
Up there, over there . . . . *Là-haut, là-bas*
Nowhere, somewhere . . . . *Nulle part, quelque part*
Everywhere, elsewhere . . . . *Partout, ailleurs*
On the right, on the left, straight on . *À droit, à gauche, tout droit*
Lower/upper (floor) . . . . *Inférieur/supérieur*
Ground floor . . . . *Rez-de-chaussée*
In front of/behind . . . . *Devant/derrière*
Inside . . . . *Dedans (also à l'intérieur)*
Outside . . . . *Dehors (also à l'extérieur)*
Under/over . . . . *Sous, en dessous/au dessus de, dessus, par-dessus*
Place . . . . . . *L'endroit, le lieu (un bel endroit, le lieu de naissance)*

GAME, SET AND PARIS MATCH!

If Brad Pitt and Angelina Jolie's twins had been born in the south of France 20 years ago, the publication most likely to have fought tooth and nail to the front of the queue for the photograph would have been *Paris Match*.

This was arguably the first celebrity magazine as we know it today. Scarcely a week went by without a deliciously intrusive photo-article on the Monaco royal family: the car cash that killed Princess Grace and injured Princess Stéphanie; Caroline's beauty and tragedy and Albert's weird secret life – was he gay or was there a certain *je ne sais quoi* about having a secret child with a Tonga-born flight attendant?

Best of all, as schoolkids, we were allowed to read *Paris Match* for study purposes. Seldom has there been so much assiduous concentration on phrases like 'gracious home', 'fifth husband', 'glittering soirée' and, especially popular, 'new bikini-fit body'.

At its peak, in the mid-to-late 1980s, the glossy sold more than a million copies a week and was noted for its scoops.

For the Brits, it was a vivid visual glimpse into the world beyond the pen and ink world of Maman, Papa, Pierre et Chantal...

DICTATION, PLEASE, MADEMOISELLE

Since some of us were clearly destined to be typists in France, it was deemed necessary to teach us the equivalent of 'The quick brown fox jumps over the lazy dog' in French. The sentence, made up of all the letters of the alphabet, enabled us to spot keys that were not working.

The French version was: '*Allez porter ce vieux whisky au juge blond qui fume un Havane*', which even by our 'quick brown fox' standards is a remarkably random 'Go and take this old whisky to the fair-haired judge who is smoking a cigar'.

A PICTURE SAYS MORE THAN A THOUSAND WORDS – IF ONLY WE HAD THE VOCAB...

English pupils will forever be haunted by those simplistic pen-and-ink line drawings from which they had to extract a story or description – in French.

For one thing, more often than not, something terrible had happened – an accident, a fire, a burglary – that involved the emergency services and maybe even parts of the body – all of which had to be expressed in *le français*. For another, they represented a criminally sanitised version of reality – there was not a black face, fractured family or obese child to be seen anywhere.

It was all families of four, with Papa at the wheel of the sedate saloon car, with Maman unpacking the sandwiches for Pierre et Chantal, grinning glassily in the rear seat, not forgetting Fifi the dog in the boot.

Forget imagination – this was not the chance to tell the examiner that Maman, Papa, Pierre, Chantal et Fifi were driving to a swingers' holiday in a nudist camp. Instead, certain observations were advised.

You had to include what season it was in the picture and therefore in your story, which day of the week it was and what the weather was doing. And you had to remember to give French names for your characters (*adieu* Clive and Sharon) and make sure to link your story from one picture to another if there was more than one.

Also, you had to use suitably apposite time-progression words, such as *puis, quelques minutes plus tard, bientôt*. And you were definitely not advised to end your tale with *et tout le mond vécurent heureux jusqu'à la fin des temps* (and they all lived happily ever after).

a) Où est la voiture?
b) Où est le chat?
c) Qu'est-ce qu'il y a dans le coffre de la voiture?
d) En quelle saison se passé cette scène?
e) Qu'est-ce qu'il y a à droite de la maison?
f) Combien de raquettes de tennis y a-t-il?
g) Qu'est-ce que l'homme tient à la main droite?
h) Qu'est-ce que la petite fille prend?
i) Où est le garçon?
j) Où va la famille?

QUOTE UNQUOTE

'I can speak French but I cannot understand it.'
Mark Twain, US author

CLASSIC O LEVEL VOCABULARY TOPIC: EXCLAMATIONS

Agreed, all right! .... *D'accord!*

Cheer up! .... *Courage!*

Delighted (to meet you)! .... *Enchanté*

Excuse me! .... *Pardon! Excusez-moi!*

Cheers! .... *Santé!*

That's a shame! .... *C'est dommage!*

Hello! .... *Salut!*

Fire! .... *Au feu!*

Great! .... *Chouette! Formidable! Sensationnel!*

Really? .... *Vraiment? Sans blague?*

Have a good trip! .... *Bon voyage!*

See you soon! .... *À bientôt, À tout à l'heure*

Stop thief! .... *Au voleur!*

That's it! .... *C'est ça!*

Too bad! .... *Tant pis!*

What? .... *Comment?*

THE FRANGLAIS OF MARK TWAIN

'The people of those foreign countries are very, very ignorant. They looked curiously at the costumes we had brought from the wilds of America. They observed that we talked loudly at table sometimes. They noticed that we looked out for expenses, and got what we conveniently could out of a franc, and wondered where in the mischief we came from. In Paris they just simply opened their eyes and stared when we spoke to them in French! We never did succeed in making those idiots understand their own language. One of our passengers said to a shopkeeper, in reference to a proposed return to buy a pair of gloves, "Allong restay trankeel – may be ve coom Moonday"; and would you believe it, that shopkeeper, a born Frenchman, had to ask what it was that had been said. Sometimes it seems to me, somehow, that there must be a difference between Parisian French and Quaker City French.'

Mark Twain, *The Innocents Abroad*

How to say the letter 'r' in French

This growly, 'back-of-the-throat' sound argues the toss with 'u' as to which is the most difficult letter to pronounce properly in French, but here goes. Open your mouth. Close your throat (do a swallow and stop halfway through) and carefully enunciate the sound 'k', several times.

Concentrate on where in your throat that 'k' sound, referred to as the 'k part' from now on, is made. Keep feeling the 'k part', still imagining that you are halfway through swallowing, and tensing those muscles. Then gently push some air through, saying 'Ra-ra-ra' to practice. Don't panic that the sound produced is nothing like an English 'r' – the French 'r' is closer to the 'ch' in 'loch' and the 'kh' in Arabic, eg Akhmed.

ANIMAL PASSION

We are told that French is the language of love and certainly it seems that way when Serge Gainsbourg and Jane Birkin are growling their stuff in *Je t'aime... moi non plus* (although this isn't as sexy as you think it is when you realise that Jane Birkin is actually sighing about feeling Serge's love *entre mes reins...* (Sorry, you'll have to look that up because this is a family book).

Yet when we look at the terms of endearment that are listed as being habitual, a different picture emerges. From *ma biche* (my doe) to *mon lapin* (my rabbit) to *ma loutre* (my otter) and *ma puce* (my flea), the sentiment doesn't quite translate to English sensibilities. How romantic is an insect that bites you and makes you scratch? Even less appealing are the supposed endearments, *mon coco* (my coconut) and *ma crotte*, which is translated as 'my dropping' or 'doggy-do'.

Remember too that the possessive adjectives *mon* and *ma* (my) have to agree with the gender of the expression, *not* that of the person you're talking to/about (although it is a rule of thumb that *ma* and *mon* go with girls' and boys' terms respectively).

Hmm, the idea of boning up on our romantic French doesn't quite appeal suddenly. Some things just don't travel – we think we'll stick with a simple *'chéri(e)'*. So there.

Correct personal form?
Have you used the right tone of formality/informality with tu/vous?
The right 'person'? ie je/nous, il/elle, ils/elles

Verbs
Have you used the right tenses?
Do they agree with their subject?
Do the past participles agree (when with *être*)?

Nouns and Adjectives
Do they agree?
Are they in the right position?

Adverbs and Prepositions
Are they in the correct position?
Are they the right ones to use?

OH, I MEAN, REALLY: HOW ALL -OIR VERBS ARE IRREGULAR

We know perfectly well that *avoir* is a tricky, wee thing but did you remember that all verbs ending in -*oir* are irregular and ornery in their own special way?

Take *voir* and *devoir* – a logical person might think that *voir* would behave in the same way as *devoir* (just without the de, obviously) and, yes, they start off roughly the same – *je vois, je dois, tu vois, tu dois* (dizzy yet?). But just as we get into the first person plural – the 'we' person – they deviate and *nous devons* waves goodbye to *nous voyons*.

We'll tell you which are the more common -*oir* verbs – *avoir,* *s'asseoir, devoir, pouvoir, recevoir, savoir, pouvoir, voir* and *vouloir* – but declining them all would transport us back into that classroom a little too literally.

Instead we shall leave you with one more -*oir*ish moment: two -*oir* verbs exist only in the third person singular. They are *falloir* (to be necessary) and pleuvoir (to rain) – declined solely as *il faut* and *il pleut* respectively.

Before we roll our eyes however, think for a moment about 'you are raining' and 'we are raining', and you'll see the problem.

WORDS THAT ACTUALLY MAKE
YOU SOUND FRENCH

(rather than straight out of a classroom)

Je n'en reviens pas	*I can't believe it*
C'est pas vrai!	*You're kidding!*
En avoir marre/ras-le-bol	*To be fed up, angry*
J'en ai marre de ces pubs!	*I'm so sick of these ads!*
Tu te fous de ma gueule?	*Are you kidding me?/ Do you think I'm an idiot?*
Tu me prends pour qui?	*Who do you think you're dealing with?/ Do you think I'm stupid?*
Lâche-moi les baskets!	*Give me a break! Leave me alone!*
Casser les oreilles à quelqu'un	*To talk someone's ear off*
Ça coûte la peau des fesses!/Ça douille!	*That's really expensive!*
Beurk!	*Yuck!*
C'est dans la poche	*It's a sure thing*
Ça va être chaud!	*It's going to be tough!*
Ça gaze?	*How are things? What's up?*
Carrément	*Completely*
Rudement	*Very/terribly*
Pas mal de/un paquet de	*A lot of*
Super/mega/hyper	*Very/ultra*
Vachement	*Very/really*
Foutrement	*Extremely*
Oh, la vache!	*Oh, wow!*
Être de mauvais poil	*To be in a bad mood*
Péter les plombs/un cable	*To go crazy*
Perdre la boule/les pédales	*To lose one's mind*

QUOTE UNQUOTE

Liberté! Égalité! Fraternité!
(Liberty! Equality! Brotherhood!)
The slogan of the French Revolution

VI

CLASSICS

*If the Romans had been obliged to
learn Latin, they would never have
found time to conquer the world.*

Heinrich Heine, German poet

CHECKLIST OF GREEK AND ROMAN DEITIES

The Romans' mix-and-match pantheon of gods and goddesses chimed with their empire-building mentality. As can be seen by the close mapping of the Greek deities, Roman mythology becomes a slippery eel, a big piece of spin bent on legitimising the Roman past and manoeuvring the Roman future...

Greek	Roman	Role
Zeus	Jupiter/Jove	King of the Gods, God of Skies
Hera	Juno	Wife of King, Goddess of Marriage
Poseidon	Neptune	God of the Sea
Cronos	Saturn	King of the Titans
Gaia	Gaea	Goddess of the Earth
Hades	Pluto	God of the Underworld
Hephaestus	Vulcan	God of the Forge
Demeter	Ceres	Goddess of the Harvest
Ares	Mars	God of War
Aphrodite	Venus	Goddess of Love
Apollo	Apollo	God of the Sun, of Music
Artemis	Diana	Goddess of the Moon and Hunting (Apollo's twin sister)
Athena	Minerva	Goddess of Wisdom
Hermes	Mercury	Messenger of the Gods
Dionysus	Bacchus	God of Wine
Persephone	Proserpine	Queen of the Underworld
Eros	Cupid	God of Love

The blame for the collapse of the Roman Empire can almost, some historians agree, be traced back to the door of one lone individual's over-arching ambition and staggering incompetence as early as AD9.

Publius Quinctilius Varus's name may sound more like a sexually transmitted disease than a military leader's, but it doesn't sound as ugly as the man himself – this 'historic cock-up artist' described by Boris Johnson as having a 'big protuberant Roman snout, thick boobyish lips and a pudding-basin haircut'. Appearance and name aside, there wasn't much going for PQ Varus, responsible as he was for the biggest military disaster in the history of the Roman Empire: the battle of Kalkriese. Up to 30,000 soldiers, women and children were slaughtered; not one but three of the inestimably morale-significant sacred eagles of the legions were lost; Varus himself committed suicide – and never again did

Rome attempt to colonise beyond the Rhine. What had been an unstoppable spread had just come up against a brick wall of disaster and then fear.

Had Rome not failed, had Tiberius later pushed on into Germany, then history might have been very different: there would not be the cultural fissure down the middle of Europe between Latin and Northern, between wine sippers and beer sloshers. The people of Germany would now, like other ex-Roman Europeans, be speaking a Romance language; there would have been no Saxons – and hence no Anglo-Saxons to invade England and muddy the waters of our own Latinate areas of language. We might even be Latin-based speakers ourselves. Pause a minute and imagine a world of *Lapides Provolventes* (The Rolling Stones), *Ille Quis* (The Who) and *Pretium Iustum Est* (The Price is Right)...

QUOTE UNQUOTE

Status quo, you know, that is Latin for 'the mess we're in'.

Ronald Reagan, former US president

SHAKE IT ALL ABOUT

So these cases, what are they all about then? Is nominative when you choose a name? Accusative when you start getting stroppy and pointing fingers? No, no, no.

- **Nominative** is the subject: The blackboard was the absolute bane of our existence.

- **Vocative** is the case of address: O blackboard, I shall wipe you any minute!

- **Accusative** is the object: The teacher whacked the blackboard with his long pointer.

- **Genitive** is the 'of' case: The top of the blackboard was littered with all kinds of graffiti.

- **Dative** is the 'to' or 'for' case: The dunce talked to the blackboard, as if hoping it would help.

- **Ablative** is the 'from', 'by', 'in' or 'with' case: Right by the blackboard was the bell that would finally signify the end of the class.

KVESTIONS, KVESTIONS

The good news is that although the interrogative pronouns also have feminine and plural forms, the powers that be decided that they would let us off the hook about having to use them. The other good news is that, for once, the rules are clear: the question word in Latin always, always comes first in the sentence with no English-style word inversions (he has come?). *Quis* (who?), *quem* (whose?), *cuius* (whose? Of whom?), *cui* ('to whom?') and *a quo* (by whom?) are simply used as adverbs, bunged at the front and the rest of the sentence treated as usual. Phew. The only marginally tricky ones are which and what (*quid*) which is used as an adjective, agreeing with that noun, and therefore declining:

Nom	Qui	quae	quod	qui	quae	quae
Acc	Quem	quam	quod	quos	quas	quae
Gen	Cuius	cuius	cuius	quorum	quarum	quorum
Dat	Cui	cui	cui	quibus	quibus	quibus
Abl	Quo	qua	quo	quibus	quibus	quibus

And no quibbling at the back.

Who am I from Roman and Greek mythology?
I tackled a labyrinth and slayed a bull-like creature...

Answer on page 312

I SHALL SAY THIS ONLY ONCE

Only a true sadist could have decided that the Goddess of Memory should be called Mnemosyne, a name that most of us used up precious parts of our own memory trying to remember how to spell. Why not her sister Leto or niece Hera? Nice easy names that anyone can remember. It is doubly ironic, then, that it is the word mnemonic that means 'a pattern of letters or ideas which aids the memory'. Mnemonics were the very mainstay of Victorian Classics education: educational publishers thrived on pumping out ever more handbooks of doggerel that were then parroted faithfully by generations of Empire schoolboys in an attempt to remember all the fiendish exceptions in Latin.

One of the earliest uses of mnemonic verse to teach Latin was the *Doctrinale,* produced in 1199 by Alexander of Villedieu, which was an entire grammar of the language comprising 2,000 lines of doggerel verse. Despite sounding more like a punishment than a cure, it was used as a standard Latin grammar textbook across Europe for three centuries. Critics of Alexander at the time considered it to be 'a monstrous idea to squeeze an entire grammar into verses', but the verse form of *Doctrinale* in fact arose by accident. Alexander had been employed by the bishop of Dol-de-Bretagne to teach Latin to his nephews. He had noticed that the boys could not remember Priscian as prose, so he translated its rules into verse form. When Alexander was away one day, the bishop asked his nephews a grammar question, and was surprised when they answered in verse. The bishop persuaded Alexander to compile and to publish an entire book of such verses, which became the *Doctrinale*. From that point onwards, it was rare for a grammatical work to not at least contain the principal rules as mnemonic verses. Even the new humanistic grammars of the 15th century included the verses excerpted from *Doctrinale* or other versified grammars. This method of Latin (and Greek) grammar instruction was used by teachers well into the 20th century, and though frowned upon now as being too unthinking, too regimented, we happen to know that Classics pupils still value the occasional helping hand.

EVERYDAY IDIOMS – BUT WHAT DO THEY MEAN?

1. **A priori** . . . . from what comes before
2. **Ad hoc.** . . . . for a particular purpose
3. **Agenda** . . . . things to be done
4. **Alibi** . . . . elsewhere
5. **Caveat (emptor)** . . . . . . let him (the buyer) beware
6. **Curriculum vitae** . . . . . the course of one's life
7. **Deus ex machina.** . . . . . 'a god from a machine', a contrived or artificial solution
8. **Ex tempore** . . . . without premeditation
9. **In flagrante delicto.** . . . 'while the crime is blazing', caught red-handed (no sex inference)
10. **Habeas corpus** . . . . . . 'you must have the body', ie in law, you must justify the charge with physical evidence
11. **Ipso facto** . . . . by that very fact
12. **Mens rea.** . . . . guilty mind
13. **Moratorium** . . . . delay
14. **Ne plus ultra.** . . . . no further, impassable
15. **Nulli secundus** . . . . . . second to none
16. **Per se.** . . . . by, in itself
17. **Persona (non) grata.** . . (un)welcome person
18. **Post hoc.** . . . . after this
19. **Prima facie** . . . . at first sight, on the face of it
20. **Pro bono.** . . . . for the good of the public
21. **Res inter alios.** . . . . . . a matter between others (it's not our business)
22. **Sic** . . . . thus, just so
23. **Sui generis.** . . . . of his/her/its kind
24. **Veto.** . . . . I forbid
25. **Vice** . . . . in place of (ie vice versa – in place of this, reversed)

TICK, TOCK, TICK, TOCK

For the duration of time – for six months, for many years – just use simple accusative – *sex menses multos annos*. Almost all other time – in six months, at the fifth hour, on the sixth day, in a few years – is expressed by a simple ablative, again with no prepositions: *sex mensibus*, *quinta hora*, *sexto die*, *paucis annis*. Seems suspiciously easy...

A gentleman need not know Latin, but he should at least have forgotten it.

Brander Matthews, US writer

LET'S START AT THE VERY BEGINNING...
IT'S A VERY GOOD PLACE TO START

Say 'Latin' to anyone and they can spout *amo, amas, amat* at you, but a) can they finish conjugating and b) can they tell you what conjugating actually means? How about declensions? Indicative tenses? Participles? They're quiet now, aren't they? Well, along gallops *The Universal Crammer* to the rescue!

We are going to presume you know what nouns, verbs, adjectives are, so we shall skip condescension for 'declension': a grouping of the forms of nouns, adjectives and pronouns, according to numbers and cases.' As page five of *Kennedy's Shorter Latin Primer* (the Cliff Notes equivalent of the Bible of Latin grammar) states baldly: 'Latin has five declensions. The numbers are two, singular for one – *mensa*, a table. Plural for more than one – *mensae*, tables. The cases are six: nominative (the subject), vocative (the case of address), accusative (the object), genitive (the possessive 'of' case), dative (the 'to' or 'for' case) and ablative (the 'from', 'by', 'in', or 'with' case). Now go back and read that all again because it is truly the meat and two veg of the nouns/adjective/pronoun world.

Then we skip boldly over to the world of verbs, which are conjugated – in their finite form – according to their person, number, tense, mood and voice. The three persons – first ('I' in singular number, 'we' in plural), second ('you') and third ('he/she/it' or 'they') combine with their six tenses (present, future simple, past imperfect, perfect, future perfect and pluperfect), their three moods (indicative, imperative and subjunctive) and their voice (easy this: active or passive) to create technically elegant and exact phrasings that should have been the delight of every British schoolchild set to parse them.

The trouble was, there were those exceptions: hundreds of them littered balefully across the pages of primers, lurking around every grammatical corner. Suddenly we knew all about tricky language learning and felt sorry for those poor sewers who had to learn English...

Their heyday was around 1500-1200BC, they were the staples of Greek writers and then Greek playwrights, they were generally half-man, half-god but usually had less than godlike qualities when it came to their home lives and, strangely for such hunks, more often than not relied on their womenfolk's wiliness to get them out of trouble.

Perseus

Fathered by Zeus (who wasn't?) dressed up as a golden shower, then set adrift by nervous grandpa Acrisius; he killed Medusa the Gorgon (hair of snakes, turned men to stone, you remember her) with the help of Hermes' magic sword, Athena's shiny bronze shield and the winged sandals, invisible-cloaking cap and magic 'head'-bag from the nymphs of the North – by only looking at her reflection in his shield. Fell in love with Andromeda in Ethiopia on the way home, saving her from dread (then dead) sea monster but, once home, he accidentally killed King Acrisius, having gone to make up with him.

Heracles/Hercules

Another son of Zeus (but really got it in neck from jealous Hera) and great-grandson of Perseus. Mighty and brilliant from the moment he strangled two snakes in his cot (thanks, Hera) and then killed the mighty Thespian lion at 18; Hera then maddened him into killing his wife and children – the famous 'Twelve Labours' were a penance. Slept with 50 sisters in 50 days but his Lothario ways did for him when wife Deianira poisoned him. On his funeral pyre a thunderclap took him up to the gods, where Hera finally kissed and made up, giving him daughter Hebe as yet another wife.

Theseus

Home-grown hero credited with turning Athens into most powerful democratic city-state. Classic boy-impressing-dad life story; Theseus, product of King Aegeus and one night stand, volunteers for yearly tribute sacrifice of seven boys and seven girls to rulers Crete. Evil King Minos' daughter Ariadne fell in love at first sight, helped him defeat fearsome Minotaur (half man, half bull) and escape Labyrinth with a cunning ball of string. But true love didn't run smooth – whether by mistake or not, Theseus left Ariadne on Naxos, then returned to Athens without hoisting prearranged white sail of success. Heartbroken Aegeus duly hurled himself into sea (then called Aegean after him); later Theseus joins him after a chequered later life as great Athenian ruler and rubbish husband leads to an ignominious death falling off a cliff.

ROMAN VILLA

Living in a Roman villa would be comparable to living in a large country by today's standards. Comfort was important, as well as Roman mosaics that reflected their owners' personalities or accomplishments.

VIRGIL THE SPIN-DOCTOR

The name Virgil may strike fear into the hearts of many a Latin student (that and Caesar, whose interminable passages on war after war after war were learnt off by heart in translation rather than trying to translate them properly ourselves) but it turns out that it was he who came up with the idea of doctoring the 'history' provided by Homer in *The Iliad* and *The Odyssey* and Naevius' *Punic War*, and produce a ready-made hero to legitimise Rome: Aeneas. Virgil's *Aeneid*, written between 29-19BC, was a big fat piece of propaganda that told the story of Aeneas, who did reach the Tiber River that was to flow through Rome but that was about it. Woven through it were 'prophesies' (easy to bill them as such, 1,000 years after all the events) about how his 'founding' of the Rome dynasty would come to its most glorious fruition with Caesar Augustus. No prizes for guessing who Virgil's boss was...

DON'T MAKE A MOVE

The 'movement towards' rule always sounded rather threatening (perhaps because so much of the Latin we learned was martial and warlike in nature) but just turned out to be merely irritating. Just when we thought we had worked out the difference between the ablative and dative case, it transpired that there were rules about how direction or movement alter cases. And rules is rules. So here they are:

- When the movement is about common nouns and, at the other end of the grandness scale, whole nations – then use prepositions + accusative – ie *ad silvas*, to the woods; *ad Italia*, to Italy.

- When the movement concerns names of towns – no prepositions, accusative only – ie *Romam*; to Rome, *Athenas*, into Athens.

- The dreaded 'special words' are those exceptions that also take no prepositions and the accusative: ie *domum*, to home; *rus*, to the countryside; *humum*, to the ground.

- 'In' or 'At' obviously has no movement towards or away from – so is signified by the Latin 'in' and the noun in the ablative – except for names of cities or towns, which take the little used locative (1st and 2nd person singular = same as genitive, rest = same as ablative, so not that different – *in Romae, in Londinii, in Carthagine*).

OH, BRING ON THE DRAG QUEENS
WHILE YOU'RE AT IT

Most of the legwork in Latin had to do with figuring out what gender a word could be – because of all the declining that then had to be done (if only one could have declined to decline) – and trying, more out of hope than experience, to remember all the weird ones. The general rules of thumb were easy enough: all nouns showing sex (ie people and animals) have that gender; nouns ending in –a or –ae (1st declension) are feminine except male professions – like *agricola*; and nouns ending in –us are masculine, except *domus* (home), *manus* (hand) and various types of trees which are feminine and a far few, like *onus* and *tempus*, which are 'big intangibles' and neuter. Then we enter a whole world of hurt with all the exceptions in the other declensions… but we're not here to bring you pain, so we'll spare you that…

HOW DID THEY GET THIS MNEMONIC PAST US FILTH-MERCHANTS AT SCHOOL?

Gender in IV Declension
Feminina, trees in us,
With tribus, acus, porticus,
Domus, nurus, socrus, anus,
Idus (iduum) and manus.

HOW THE DINOSAURS SPOKE GREEK

They didn't, of course, but more than a passing rubric of Greek can be drummed into one's consciousness if you cram in a few dinosaurs' names – which then makes you look very cool with your three-year-old son...

- **Brontosaurus** *Greek* – 'Bronto' = thunder; *Greek* – 'saurus' = lizard, reptile

- **Megalosaurus** *Greek* – 'mega' = long, large, great

- **Pachyderm** *Greek* – 'pachy' = thick; *Greek* – 'derm' = skin

- **Protoceratops** *Greek* – 'protos' = first, earliest; *Greek* – 'cera, ceras' = horn; Greek – 'tops' = face

- **Pterodactyl** *Greek* – 'pteron' = feather, wing; *Greek* – 'dactylos' = finger

- **Rhinoceros** *Greek* – 'rhinos, rhino' = nose, snout; *Greek* – 'cera, ceras' = horn

- **Stegosaurus** *Greek* – 'stegos' = roof, cover

- **Triceratops** *Greek* – 'tri' = three

- **Tyrannosaurus rex** – a mixed-up kid; *Greek* – 'tyrannikos' = tyrant, *Greek* 'saurus' again; *Latin* – 'rex' = king

- **Velociraptor** *Latin* – the Roman one; 'veloci' = speedy; *Latin* – 'raptor' = robber, plunderer

WORK IT OUT

Find the odd one out:
- Os
- Fenestra
- Caput
- Lingua
- Laeva

Answer on page 312

ROMAN GODS: THE PREQUEL

It's not too much of a stretch to remember that the Romans played fairly fast and loose with their mythology, grafting what they had – some gods (Jupiter, Mars, Romulus-turned-Quirinus), a system of highly superstitious rituals and a love of animal sacrifice and entrail-gazing – onto the more developed Greek mythology and ending up with a remarkably similar castlist, just with different names (see page 136). But how much was native to them, and how much was borrowed from all the others they colonised in their 1100 years as a world Empire?

For the Romans it was all about syncretism, bringing together the gods, stories, rituals and emblems of various cultures, splicing them in with the 'numena' the original Italian gods, and making them Roman-owned. As Dr Blackwell says in *Mythology for Dummies*: 'A Roman might nod to his Lares and Penates (original Roman gods) in the morning, pray to Isis (Egyptian goddess) at lunchtime and attend a feast in honour of Heracles (Greek hero). In the afternoon, have his future told by a haruspex (priest trained in ancient Etruscan art of liver-based fortune telling) and end the day attending a meeting of the cult of Mithras (Persian deity whose followers met in caves).'

But it was the likes of Livy (c 284-207BC) who was the real spin-doctor; his Odyssia is much more than just a re-telling of Homer's *Odyssey* (written hundreds of years before), Livy substituted in some Roman gods and goddesses and changed the names of the others into their Roman counterparts, thereby creating a real Latin epic poem. Plutarch, Greek by birth but a Roman citizen, dabbled outside both of his 'native' cultures with treatises on both Isis and Osiris and two (Persian) Zoroastrian gods, one of whom, Mithras, went on to be a real hit with Roman citizens and a fully-fledged Roman god superstar.

MODERN LATIN

(With thanks to Henry Beard)

Ain tu?	Is that so?
Apudne te vel me?	Your place or mine?
Da mihi sis	I'll have a…
cerevisiam dilutam	lager
poculum vini albi	glass of white wine
spiculum argenteum	Martini
Dic itane est	You don't say!
Die dulci fruere	Have a nice day!
Fors fortis	Fat chance
Labra lege	Read my lips
Lege atque lacrima	Read 'em and weep
Noli me vocare, ego te vocabo	Don't call me, I'll call you
Non sum paratus me committere	I'm not ready to make a commitment
Nonne macescis?	Have you lost weight?
Nullo modo	No way!
Podex perfectus es	You are a total a**hole
Prandeamus	Let's have lunch!
Quid fit?	What's happening? Whassup?
Raptus regaliter	Royally screwed
Totus anctus	In a world of hurt
Tuos iube meis dicere	Have your people talk to my people
Visne saltare?	Do you want to dance?
Volo pactum facere	I'd like to cut a deal

HOW TO READ LATIN

To read Latin well is not so difficult, if you begin right. Correct habits of reading should be formed now. Notice the quantities carefully, especially the quantity of the penult, to insure you're getting the accent on the right syllable. Give every vowel its proper sound and every syllable its proper length. Then bear in mind that we should read Latin as we read English, in phrases rather than in separate words. Group together words that are closely connected in thought. No good reader halts at the end of each word.

Latin for Beginners, by Benjamin Leonard D'Ooge (1860-1940)

1. Nemean Lion: could not be hurt by weapons: Hercules choked it to death.

2. Lernian Hydra: nine heads, growing two new ones for each one chopped off. Not a problem: Hercules cauterised each stump as he beheaded each and then buried the last, immortal, one under a rock.

3. Golden Hind of Cerynitia: horns of gold and couldn't be killed because it was sacred to Artemis. Took a year to track it down and catch it (with tacit help of Artemis).

4. Erymanthian Boar: One of the easier tasks, but Hercules wasted time dawdling; finally cornered the boar in the snow of Mt Erymanthus.

5. Augean Stables: Hercules cut deals all round to clean the famously filthy stables of King Augeas (Poseidon's son) in one day – by diverting a nearby river.

6. Stymphalian birds: Athena came to the rescue with a pair of Hephaestus-forged bronze castanets with which Hercules noisily flushed the birds out from their forest in Arcadia.

7. Cretan Bull: the Daddy of the Minotaur, this white bull had impregnated a bewitched Pasiphae, wife to King Minos, via a cunning hoist devised by Daedalus; Hercules brought it back to Mycenae but no one actually wanted it so it just roamed the countryside.

8. Mares of Diomedes: strange man-eating horses belonging to the son of Ares; Hercules beat him at arm-wrestling, killed him and fed him in little bits to the mares, who promptly lost their taste of human meat…

9. Belt of Hippolyta: Hippolyta had agreed to give our boy her belt, but Hera spread the word that the Hercules Gang were actually after the Amazonians' bodies; when Hippolyta showed up armed to the teeth, Hercules assumed she was doing the dirty on him and killed her, stealing the belt.

10. Cattle of Geryon: herd of cattle guarded by three-bodied monster on a far flung western island. Getting them was easy enough; bringing them back as a complete herd proved more of a headache.

11. Golden Apples of the Hesperides: Hercules did his usual fast-talking with Atlas, saying he would hold the earth for a sec while Atlas popped up to get the apples; Atlas did so but, not surprisingly, wouldn't take the earth back again saying it was now Hercules' turn. Thinking quickly, Hercules agreed but asked if he could just quickly hand earth back to Atlas while he got a more comfortable forehead pad… and promptly legged it.

12. Hound of Hades: Cerberus had just the three heads and, having promised Hades that he wouldn't use weapons, Hades simply flung his arms around all three necks and hung on for grim death until the fearsome dog eventually capitulated.

Rident stolidi verba Latina
(fools laugh at the Latin language).
Ovid, Roman poet

ROMAN GLADIATORS

The net fighter *retiarius* versus the heavily-armed *secutor*
Net fighter gladiators were the most vulnerable, only having a shoulder guard
to protect them, but they could move more nimbly than the heavily armoured
retiarius and inflict deadly blows with their tridents.

Just as nouns fall into declensions, verbs are grouped by conjugations: four regular types of verbs distinguished by the final sound of the Present stem before the suffix of the present infinitive active is added. In layman's terms, all Latin verbs in their infinitive form (to be, to go, to howl at the moon) end in –re; it's the connecting vowel just before that signposts the differences: add to that the other principal parts and this is your launch pad into how all regular verbs 'react' to all differences of person, tense, mood and voice.

Active voice principal parts:

Conj	Stem	1st Pn	Inf Pres	Perfect	Supine	English
1st	-a	amo	amare	amavi	amatum	To love
2nd	-e	moneo	monere	monui	monitum	To warn
3rd	cons't or u	rego	regere	rexi	rectum	To rule
4th	i	audio	audire	audivi	auditum	To hear
		I hear	*To hear*	*I have heard*	*In order to hear*	

Passive voice principal parts:

Conj	Stem	1st Pn	Inf Pres Participle	Perfect	Gerundive
1st	-a	amor	amari	amatus	amandus
2nd	-e	Moneor	moneri	monitus	monendus
3rd	cons't or u	regor	regi	rectus	regendus
4th	-I	audior	audiri	auditus	audiendus
		I am heard	*To be heard*	*Heard*	*Fit to be heard*

Ignoring for a moment all the irregular exceptions to the above, this table now means that you can bring all manner of verbs here by the scruff of their neck, wriggling and protesting, and wrestle them into one of the conjugations above according to that connecting vowel.

Amor vincit omnia (love conquers all)
Virgil, Roman philosopher and poet

BOTH FEET IN THE PAST

When one is droning through the fourth declension complement second accusative, it's hard not to get sulky about Latin and wonder what the point of it all is… but the simple truth is that once you know a bit of Latin, you can read almost any Romance language just by recognising the stem. So test yourself on a few of the words below and start planning that continental mini-break:

1. **anthropos:** man, human being *anthropology, misanthrope*
2. **brevis:** short *brevity, abbreviate*
3. **cognito:** know *cognisant, recognise*
4. **credo:** believe *credible, incredulous*
5. **culpa:** blame *culpable, culprit*
6. **dominus:** a lord, master *dominate, dominion*
7. **fido:** to trust, believe *confide, infidel*
8. **genus:** kind, origin *generic, congenital*
9. **lego, lectum:** read, thing read *intellect, legible*
10. **locus:** a place *local, dislocate*
11. **morior:** die *mortal*
12. **nihil:** nothing *nihilism, annihilate*
13. **pathos:** suffering, feeling *sympathy, apathy*
14. **pendo:** weigh, hang *depend, pendant*
15. **per:** through *perceive, persist, persevere*
16. **phobos [g]:** fear *phobia, claustrophobia*
17. **porto:** carry *transport, export*
18. **sanguis:** blood *sanguine*
19. **satis:** enough *satisfy*
20. **solus:** alone *solo, desolate*
21. **spiritus:** breath *inspire, spirit*
22. **tractum:** drawn, pulled *distract, tractor*
23. **usus:** use *abuse, utensil*
24. **vacuus :** empty *evacuate, vacuum*
25. **via:** way, road *deviate, viaduct*

TROJAN HORSE, ROMAN WOLF
OR COCKAMAMIE?

The story of how Rome was founded was one of the more enjoyable lessons we had, with its mix of Mowgli-style feral sucklings, murder, rape and mystery. In what was already a classical cliché, baby twins (and apparent descendants of Trojan Aeneas) Romulus and Remus fall foul of a succession issue and are thrown abandoned into the Tiber in a basket. River god Tiberius saves them; they are then suckled by a she-wolf before being brought up by local good-hearted shepherd to be knockabout strapping youths who realise their birthright, knock off Bad Uncle Amulius, then scrap over which hill to found their new city on. Remus gets his head bashed in with a spade, leaving Romulus sole victor but in a woman-free city; so his merry men kidnap (and rape) 700 Sabine women in an exercise of forcible-populating; by the time their Sabine menfolk really get their act together, the Sabine women have already starting producing Roman babies so, eminently sensible as women are in these circumstances, persuade both sides to lay down weapons and live together.

Romulus rules for 38 years but gets high-handed towards the end, leaving his Senate unconsulted, toothless and frustrated; cue mysterious death of Romulus when he disappears during a vicious storm never to be seen again. A wily Senator claims he saw him going up to heaven asking to be remembered in godly form as Quirinus, so with a sigh of relief the Romans abandon sticky issue of Romulus' disappearance and opt for deification and getting on with the everyday business of colonising the rest of Italy.

From beginning to end, Rome's founding is gripping and who cares if the she-wolf aspect turns out to be a mistranslation (more likely, she was a foxy prostitute-turned-shepherd's wife and the twins' inadvertent wet nurse); who cares if there is more than a whiff of home-grown traditions being grafted onto Greek heroic legend (making the Trojans the ancestors of the Roman people) in an early example of epic spin by Roman chroniclers: why else would Roman centurions have taken a uniform based so closely on the Greeks' drawings of the Trojans? Without the drama and mythology we'd have got just another hilltop town.

With Aeneas, fated twins, murder and mysterious disappearances, we got the launch of the Rome phenomenon.

WORK IT OUT

I am the Titan of light, the father of the sun, the moon, and the dawn. Who am I?

Answer on page 312

NEVER TICKLE A SLEEPING DRAGON

Or, *Draco dormiens nunquam titillandus...* showing us that JK Rowling really knew her stuff when it came to the classics. She didn't stop here: the Harry Potter series is woven through with cod Latin and classical references; now you can even read her books all the way through in Latin (we think we hear the death-knell of Caesar as a set text...), starting with *Harrius Potterus et Philosophi Lapis*. See below for the genuine Latin articles:

accio . . . . I summon, call to me
arduus . . . . steep, high
arma . . . . weapons, armour
augeo . . . . I increase
dens . . . . a tooth
dormio . . . . I sleep (*dormiens* is a present participle: sleeping)
draco . . . . a snake or dragon
ex . . . . out of, from
expello . . . . I send away
expectoro . . . I send out from my chest / heart (*pectus* means chest or heart)
exspecto . . . . I wait for / expect / need
Hermes . . . . the (Greek) name of the Messenger god
(his Roman name is Mercury)
imperium . . . . power, area of supreme authority
impero . . . . I order or command
incendium . . . . a fire
incendo . . . . I kindle, set alight
levo . . . . I make light (*levitas* = lightness)
lumen . . . . light
ludo . . . . I play
nox . . . . night, darkness
nunquam (or numquam) . . . . never
patronus . . . . a protector or sponsor
Sirius . . . . the Roman name for the star known as the Dog-star

The decline and fall of Rome in a nutshell

In AD417, the Gallic pagan poet Rutilius Namatianus said of Rome: 'You have made out of diverse races, one patria, one country. You have made a city out of what was the world'. Ironically, the Empire was beginning to tumble down past Rome's ears – the capital itself had already momentarily fallen to Alaric and his Visigoths in AD410 – but in a way this makes the praise all the more encompassing: such was the power and might of Rome that nobody could seriously believe that her shadow wasn't permanently laid over what was then considered the very limits of the civilized world.

Since its foundation in 753BC (and after the early centuries of merely duffing up those tribes around them), Rome had been both scourge and saviour of Europe, Asia and Africa for centuries, to the point where the inhabitants of those many countries could hardly believe in any possible opposing power; where fear mingled with admiration, awe and even worship. By the 5th century, the idea of Rome had outstripped herself as a symbol of irresistible force as the Romans juggernauted through three continents to become something more elevated, almost deified – the Queen of Civilisation, the giver of enlightenment and happiness. The Roman approach of assimilation and intermarriage – the view was that anyone was a potential Roman citizen – had the happy effect of creating a universal sense of Romanness, so that it wasn't just the military might, or the drill and discipline – it was the undeniable economic success and thereby the peacefulness of this rich and varied but connected monoculture that made it the Greatest Empire Ever. At the height of power, about 1 million people lived in Rome itself, with over 50 million in the Empire as a whole.

In the end, of course, Rome fell – collapsed on all fronts – political, economic and cultural, on an unparalleled scale, even though most of the invading Goths, Vandals, Huns and Franks actually wanted to ape Rome. In parcelling up the spoils – the Ostrogoths got Italy, the Vandals got Spain, etc – the new arrivals lost sight of the 'one-ness' of Rome. Only in the East (the Byzantines never called themselves such but stuck to Rhomoi, 'Roman citizens'), did the Roman culture survive longer.

There were other effects too. As Boris Johnson writes in *The Dream of Rome*: 'The army disintegrated. The population shrank. Plagues raged... Above all, it was the end of the amazing Roman literacy: it was not just Virgil who was buried in the night of the Dark Ages, it was reading and writing'.

Rome was dead, long lived nothing like it thereafter.

THE GREEK GOD ZEUS

In ancient Greek religion Zeus was the chief deity of the pantheon, a sky and weather god who was identical with the Roman god Jupiter. Zeus was regarded as the sender of thunder and lightning, rain, and winds, and his traditional weapon was the thunderbolt. He was called the father of both gods and men.

WAY TO GO

When Caesar conquered Britain in AD43, the Romans brought with them their famous straight roads (the Britons were idle farmers, not moving much). They built them on raised embankments – in Old English, they were called highways – and in between the towns developed for trade and markets, they built layered roads (stratum) that were called 'straets' by the English, or 'streets'. Hundreds of miles of streets and roads were created, with the word 'mile', coming from mille, meaning 1,000, because the Roman mile was measured by 1,000 paces; a rather shorter mile than today's measurement.

VII

RELIGIOUS EDUCATION

Religion is a culture of faith;
science is a culture of doubt.

Richard Feynman, US physicist

'Religion is the sigh of the oppressed creature, the heart of a heartless world, the spirit of unspiritual conditions,' said Karl Marx, before going on to comment, 'It is the opiate of the masses.' Whether you are a Marxist or a Jehovah's Witness, schooldays' enthusiast or grown-up atheist, the chances are you'll have a view on religion, a set of beliefs and practices, often associated with a concept of supernatural power, that shapes or directs human life (and death) or a commitment to a system of ideas that provide coherence for one's existence. Even communities that seem cut off from the rest of the world seem to have a religion in the first place.

Religions can be monotheistic or polytheistic – that is, worshipping one or many gods – or pantheistic, which basically means there's a deity in everything. Polytheistic religions believe that each god controls one aspect of nature or human activity – fertility, agriculture and hunting being the usual contenders for the top spot – while some are non-theistic and do not follow a supreme creator or creators at all – like Buddhism or Jainism.

Interestingly, the lion's share of the world's religious choice goes to the monotheistic religions – eg Islam, Christianity and Judaism – all of which, despite their huge ideological differences, developed in the Middle East and share many rituals, festivals, mythology and an often similar-sounding God. Jesus, for example, is considered a prophet by Muslims. Today, it is this melting pot that informs the religious studies syllabus – but most of us were taught about religion according to the school we attended; and our religious studies exam reflected the largely Christian bias of that education, with little gobbets of 'other' religions merely thrown in for a bit of colour. Of course, all this went over our heads at the time – we just focused on the fact that if you did RE, you got to watch that film about the lifecycle of a sperm. Remember that?

QUOTE UNQUOTE

If we have to give up either religion or education, we should give up education.
William Jennings Bryan, US politician

IN A NUTSHELL: THE LIFE OF JESUS

- **Born in Bethlehem** during a census; returned to Nazareth with mother Mary and Joseph.
- **Taken to the Temple** at the age of 12; found in discussion with rabbis, 'advanced in wisdom and favour with men'.
- **Baptised** by John when about 30 years old.
- **Followed by 40 days' fasting** in the wilderness; devil tries to tempt him.
- **Next three years:** early Ministry in Galilee and gathering of disciples: Peter, James and John chosen first.
- **Miracles,** Parables and Sermon on the Mount.
- **Transfiguration,** seen with Moses and Elijah.
- **Journey to Jerusalem**
- **Entry to Jerusalem:** Palm Sunday.
- **Monday:** threw the moneychangers out of the Temple.
- **Tuesday to Wednesday:** teaching, healing, annoying the Pharisees.
- **Thursday:** The Last Supper.
- **Friday:** trials, crucifixion, death at 3pm.
- **Sunday:** resurrection.
- **40 days later:** ascension.

FENDING OFF 'THE ENEMY'

Starting RE early will build a barrier against the Man Downstairs, according to Timothy Dwight:
Religious Education should be begun in the dawn of childhood. The earliest days, after intelligence is fairly formed in the mind, are incomparably the best for this purpose. The child should be taught, as soon as he is capable of understanding the Instructions, which are to be communicated. Nothing should be suffered to pre-occupy the place, which is destined to truth. If the intellect is not filled with sound instruction, as fast as it is capable of receiving it, the enemy, who never neglects to sow tares when parents are asleep, will imperceptibly fill it with a dangerous and noxious growth. The great and plain doctrines of religion should be taught so early, that the mind should never remember when it began to learn...
From *Theology: Explained and Defended in a Series of Sermons* (1830)

This is the way the disciples run.
Peter, Andrew, James and John
Philip and Bartholomew
Thomas next and Matthew too
James the less and Judas the greater
Simon the zealot and Judas the traitor.

KNOWING YOUR TERMS: DIASPORA, ASHKENAZIM, SEPHARDIM

Often blamed on the Romans' sacking of Jerusalem in AD70 and the mass suicide of Masada in AD73, after which the Jews actively scattered from the homeland they had lived in for over a millennium, the Jewish Diaspora (literally, 'dispersion' or 'scattering') had begun long before; in fact, by then there were already four or five times as many Jews outside Palestine as within. When the Assyrians conquered the Promised Land in 722BC, the Hebrews scarpered all over the Middle East and disappeared almost entirely from the pages of history. So it is from 597BC, when Nebuchadnezzar allowed the Judaeans he had deported to live in a unified community in Babylon, and when another fleeing group settled in the Nile delta, leaving a tight group back in Judaea, that the Diaspora is usually dated, bringing with it the dual meaning of both scattering and consolidating: all three communities were, by and large, allowed to keep their religion, laws and customs. Since then, the diaspora has taken in every continent, every country and every border. The Ashkenazi Jews are those descended from the medieval Jewish communities of the Rhineland who spread into Central and Eastern Europe and beyond, via emigration, to the Americas – today they make up about 80% of all Jews worldwide. Often mentioned as the counterpoint to the Ashkenazim are the Sephardim, the Jews that spread from the Middle East into the Iberian Peninsula.

- **Anger management**: 'Let not the sun go down upon your wrath.' *Ephesians 4:26*
- **Being pushy**: 'Ask and it will be given to you; seek and you will find; knock and it will be opened to you.' *Matthew 7:7*
- **Birth and death**: 'For everything there is a season, and a time for every matter under heaven: a time to be born, and a time to die.' *Ecclesiastes 3.1-4*
- **Divorce**: 'Jesus replied: "Moses permitted you to divorce your wives because your hearts were hard. But it was not this way from the beginning. I tell you that anyone who divorces his wife, except for marital unfaithfulness, and marries another woman commits adultery."' *Matthew 19:8-9*
- **Gardening**: 'Then the Lord God placed the man in the Garden of Eden to cultivate it and guard it.' *Genesis 2:15*
- **Joy**: 'Tell the heavens and earth to celebrate and sing! Command every mountain to join in song!' *Isaiah 49:13*
- **Kindness**: 'And be kind to one another, tenderhearted, forgiving one another.' *Ephesians 4:32*
- **Love**: 'Beloved, let us love one another: for love is of God; and every one that loveth is born of God and knoweth God... God dwelleth in us, and his love is perfected in us.' *John 4:7, 11-12*
- **Marriage**: 'Husbands ought to love their wives as their own bodies. He who loves his wife loves himself.' *Ephesians 5:28*
- **Money**: 'Happy is the man who finds wisdom and understanding, for the gain from it is better than gain from silver and profit better than gold.' *Proverbs 3:13, 14*
- **Parents**: 'Listen to your father who gave you life and do not despise your mother when she is old.' *Proverbs 23:22*
- **Peace**: 'Do not overcome evil by evil, but overcome evil with good.' *Romans 12:21*
- **Prejudice**: 'There is neither Jew nor Greek, there is neither bond nor free, there is neither male nor female: for ye are all one in Christ...' *Galatians 3:28*
- **Sadness**: 'For thou shalt forget thy misery; Thou shalt remember it as waters that are passed away.' *Job 11:16*
- **Teenagers**: 'And why are you anxious about what to wear? Consider the lilies of the field, how they grow; they toil not, neither do they spin. And yet I say to you, that even Solomon in all his glory is not arrayed like one of these.' *Matthew 6:28-29*
- **War**: 'Prepare for war; rouse the warriors; let all the fighting men draw near and attack.' *Joel 3:9*

BREWING UP A GOOD CUP OF RELIGION

The point at which the Hebrew religion is said to start (up to that point Man was too busy being Created, Falling, being Flooded and generally finding his feet with God to set about organising a religion) is in about 1,700BC when Abram, son of a man called Terah who lived 240km/ 150 miles north of the Dead Sea, received a direct call from God to go to a new land which he and his descendants would make into a nation. The fact that Abram upped sticks and went across the Jordan to Canaan where he and family became known as the 'Hebrews' – those who had crossed the river – is evidence of his real faith in God. Whereas the covenant with Noah was between God and all mankind, the covenant between God and Abram was between God and his 'chosen people'– the 'mark' of being chosen was the act of circumcision, in return for which God would care for and protect Abraham (as he was now re-named) and his descendants, 'as many as the stars in the sky'.

CRAFTY CRAM... ISLAM

Islam means 'submission', to the Shahada, or Profession of Faith – 'there is no god but God, and Muhammad is the Prophet of God'. Muslims believe that Islam has always existed as the way of life God intended for humankind; guidance is taken from the Qur'an (Koran) and the Hadith – the words and deeds of Muhammad, born AD570, who went from 40-year-old merchant to enlightened preacher of Allah, the one god, as well as prophet and social campaigner, who died in the arms of his favourite wife, A'isha, in AD632. Nearly 90% are Sunni (sunna means path, the way of Muhammad), with splinter groups thereof – most of the remaining 10% are Shi'i

(from Shi'at Ali, meaning party of Ali, the Prophet's cousin and son-in-law, more emphasis on suffering and martyrdom). Islamic fundamentalism, with its jihad ('holy war') is the extreme end of both branches, but shunned by the vast majority. The five Pillars of Islam are the cornerstones: Shahada, the Creed; Salat, prayer (five times, facing Mecca); Saum, fasting (from dawn to dusk during Ramadan); Zakat, gift-offering (at least 2.5% should be given to the poor) and Hajj, pilgrimage (at least once, Muslims must go to the Ka'ba at Mecca).
Worship in: mosque.
Spiritual centre: Mecca (in Saudi Arabia).

Few religions are totally new but tend to concentrate on and develop one facet in tandem with the personal vision of their founder...

Baha'ism

Peace-loving sect founded in 1860s by Persian self-declared prophet and 'incarnation of God' Baha'u'llah – now with more than seven million followers in 200 countries.

Cao Dai

Colourful South Vietnamese blend of Christianity, Buddhism, Taoism and Confucianism, founded in 1920s and based on strictly ascetic practices.

Jehovah's Witnesses

Founded in the late 19th century, with millenarian belief that Christ will return to Earth and save the Chosen Few. Dependent on missionaries to spread the word.

Mennonites and Amish

Pacifist, non-modernising separatist communities in the US, originally based on New Testament Dutch reform pioneers fleeing to the New World.

Mormons

Church of Jesus Christ of the Latter Day Saints, set up when its founder, Joseph Smith had a vision in 1822, with millenarian belief that Christ will establish a new Jerusalem in America. No longer practises polygamy.

Quakers

Pared-down Christian movement, aka Society of Friends, founded by George Fox in the 17th century, with no priests or sacrament – God is just present when Friends meet.

Rastafarianism

Originated in Jamaica in 1930s after the coronation of 'new messiah' Prince Ras Tafari as emperor of Ethiopia with the title Haile Selassie. Rastafarians see themselves and those of African descent as the Israelites of the Old Testament. The Bible plays a central role, as does diet and smoking 'ganga'.

Scientology

Developed in 1950s by L Ron Hubbard. Beliefs include the theory that guilt feelings build up over several reincarnations. Scientology is loaded with money, but weighed down by suspicion over its secrecy and recruitment methods.

Seventh Day Adventists

William Miller founded this in the US with the prediction that the world would end in 1843-44... when it didn't, they concluded not enough people were keeping the Sabbath.

What is the other name for the 10 Commandments?
Answer on page 312

THE GOSPEL ACCORDING TO...?

In the still tumultuous and truth-seeking hurly-burly that is the world of scriptural research, the traditional view of the Synoptic Gospels ('Syn-optic' because the first three books of the New Testament – Matthew, Mark and Luke – all describe the life of Jesus from the same point of view) was that they were largely biographies written by well-known Christian authors, recording the life of Jesus as a story with some regard for chronological sequence. Each has its own 'voice', discipline, and particular 'beef' – eg Matthew is surmised to be a Jewish convert to Christianity, intent on defending his new faith against Jewish opponents and invoking Old Testament precedent to make the point that Jesus was the fulfillment of Old Testament prophecy.

In the last hundred years, however, it has become the view (not universally accepted) that, of the three, only Mark's is truly the original source (and even then, is written nearly 70 years after the events he is describing, although that dating has also been questioned). Both Matthew and Luke improve Mark's style, refine his slangy language and reject his use of Aramaic for direct quotes from Jesus and tend to treat the Apostles with a reverence that Mark, who was closer to the nitty-gritty days of the disciples, hadn't bothered with.

This white-glove treatment goes for Jesus as well; where Mark describes him as a straight 'carpenter', Matthew and Luke distance their Lord from getting his hands dirty, calling him the 'carpenter's son'. But then it all starts to get a bit James Bond: after totting up the verses that are repeated from Mark by Matthew and Luke, it becomes clear that there are a good 250 verses that are so identically shared by the pair that a second written source must have been copied...

This mysterious 'other' voice is always referred to rather portentously as 'Q' (but with no gadgets up his sleeve), thought to originate in Antioch, in Syria, as early as 30AD so even closer to the action than Mark. Last but not least is the Gospel of John, written later, around AD100. John represents a very different perspective and is heavily influenced by Platonic philosophy.

THE LAST SUPPER

Based on *The Last Supper* by Leonardo da Vinci

The painting depicts the moment that Jesus said to his disciples:

Now when the even was come, he sat down with the twelve.
And as they did eat, he said, Verily I say unto you, that one of you shall
betray me.
And they were exceeding sorrowful, and began every one of them to say
unto him, Lord, is it I?
And he answered and said, He that dippeth his hand with me in the
dish, the same shall betray me.
Matthew 26

The disciples are all reacting in horror at the thought that someone at the
table would betray their master.

KEEPING US IN CHECK

Man's rebellious streak provides the need for religious education, according
to Charles Grandison Finney, writing in the mid-1800s:
Religion is the work of man. It is something for man to do. It consists in
obeying God. It is man's duty. It is true, God induces him to do it. He
influences him by his Spirit, because of his great wickedness and reluctance
to obey. If it were not necessary for God to influence men – if men were
disposed to obey God, there would be no occasion to pray. 'O Lord, revive
thy work.' The ground of necessity for such a prayer is, that men are wholly
indisposed to obey; and unless God interpose the influence of his Spirit, not a
man on Earth will ever obey the commands of God.
From *Lectures on Revivals of Religion* (1835)

I know God wouldn't give me anything I couldn't handle. I just wish he didn't trust me so much.

Mother Theresa, Roman Catholic nun

A PILGRIM'S PROGRESS

Obsessed as we were with collecting badges in our schooldays – from Scouts and Girl Guides to the CND logos and punk exclamations that we pinned all over bookbags and rucksacks – we were merely following in the footsteps of some truly dedicated badge-collectors: Christian pilgrims. From as early as the 3rd century, Christians set out on foot, horseback or by cart. The sun of Our Lady of Walsingham, St Catherine's wheel, the bell of St Thomas a Becket, the eagle of St John and the shell of St James that went on to become the generic emblem of pilgrimage – all represented a lively market in small lead badges that pilgrims wore pinned to their hats as a visible 'map' of where they'd been and, by association, how blessed holy they were. Pilgrimage was by no means just a Christian pastime: all major religions, past and present, have had their holy centres to which believers are drawn, not just for a quick sightsee but as a physical manifestation of their faith, like Mecca for Muslims, Buddha's birthplace at Kapilavastu, or Karnak for Ancient Egyptians. The Holy Land, for example, acts as a focal point for both Jews, Christians, Muslims and those of the (slightly lesser-known) Baha'i faith. The journey alone has as much significance as the final destination – as can be read in Bunyan's *Pilgrim's Progress* or Chaucer's *Canterbury Tales* – but often created unexpected side effects: flourishing trade routes or, in the Middle Ages, a 'holy' excuse for the slaughter of the Crusades. Ironically, for people who disdained and banned religion, the personality cults encouraged by communist leaders led to quasi-religious pilgrimages of the modern age, as anyone who had seen the snaking queues around the tombs of Lenin or Ho Chi Minh would agree.

A SHOPPING BASKET OF MIRACLES

- **Healing:** the Paralysed Man (*Mark 2:1-12*). Man on litter is brought to Jesus, told to pick up his bed and walk. Thrown into the bargain is the news from Jesus that his sins are forgiven – this presumption of the authority to do so maddened the Pharisees.

- **Healing on Sabbath:** the Man with the Withered Hand (Matthew *12:9-14*). Healing him enraged and united previous enemies, the Pharisees and Herodians: Jesus argued that to do good could not be wrong at any time and yah-boo-sucks to Sabbatarian niceties.

- **Raising the Dead:** the Daughter of Jairus (*Luke 8:40-56*). Messengers tell Jesus that the girl is dead, he says she's sleeping and rouses her with words: 'Talitha cum' meaning, 'Get up, my child'. Coma or miracle? Seen as Act of God: death is no longer final.

- **Raising the Dead:** Lazarus (*John 11:1*). A close friend of Jesus is being mourned by his mother and sister, having been dead for four days. Jesus commands him to: 'Arise, Lazarus!' So he does.

- **Restoring Sight:** Blind Bartimaeus (*Luke 18:35-45*). This marks the point where Jesus's miracles stopped being private and offhand but public and deliberate; the time for secrecy is past – Bartimaeus is healed instantaneously with a word and then invited to become a follower.

- **Exorcism:** Madman and the Gadarene swine (*Mark 5:1-20*). A lunatic's demons are exorcised by Jesus and sent into a herd of pigs, whereupon they promptly all go mad, hurl themselves off a cliff and drown in the sea. Everyone is happy – swine are unclean so who cares about the pigs?!

- **Controlling Nature:** Stilling of the Storm: (*Matthew 8:23-27*). Jesus is asleep in a boat on the Sea of Galilee, woken up by panicking disciples during a storm; rebukes storm and calms it, then rebukes disciples for panicking – ie keep your nerve, keep your faith.

- **Controlling Nature:** Feeding of the Five Thousand: (*Luke 9:10-17*). The only miracle recorded in all four gospels so must have seemed important. Jesus, praying to God and with only five loaves of bread and two fish, feeds a large crowd of listeners in precursor to Eucharist bread-as-body phenomenon.

The story of Moses is one that we've heard from the days of our own Moses basket – first, the miraculous escape from a massacre of Hebrew first-borns where a baby Moses is found in a basket in the reeds of the river by an Egyptian princess and, ironically, brought up in the palace of the man who meant to kill him. Then we have the Burning Bush, the plagues and the miraculous 'pass-over' of the Angel of Death – all fantastical elements of another thumpingly good Bible story. But they saved the best for last – the parting of the sea as the Israelites flee Pharoah's charioteering army. Seldom have so many academics been so exercised by a Bible passage: was it the Red Sea? Could it possibly have really been parted by a bit of strong wind? Probably not – some insist that the original Hebrew read 'yam suph', which should

have been translated as 'Reed Sea' ie more of a shallow inland lake – while others say that though it wasn't the Red Sea, it was more likely an extension of the Gulf of Suez. Then the creationists insist that, hell yes, with the cited strong east wind, a shallow-ish sea could have been blown off shallow sandbanks, allowing the Israelites through, only to slacken when the Egyptians followed – causing the waters to swirl back again and catch them like sitting ducks. Whatever the 'truth', the story of the Exodus is a great one and one in which it was specifically believed to be the hand of God that intervened in the Israelites' favour – as can be seen in the ancient fragment of the 'Song of Miriam', the sister of Moses and Aaron: 'I will sing to Yahweh for He is exalted gloriously; Both horse and chariot rider He has cast into the sea!'

WANT TO GET SOMETHING OFF YOUR CHEST?

Would you like to email the Pope? Try benedictxvi@vatican.va. Want to beard the Archbishop of Canterbury? Contact him through www.archbishopofcanterbury.org. Or how about the Dalai Lama? You could try transcendental meditation but it's probably easier to click on ohhdl@gov.tibet.net. Though not available in our schooldays (by snail mail we had as much chance of contact with holiness as we had with *Jim'll Fix It*), God is now but one mouseclick away...

WORK IT OUT

What two books of the Bible are named after women?
Answer on page 312

RECIPE FOR DISASTER

Water that changed into blood, frogs, maggots, flies, mad sick cows, boils, hail, locusts, darkness and the death of every first-born in the country.... Is this an Apocalyptic, slasher horror novel or the Bible story of the plagues visited upon the poor old Egyptians?

ALWAYS LOOK ON THE BRIGHT SIDE OF LIFE

Life of Brian, Monty Python's utterly brilliant (an obviously objective view) pastiche of the Jesus Story, was released in 1979, so was very much a feature of our schooldays. Blessed was the RE class that had an enlightened enough teacher to play the video to the class so that we could show off our understanding of all its in-jokes. But it was only recently, when the *Secret Life of Brian* TV documentary was re-aired that most of us got to realise the scale of the real-life controversy that was unleashed upon the Monty Python team. In a hilarious interview with an outraged Malcolm Muggeridge and a frothing Bishop of Southwark, the Pythons were accused of everything from godlessness to outright blasphemy, despite the constant reminder from the foursome that, doh, the film really was about someone called Brian and the only time Jesus was actually mentioned was the throwaway line: 'oh, *that* do-gooder' which was hardly worthy of such heaped censure. How we laughed when it was revealed that neither critic had actually watched the film; how we sniggered when Terry Jones said that he couldn't understand why so many people found the film offensive, given that the film was poking fun at people who couldn't think for themselves; how we cheered when, for the first time in living history, Michael Palin actually seemed to lose his temper with the boorish bluster of his inquisitors. As if we needed more of an excuse to worship at the altar of the *Life of Brian*...

STICKS AND STONES

Being an early Christian was no beach party. Martyred as we felt by having to study them all, the grisly roll-call of Christian suffering during the first few centuries (and, in the name of religion, sporadically, ever since) was a tad sobering. From the first martyr, St Stephen, being stoned by his own people, the Jews, on through the steady dimunition of the Apostles (all were killed except John) to St Polycarp, speared and then burnt alive; Apollonius, sewn alive into a sack and then thrown into the sea; Perpetua of Carthage, still breastfeeding when she was gored by a bull (she survived that, so was then put to the sword); Ignatius, killed by lions in the Roman arena; Justin (thereafter called Justin Martyr, lest we forget), scourged and beheaded; Pope Sixtus, executed by Emperor Valerian along with six deacons; to the likes of Cecilia, Agatha, Agnes and Lucy, who died being raped and tortured brutally, simply for rejecting pagan suitors. Even in the casual brutality of the times, the spilled blood of the martyrs impressed their peers and helped lead to waves of conversions throughout the Roman Empire and beyond. They didn't die in vain...

CRAFTY CRAM... JUDAISM

One of the oldest religions to believe in one single, omnipotent, omniscient God, Jews believe that God selected them as his Chosen People. Precedent and learning, liturgy and tradition – these are all summed up in the Tanakh, the Jewish Bible: containing the Torah (The Word of God, means 'guidance' and 'law': the first five books of what we call the Old Testament, sometimes called the Books of Moses, and 613 commandments on which Jewish life is based); the Nevi'im (The Prophets: spiritual lessons and prophetic speeches); the Ketuvim (The Writings: 11 books of poetry – Song of Solomon – alongside psalms and proverbs) and the Apocrypha (everything that fell outside the Jewish mainstream). Finally, throw in the Talmud (combination of the 'oral Torah' Mishna and resulting teachings, the Gemara) – the next most important Jewish text. Talmudic law derives from rabbinic discussions and interpretation of the Torah which lays down laws on everything from food to a woman's menstrual cycle. Observing Jews follow strict dietary rules. At 13, children are brought to Judaism through the bar mitzvah ('son of the commandment') for boys, bat mitzvah for girls.

Worship in: synagogue ('assembly').
Spiritual centre: Jerusalem.

Stories to illustrate, challenge and provoke decision on matters to do with the Kingdom of God:

- **The Mustard Seed** *(Luke 13: 18-19)*. Tiny seed grows into large shrub capable of cracking rock, ie humble Jesus and a tiny band of followers can grow into a vast community.
- **The Dragnet** *(Mark 13: 47)*. Kingdom of God gathers in all kinds just as a dragnet does not discriminate between the kinds of fish it catches: sorting will be done on shore – ie God will do final sorting at the Day of Judgement.
- **Labourers in the Vineyard** *(Matthew 20: 1-16)*. One of reconciliation parables. Any labourer, who accepts the invitation to come into the Kingdom of God, no matter how late in the day, will receive an equal reward as those who have been faithful the longest (vineyard is a common symbol for Israel).
- **Prodigal Son** *(Luke 15: 11-32)*. Two sons, wayward one who's left for foreign lands (ie a sinner) and one at home behind fence of self-righteousness (ie Scribes and Pharisees). On the prodigal's return, the fatted calf is killed amid great feasting and rejoicing. God will welcome back repentant sinners.
- **Unjust Bailiff** *(Matthew 18: 23-35)*. Chimes with Jesus's advice to disciples to be 'as wise as serpents and harmless as doves'. Though the bailiff is the one cheating his master – master and servants are also dishonest in some way, so there is something to be learned about shrewdness.
- **The Mote and the Plank** *(Matthew 7: 5)*. Don't pull the speck of dust from your brother's eye before pulling the large plank from your own – ie before judging others, look to your own faults.
- **The Good Samaritan** *(Luke 10: 30-37)*. A traveller is left half dead and the priest and Levite just walk on by. The despised Samaritan crosses the road to rescue him, bind wounds etc – love God, love your neighbour, anyone in need, irrespective of religious, racial, social or political divisions.
- **The Talents** *(Matthew 25: 14-30)*. Three servants are given money by master; one got five, made five more; next got two, made two more; last just buried his, he is berated as being lazy and wicked and thrown out – ie don't keep Word of God to yourself but spread to all mankind.
- **The Barren Fig Tree** *(Luke 13: 6-9)*. Fig tree is a symbol of Israel; Jesus is the man who came in search of fruit, found none, and cursed the tree – ie Israel's time for repentance is short, its people are being given one last chance.
- **The Sheep and the Goats** *(Matthew 25: 31-46)*. Sorting the sheep from the goats. Last Judgement is to involve all nations and peoples; they will be judged by the compassion they have shown to those in need – to serve the needy is to serve Jesus.

Christianity: In the beginning... there were the Seven Days of Creation, Seven Deadly Sins, Seven Cardinal Virtues and, in Catholicism, the Seven Sacraments. On the seventh day of the siege of Jericho, Joshua and seven priests marched around the walls of the city seven times and were duly able to collapse the impregnable walls. In the Bible, the number seven is used over 700 times, 54 times in the Book of Revelations alone. There are seven churches, seven Spirits, seven stars, seven seals, seven trumpets, seven vials, seven personages, seven dooms and seven new things.

Ancient Greeks: Aristotle said: 'Every action must be due to one or other of seven causes – chance, nature, compulsion, habit, reasoning, anger or appetite.'

Folklore: Seven is the age of reason, 14 the age of puberty; 21 the traditional age of legal adulthood. Running round a grave seven times will raise a ghost. The seventh son or daughter is widely credited as having healing powers. In the tale of Thomas the Rhymer he went to live in the faerie kingdom for seven years.

Hinduism: In mythology, there are seven worlds in the universe, seven seas in the world and a celestial group of seven stars, the 'Sapta Rishi', based on the seven great gurus (whose mothers are known as the Seven Goddesses). Hindu weddings contain seven promises; reincarnation has seven manifestations. There's music at this seven party too: Hindu music has seven-note 'Sapta Swaras' instead of our eight-note octaves, from which hundreds of Ragas are composed.

Islam: Muhammad reputedly ascended into the Seven Heavens in Jerusalem; Hajj pilgrims walk around the Ka'aba seven times and, on the way there, stone the statues of devils three times using seven stones each time. The fundamental expression of Muslim faith, the shahada: 'There is No God but God and Muhammad is the Messenger of God' has seven words in Arabic. There are 25 references to the number seven in the Qu'ran. There were Seven Voyages of Sinbad and part of the Muslim wedding ritual is for seven happily married women to touch the bride's dress for good luck.

Shinto: Shichi Fukujin is no Japanese invocation or curse, but the Seven Gods of Good Fortune, popular deities said to bring good luck.

Sumerian and Babylonian: Thinkers in these ancient civilisations identified seven planets (still the most that can be seen with the naked eye) and framed the seven days of the week around them – a structure we use to this day.

The Hindu God Ganesh
The elephant deity riding a mouse has become one of the most common symbols for anything associated with Hinduism. He is one of the five prime Hindu deities (Brahma, Vishnu, Shiva and Durga being the other four) and is the Lord of success and destroyer of evils and obstacles. He is also worshipped as the god of education, knowledge, wisdom and wealth. Devotees of Ganesh are known as 'Ganapatyas', and the festival to celebrate and glorify him is called Ganesh Chaturthi.

AN IMMACULATE PRECONCEPTION

Forget the *Da Vinci Code*, the biggest shocker of religious dogma is about the Immaculate Conception. This is because when we talk about Immaculate Conception, it refers not to the birth of Jesus (for which the Virgin Mary became pregnant through the Holy Spirit), but to the birth of Mary herself. The idea being that when Mary was conceived, she was destined to be the Virgin Mother of Jesus, and so was effectively granted immunity from original sin, making her uniquely 'immaculate'.

*Two little dicky birds, sitting on
a wall.
One named Peter, one named Paul.
Fly away Peter, fly away Paul.
Come back Peter, come back Paul.*

If only the path of the early
Christian Church had been as
simple as this nursery rhyme
suggests. For one thing, neither of
the men credited with building the
foundations of the Church had a
simple path to Jesus themselves.
Peter (born Simon but nicknamed
'Peter' or 'rock' by Jesus) was one of
the disciples but had denied being a
follower of Jesus not once but three
times; Paul (born Saul of Tarsus, a
hard-nosed Pharisee) hadn't even
met Jesus and had not only been
at the stoning of Stephen but had
actively persecuted early Christians
before his dramatic conversion. Yet
each managed to do marvellous
things, as detailed in Acts.

Peter's particular strength was
to act as steadfast witness to the
Jews that their Messiah had indeed
come, died and risen again, and
soon emerged as the clear leader
of the remaining Apostles. He
did indeed 'fly away' – travelling
widely, preaching in Palestine,
Antioch, the Middle East and, of
course, Rome. He was the first Pope
(in ancient Greek, an affectionate
term for 'father'), after whom
St Peter's Basilica was named – and
is hailed as the father of the Church.

Paul's calling was to enlist not just
Jews but Gentiles too, extending
the remit of Christanity beyond the
'chosen people' – something that
seems natural to us now, but was
a radical notion then. From here,
Christianity developed as a world
religion, spreading along the
pre-existing communication lines
of the Roman Empire, unshackled
from its racial and legalistic
origins – even surviving the fall
of Jerusalem in AD70. Paul too
travelled (when not writing letters)
and, like Peter, ended up in Rome.
It is speculated that Peter and
Paul did indeed come back to each
other, with some scholars insisting
that they were both executed on
the same day by Emperor Nero in
AD64 or 67.

But for the ultimate comeback,
the Christians were going to have to
wait. Early leaders were expecting
the second coming of Jesus at any
minute so, in the beginning, the
drive to pray and work together for
the advancement of their faith was
given urgency by this expectation:
'And all that believed were together,
and had all things common. And
sold their possessions and goods,
and parted them to all men, as
every man had need. And they,
continuing daily with one accord
in the temple, and breaking bread
from house to house, did eat their
meat with gladness and singleness
of heart' (*Acts 2:44-47*).

What were the names of the Three Wise Men?
Answer on page 312

HOW MANY BOOKS IN THE BIBLE?

To remember how many books are in the Old Testament, put together the number of letters in 'Old' and 'Testament' – ie 3 and 9 = 39. This is the first sum (the Old Testament coming first). Then, to remember how many books are in the New Testament, just multiply the numbers of the Old Testament (3 and 9) and you have the answer. New Testament = 3 x 9 = 27 books. Isn't that neat?

AND ON THE THIRD DAY, HE ROSE AGAIN... AS DID HE... AS DID HE

The resurrection of Jesus Christ after he died on the Cross is obviously one of the seminal moments of both Christianity and of our religious education. But resurrection – as clearly distinct from both immortality and reincarnation – is by no means an exclusive feature of the Christ story. Even before Jesus shuffled off, a recurring dying-and-rising god motif threads through ancient Mesopotamian culture – Osiris has a stab at it in Egyptian mythology and the Canaanite Ba'al myth has definite resurrectionist overtones. In the New Testament, Elijah and Moses individually vanish and after hundreds of years are briefly seen again, walking together with Jesus.

Afterwards, the resurrection crops up in Islam – one of the reasons Muhammad was sent to us as the Prophet was apparently to explain the 'doctrine' of resurrection and there is a traditional spot in Jerusalem from where both Muhammad and his horse ascended into the sky; meanwhile, the body of first guru of the Sikhs, Nanak Dev Ji, is reputed to have disappeared, leaving only flowers in his stead, and at the end of a popular Buddhist myth, Gesar, the saviour of Tibet, chants on a mountain top and his clothes fall empty to the ground. Nowadays, of course, we also have the myth of Elvis to cling on to. When will the King rise again?

CREATIONISM: CRACKPOT OR CREDIBLE?

Believing that every word of Genesis is literal and true is the cornerstone of creationism: it believes evolution is a made-up 'envelope' theory into which we have wedged all 'science'; carbon-dating is mostly a (wrong) assumption – the Earth is only 6,000 years old; and man co-habited with dinosaurs (creationists prefer to call them 'dragons'). But what might have stayed a debate between 'young-Earth creationist scientists', geologists and formal scientists and the vast majority of us who believe that Genesis is merely a perfectly good allegory for the might of God, has since turned into a cosmic battle for hearts and minds – specifically, young American hearts and minds. By the 1930s, creationism had caught on to such an extent that evolution (the 'Godless' antithesis of creationism) was omitted entirely from most US school textbooks until the 1960s. Since then, scientific discoveries have been dismissed by creationists under the blanket condemnation: 'the majority of scientists are sometimes wrong: just like, for over 1,000 years from Ptolemy to Galileo, scientists were wrong in thinking that the universe revolved around the Earth' – and US schools are still at the frontline of the debate. Most often it is the defence that it contravenes the constitutional separation of church and state that holds most water: reminding us Brits how lucky we are that our issues of church and state have more to do with Charles and Camilla getting married than the hot potato of education.

ONE MORE ANGEL IN HEAVEN

We can blame Andrew Lloyd-Webber for the fact that several generations of schoolchildren will forever associate the stern moral tale of Joseph with some irritatingly catchy music and a Pharoah with a pronounced Elvis complex – but the surprising thing is that the technicolour dream coat is real – well, depending on how you translate *kethoneth passim* it is. The King James Bible describes it thus: 'Now Israel loved Joseph more than all his children, because he was the son of his old age: and he made him a coat of many colours', whereas the Revised Standard Bible went for the slightly less musical-inspiring 'long robe with sleeves'.

A friendly study of the world's religions is a sacred duty.

Gandhi

THE CHURCH YEAR

Consists of six 'seasons' (following the lifecycle of Jesus) – Advent, Christmas, Epiphany, Lent, Easter, Pentecost – and 12 festival days.

Christmas	Dec 25: birth of Jesus Christ. But you knew that already.
Name of Jesus	Jan 1: the naming ceremony (and circumcision) of baby Jesus. All wince!
Epiphany	Jan 6: visit of the Three Wise Men with gifts of gold, frankincense and myrrh.
Baptism of Our Lord	1st Sunday after Epiphany.
Transfiguration	Sunday before Ash Wednesday that starts Lent: the day when Moses and Elijah appeared to an incandescent Jesus Christ.
Easter	A moveable feast based on the phase of the moon; the day Jesus rose from the dead, having been crucified on Good Friday, two days earlier.
Ascension Day	40 days after Easter; day when Jesus ascended to heaven – the end of his time on Earth.
Feast of Pentecost	50 days after Easter; the day when the Holy Ghost showed up as tongues of flame dancing on the heads of the remaining apostles.
Holy Trinity	Sunday after Pentecost; honouring the Trinity of Father, Son and Holy Ghost.
Reformation Day	Last Sunday in October, celebrated only by Protestants honouring Martin Luther.
All Souls'/Saints' Day	Distinctive feast days that fall on consecutive days and honour, respectively the dead and the saints.
Christ the King	Last Sunday of Pentecost; celebrating 'Christ Triumphant' the ruler of all.

SHORT BUT SWEET

O praise the Lord, all ye nations:
Praise him, all ye people.
For his merciful kindness is great toward us:
And the truth of the Lord endureth for ever.
Praise ye the Lord.
Psalm 117 is the shortest chapter of the Bible
and is also its central chapter.

CRAFTY CRAM... HINDUISM

While you can date developments in Hinduism, it is not possible to exactly date when the faith first started nor attribute it to any one person; it simply grew over the last 4,000 years. The name itself evolved from the name given to a people (rather than the more usual other way round) from the Persian word 'sindhu' meaning river. To the Persians, who often pronounced 's' as 'h', the people of India were 'those who lived beyond the Sindhu' (the Indus). It's a common Western misconception that Hinduism is a polytheistic faith, focusing on many different gods; in fact there is one absolute universal person or non-person, depending on the kind of Hinduism you practice, called Brahman. The confusion arises because Brahma, Vishnu and Shiva are considered to be manifestations of Brahman by the devotees that follow them. The mythology is mapped out in the Vedas and the Upanishads, the revealed scriptures, and in the 'remembered' Epics, the Mahabharata (which includes the famous 'Bhagavad-Gita' poem), the Ramayana and the Laws of Manu and the Puranas. The goal of Hinduism is to be released from the cycle of rebirth and absorbed into Brahman, but this means very different things depending on what kind of Hindu you are: the method is to 'pursue truth, practise harmlessness (most are vegetarian) and pass through the four 'ashramas' (16 stages) of life focused on amassing good 'karma' to get into a better 'caste' or social level, next time around.

Worship in: at home (puja) or in the temple, but studded with a rainbow of colourful festivals like Holi and Diwali.

Spiritual centre: pilgrimages are key for karma, especially to Varanasi (Benares) on the Ganges, the unofficial spiritual centre.

What are the Seven Pillars Of Wisdom?
Answer on page 312

WHO'S WHO OF JESUS'S JEWS

Essenes
The 'pious ones', who devoted themselves to serve God in a peaceful manner, leading lives of contemplation, prayer and study. The 'monks' of the Jews were based in a commune by the Dead Sea and may have been responsible for the Dead Sea Scrolls. Some speculate as to whether John the Baptist was an Essene.

Maccabees
A Jewish national liberation movement that fought for, and won, independence from Antiochus IV Epiphanes. They entered Jerusalem in triumph and established Jewish rule in Israel for a century, from 164BC to 63BC when Pompeii established Roman rule over Palestine, putting Herod in as puppet king in 37BC. The fact that they sound like a mix between a popular biscuit and a children's TV programme should be ignored.

Pharisees
The cartoonishly caricatured 'bad guys' of the New Testament, they cropped up about 150BC in Palestine, becoming known as 'the separated ones' for their snooty self-isolation from the Gentiles and their self-absorption in the hundreds of laws, covering every aspect of Jewish life.

Sadducees
Reputedly named after Zadok the Priest (though scholars fight over which Zadok: the Handel-inspiring High Priest or just a middle-ranking Zadok, who was a predecessor of the Rabbinical tradition), the Sadducees were an aristocratic, priestly Jewish sect who believed in following the Bible to the letter. They were likely leaders of the Sanhedrin (Jewish Council) when Jesus was doing his thorn-in-side-of-Sanhedrin impression.

Zealots
Extreme, fanatical religious party at the time of Jesus, beginning with Judas of Galilee in AD6 (not Judas Iscariot) and leading to rebellion in AD65. The Zealots had wanted to initiate a rule of God on Earth using brute force; they hated the Romans and would accept no compromise. The flip side of the coin to the Essenes.

VIII

MUSIC

Without music,
life would be a mistake.

Friedrich Nietzsche

A BIT OF THEORY

Degrees of the scale (or a clever way of saying *do, re, mi, fa, sol, la, ti*): tonic (I), supertonic (II), mediant (III), subdominant (IV), dominant (V), submediant (VI), leading note (VII).

The cycle of fifths (with relative minors) (*or, how far apart the different keys are*): C major (A minor), F major (D minor), B♭ major (G minor), E♭ major (C minor), A♭ major (F minor), D♭ major (B♭ minor), G♭/F♯ major (E♭ minor), B major (G♯/A♭ minor), E major (C♯ minor), A major (F♯ minor), D major (B minor), G major (E minor), C major (A minor).

Cadences: (*or four ways of finishing a musical phrase*): Perfect (V-I), Plagal (IV-I), Imperfect (I–V), Interrupted (V-VI or V-♭VI).

CRITICAL CENSURE

- '[He] is ripe for the madhouse.' *Carl Maria von Weber, on hearing Beethoven's* Symphony no 7.
- '[He] has finally lost all grasp of reason, and stands before us like a madman rocking on his haunches.' *Viennese critic, on hearing Beethoven's last four string quartets.*
- '... towards the end degenerating without warning into music of such appalling inanity and vulgarity that one can hardy believe it to be the work of the same man. One has the impression that Donna Anna has suddenly dried her tears and broken out in ribald clowning.' *Berlioz, on an aria from Mozart's* Don Giovanni.
- 'Everything flows, without clarity and without order, willy-nilly into dismal long-windedness.' *Eduard Hanslick on Bruckner's* Eighth Symphony.
- 'There are some experiences in life which should not be demanded twice from any man, and one of them is listening to the Brahms' *Requiem*.' *George Bernard Shaw.*
- The ultimate response to such critical carping goes to Max Reger, a German composer, conductor, pianist and organist who came to prominence in the early 20th century. He is reported to have written this reply to an annoying critic: 'I am sitting in the smallest room of my house. I have your review before me. In a moment, it will be behind me.'

A BRIEF MUSICAL TIMELINE

C14th Invention of counterpoint, the art of combining two musical lines.

1607 Premiere of Monteverdi's *Orfeo*, the first 'modern' opera.

1685 Birth of Handel (23 February) and JS Bach (21 March).

1710 First recorded mention of the clarinet.

1722 Composition of the first book of JS Bach's *Well-tempered Clavier*, showing the possibilities of writing music in all 24 keys.

1782 Publication of Haydn's seminal *Opus 33* string quartets.

1825 Design for single-cast metal-framed piano patented by Alpheus Babcock.

1827 Death of Beethoven.

1876 Premiere of Wagner's *Der Ring des Nibelungen*.

1895 First season of Henry Wood Promenade Concerts in London.

1913 Premiere of Stravinsky's *Rite of Spring*.

1923 Schoenberg's first 12-note pieces composed.

1956 Creation of Stockhausen's *Gesang der Jünglinge*, the first significant work of electronic music.

THE SECRET LIFE OF THE HEMIDEMISEMIQUAVER

Much of the joy of studying music is that it gives one access to an arcane world of symbols and terminology – a complete language, every bit as erudite and mysterious as ancient Greek.

There is the wonder of musical notation itself, with its five lines of stave, its clefs, key signatures and assorted rhythms, from the stately breve to the headlong hemidemisemiquaver.

To study music is to become an initiate, however humble, of this almost secret world of alluring symbols. For many, it seemed an impossible task to learn how to score-read alto and tenor clefs, read figured bass and become fluent in the strange shorthand of harmonic notation, with its curious algebra of I, iii, V^7, $\flat$VII and the like. And how many fully comprehended the difference between a Neapolitan and a French sixth, or succeeded in composing the perfect enharmonic modulation?

But even if one achieved only passing fluency, the pleasure of music always remains.

The power of persistence

Making yourself heard as a young talent can be tough. Here's some advice on staying the course:

'To do your best is to have done all that man can do and though your best be far beneath some others' poorest, the truthfulness of the idea remains. Therefore, young composers, do your best. Until you can calmly analyse and direct your own works, weighing their merits with a steady hand, until you can honestly say, "This is the best I can do under the present circumstances, and with my knowledge and experience," – until that time comes, beware of casting your half-fledged composition-birds on the world's care. In after years should you ever become famous, the critics will not know whether you wrote those pieces recently or not and will judge accordingly. Beware also of the critics, for they are the eyes by which that many-headed monster, the public, views the artist. The unprejudiced and honest critic will hold up both your faults and your virtues to the public gaze, therefore let the latter outnumber the former by so many, that the faults are lost sight of entirely, just as a tiny fleck on a rose leaf does not impair its beauty.'

From *Music*, by William Smythe Babcock Mathews (1837-1912)

BACH TO THE FUTURE

You had a head start in music at school if you knew how to read it, or understood how to construct basic chords and follow simple chord progressions. But even then, the attempt to harmonise a melody seemed the musical equivalent of a driving lesson from your dad.

Generally, this lesson centred on a hymn tune, usually taken from a work by Bach. To this tune students would have to fit chords, finding the correct harmonic progression and the correct layout of the four voices, while keeping a wary eye out for musical faux pas like the dreaded parallel octaves and consecutive fifths. At the end, you would have to take your freshly minted chorale to the music teacher, who would compare it to Bach's harmonisation of the same chorale.

This was, of course, meant to give one an insight into the inner workings of a great musical mind and the chance to test yourself against it. But all it usually proved was that JS Bach's harmonic and contrapuntal skills were pretty good, and that yours were utterly rubbish.

Which Oasis album title stemmed from a quote by Sir Isaac Newton?

- *(What's the Story) Morning Glory?*
- *Standing on the Shoulder of Giants*
- *Be Here Now*
- *Definitely Maybe*
- *Heathen Chemistry*

Answer on page 312

PASS NOTES: NEOCLASSICISM

1. A musical movement which began in the early 20th century by drawing inspiration from works of the past. It can be seen as a reaction against the excesses of romanticism.

2. Neoclassicism's leading figure was Igor Stravinsky, who is generally credited with starting the neoclassical movement with his ballet score *Pulcinella* (1920). This was a recomposition of works by Pergolesi and his contemporaries, although Prokofiev's well-known *Classical Symphony* had already appeared three years previously.

3. The other leading neoclassicist of the 1920s was the German composer Paul Hindemith, who also pioneered the concept of *Gebrauchsmusik*, or 'utility music'.

4. Many so-called 'neoclassical' composers (including Stravinksy) were influenced more by baroque music than by actual classical music. The expression 'neo-baroque' is often preferred to 'neoclassical'.

5. Other composers particularly identified with neoclassicism are Prokofiev, Bartók and Busoni. Much of Ravel's music also has more in common with neoclassicism than with impressionism.

6. Stravinsky's neoclassical music stood in direct contrast to the technique of his great musical rival, Arnold Schoenberg, inventor of the modernist 12-note system. Schoenberg's later works also show decided classicising tendencies in their use of traditional forms.

7. In addition to *Pulcinella* and *Classical Symphony*, other famous neoclassical works include Stravinsky's *Symphony in C* and his opera *The Rake's Progress* – and Bartók's *Concerto for Orchestra*.

THE UNUSUAL CAREER OF AUGUST BUNGERT

Of all the followers of Wagner who filled the opera houses of late 19th-century Europe with their overblown mythological creations, perhaps none is as deservedly neglected as German composer August Bungert (1845-1915).

Something of a sensation in his time, Bungert, like Wagner, succeeded in attracting patronage at the highest levels of society – in this case the Queen of Romania, whose verses Bungert set to music. In addition she founded an organisation known as the 'Bungert-Bund' to promote his work. There was also talk of building a special theatre at Bad Godesberg, à la Bayreuth, for the performance of his compositions, most notably his epic cycle of eight operas, *Der Homerische Welt* ('The Homeric World'), based on the *Iliad* and *Odyssey*.

Only the second part was ever completed, however, and this was performed more than 100 times around Europe before falling into a merciful obscurity from which it has yet to be rescued. This, despite the best efforts of the Bungert-Bund, under the leadership of Bungert's biographer and leading champion, Max Chop.

MOST (AND LEAST) PROLIFIC COMPOSERS

Georg Philipp Telemann (1681-1767): Credited by the Guinness World Records as the most prolific composer in history, Telemann is thought to have composed around 3,000 works, although only 800 have survived.

Franz Schubert (1797-1828): More than 600 songs, eight symphonies and a large body of chamber and piano music including 21 piano sonatas and 15 string quartets – all by the age of 31.

Leif Segerstam (b1944): Finnish conductor and composer and the world's most prolific writer of symphonies. To date he has penned no fewer than 203; the most recent was completed on 16 July 2008.

Henri Duparc (1848-1933): Arguably the least productive great composer of all time. Despite living until he was 85, Duparc stopped composing at the age of 37 and destroyed most of his work. His entire reputation now rests on just 13 songs. If performed in their entirety, they would not last much longer than an hour.

Nothing separates the generations more than music. By the time a child is eight or nine, he has developed a passion for his own music that is even stronger than his passions for procrastination and weird clothes.
Bill Cosby, US comedian and actor

GREAT FRENCH ECCENTRICS: ERIK SATIE

Like his fellow eccentric, Charles-Valentin Alkan (see page 201), Erik Satie (1866-1925) was a Parisian pianist; however, in all other respects the two could hardly have been more opposite.

Having been ejected from the Paris Conservatoire for a perceived lack of ability, Satie made a living by playing piano in the celebrated Chat Noir cabaret in Montmartre, dressed in his signature grey velvet suit and bowler hat. He became famous for his quirky piano pieces, among them *Pieces to Make You Run Away, Genuine Flabby Preludes (For a Dog), Three Fragments in the Form of a Pear* and the *Bureaucratic Sonata*.

He later collaborated with Cocteau on the ballet *Parade* whose music-hall style score features the sounds of a typewriter, sirens, a revolver and a xylophone made out of bottles. From it too evolved the concept of *Musique d'ameublement*, or 'furniture music'. Such pieces were typical expressions of Satie's loathing for Wagnerian romanticism – or 'sauerkraut', as he termed it.

He preferred to describe himself not as a musician, but as a 'phonometographer' (one who measures sounds). Satie's work was a precursor to artistic movements, such as minimalism, Dada and the Theatre of the Absurd. He was also a hugely original writer on musical matters, publishing works such as *Mémoires d'un amnésique* ('Memoirs of an amnesiac').

After his death the small room in Arcueil, in which he had lived for the previous 27 years, was found to hold a bizarre accumulation of personal effects including 12 velvet suits, lots of umbrellas, many unused, and numerous unpublished compositions such as the infamous *Vexations*, which demands that the same epigrammatic work for piano be repeated 840 times.

Its huge classical music repertoire is without doubt one of the glories of Western culture. And yet the modern custom of performing works from previous centuries would have seemed rather strange to composers of the past. For composers up to Mozart's time, music was essentially something to be used in the present – for a church service, a concert, a party, and so on – then set aside in favour of the next new piece.

Some works lasted longer than others, of course, but no one was immune to eventual neglect. By 1829 for example, 79 years after his death, even Bach's music had faded into relative obscurity. But then Mendelssohn organised his celebrated performance of the *St Matthew Passion* and kick-started the so-called 'Bach revival'. This reintroduced his works to the concert platform and set off a chain reaction that additionally stimulated interest in the oeuvre of other forgotten composers.

To begin with, the Bach revival and early music movement were mainly about repertoire – rediscovering Bach and Handel, followed by Monteverdi, Josquin, Ockeghem, Dufay and Machaut, as well as hundreds of other names synonymous with the baroque, Renaissance and medieval genres.

In the 20th century, however, the early music movement – led by pioneers such as instrument maker Arnold Dolmetsch – became as much about performance as about unearthing old repertoire.

It wasn't enough just to perform Bach on contemporary instruments (as Mendelssohn had done, substituting piano for harpsichord, and so on). Instead, the early music movement focused increasingly on 'authentic' performance, using the correct 'period' instruments and playing from the original score with the appropriate historical intonation, phrasing and ornamentation.

All of which has thrown up many intriguing musico-philosophical problems. For instance, is it appropriate to perform renaissance masses in a concert hall, or only in a church? Is it correct to perform Beethoven's piano sonatas on instruments from Beethoven's era, even though the composer himself expressed repeated dissatisfaction with what was available in his time and would probably far rather have had his music played on a modern concert grand?

The arguments rumble on, although the unfortunate fact remains that there will always be limits to the authenticity of any musical performance. For example, one may give a historically informed performance on authentic instruments in a historic house lit by candlelight, and with everybody dressed in period costume.

But even this won't get you the last but most important piece of the puzzle: an authentic audience.

MUSICAL NOTATIONS

Semibreve (whole note)   Minim (half note)   Crotchet (quarter note)

Quaver (eighth note)   Semiquaver
(sixteenth note)   Demisemiquavers
(thirty-second note)

RICHARD WAGNER:
TOTALITARIAN VEGETARIAN

Despite his unceasing egomania and offensively anti-Semitic writings (which notoriously inspired Adolf Hitler), there is a gentler but little-known side to the work of Richard Wagner. Late in life, stimulated by the example of philosophers Schopenhauer and Nietzsche, Germany's foremost musical megalomaniac became a staunch vegetarian, insisting that 'the world would be saved if everybody ate vegetables instead of meat'.

Even Hitler was impressed; apparently he adopted a largely vegetarian diet for much of his life as a result of Wagner's teachings. Indeed, in 1941 he is quoted as saying: 'There's one thing I can predict to eaters of meat: the world of the future will be vegetarian.'

If only Wagner had instilled in him a similar regard for human life.

A BIT MORE THEORY: CHORDS

Triads (*the four simplest chords*): major (C-E-G), minor (C-E♭-G), augmented (C-E-G♯), diminished (C-E♭-G♭).

Sixths (*more complicated chords – handle with care*): Italian sixth (A♭, C, F♯), French sixth (A♭, C, D, F♯), German sixth (A♭, C, E♭, F♯), Neapolitan sixth (F, A♭, D♭).

Sevenths (*chords for modulating with, and other fancy harmonic effects*): dominant seventh (G-B-D-F), major seventh (C-E-G-B), minor–major seventh (C-E♭-G-B), minor seventh (C-E♭-G-B♭), diminished seventh (G-B♭-C♯-E), half-diminished seventh (B-D-F-A), augmented major seventh (C-E-G♯-B).

Special chords (*rare and special chords, seldom encountered in the wild*): 'Tristan' chord, Wagner (F-B-D♯-G♯), 'Mystic' ('Prometheus') chord, Scriabin (C-F♯-B♭-E-A-D), fourths chord, Schoenberg, Bartók (C-F-B♭-E♭-A♭), all-interval tetrachord, Elliot Carter (C-D♭-E-F♯ and C-D♭-E♭-G), overtone chord (C-G-C-E-G-B♭-C-E-F♯).

EXCEPTIONAL INSTRUMENTS

- **Highest:** The piccolo. The D note is two-and-a-half octaves above the treble clef (one note higher than the standard piano keyboard).
- **Lowest:** The double bassoon. Eighteen feet of tubing produces a bottom note of B-flat that is one-and-a-half octaves below the bass clef (the second lowest note on a standard piano keyboard).
- **Most expensive:** A Guarneri violin, sold at Sotheby's for an undisclosed sum believed to be around US$3.9m (around £1.9m) in February 2008. The previous record was US$3.54m (about £1.8m) for a 1707 Stradivarius violin sold at Christie's in 2006.
- **Biggest:** The Telharmonium, a kind of early synthesiser patented by Thaddeus Cahill in 1897. The Telharmonium Mark II was 18m/60ft long and weighed 180,000kg/180 tonnes, while the operating mechanism alone occupied an entire room.
- **Longest conventional instrument:** The *trembita*, a kind of Ukrainian alphorn. The *trembita* can reach up to 4m/13ft in length, while its sound is said to carry for distances of up to 10km/6 miles.

Unravel these musical anagrams:

- See Sign
- Six Men Under Dry Things
- Help Child Properties
- Spy Brain Trees

Answers on page 312

MYTHBUSTERS: MOZART, NEGLECTED GENIUS

Myth: Mozart was a naïve and neglected genius who died in penury and was buried in a pauper's grave.

As touching as the popular belief is, Mozart was – or at least should have been – extremely wealthy. The music maestro earned around 10,000 florins a year – an enormous salary in 18th-century Vienna where a labourer's annual income was around 25 florins.

Mozart once wrote to his father that he had just earned 1,000 florins for a single concert. In addition, in his position as court chamber composer, he received a yearly stipend of 800 gulden (around £17,500 in modern money) just for providing a few dances during carnival season.

He lived for most of his time in Vienna in a seven-room apartment next to the cathedral, complete with parking space for his personal horse-drawn carriage.

Mozart's financial problems – which led to him writing pitiful begging letters to friends – were probably down to his lifestyle and gambling debts. As for the supposed miserable death at the age of 35 and subsequent, legendary 'pauper's grave', the reality is that Mozart was treated by the best doctors in Vienna, while the memorial service was held in St Stephen's Cathedral and attended by hordes of people.

True, he was buried with four or five others in a communal plot but that was standard, contemporary Viennese funerary practice. Only the exceptionally wealthy were accorded the privilege of individual burial, but Mozart's final resting place certainly wasn't the 'mass grave' that many have been led to believe.

Undoubtedly, the composer's actual standing is more truly represented by the wave of enthusiasm for his music which followed his death, and by the fact that two biographies of him were published in the seven years after his tragically premature demise.

ESSENTIAL REPERTOIRE: EARLY MUSIC

1. Machaut, *Messe de Notre Dame*
2. Dufay, *Missa Ecce Ancilla Domini*
3. Ockeghem, *Missa Fors Seulement*
4. Josquin, *Missa Pange Lingua*
5. Taverner, *Western Wind Mass*
6. Tallis, *Spem in Alium*
7. Gesualdo, *Madrigals, books 5 and 6*
8. Monteverdi, *Vespers*
9. Purcell, *Ode for St Cecilia's Day*
10. Dowland, *First Booke of Songs*

PASS NOTES: IMPRESSIONISM

1. In music, 'impressionism' is a loose term generally used to refer to certain French composers of the later 19th and early 20th centuries, most notably Claude Debussy.
2. Impressionism in music is much less clearly defined than impressionism in the arts. Debussy himself rejected the label, and many writers prefer the term 'symbolist'; symbolist poets such as Mallarmé and Maeterlinck, for instance, exerted far more influence on Debussy than any of the impressionist painters.
3. Impressionism began as a reaction against the overblown romanticism of Wagnerian opera, placing emphasis on shorter forms such as Debussy's numerous, relatively brief piano works, although he also succeeded in writing one great opera, *Pelléas et Mélisande.*
4. Impressionism is associated with novel types of harmony, particularly the whole-tone scale and pentatonicism. It places new emphasis on the particular sonority of individual chords and instrumental colours, just as impressionist painters highlighted the play of light and colour rather than traditional painterly forms.
5. Debussy's *Prélude à l'après-midi d'un faune* is regarded as the first great work of musical impressionism.
6. Debussy's great French contemporary, Maurice Ravel, is often described as an impressionist, although much of his music is neoclassical rather than impressionist in style.
7. The influence of impressionism can be seen in the work of composers as diverse as Paul Dukas, Manuel de Falla, Frederick Delius, Isaac Albéniz, Ottorino Respighi and Arnold Bax.

THE UNUSUAL LIFE OF CARLO GESUALDO

Unique for all the wrong reasons, Carlo Gesualdo, Prince of Venosa (1566-1613) holds the dubious record of being the only great composer in history to be an acknowledged murderer.

Born into an aristocratic family at Venosa, Italy, in 1566, Gesualdo was married at the age of 20 to his first cousin, Donna Maria d'Avalos, daughter of the Marquis of Pescara. But Donna Maria subsequently began an affair with Fabrizio Carafa, the Duke of Andria.

In October 1590, at the Palazzo San Severo in Naples, Gesualdo (with help from his servants) caught them in *flagrante*, after pretending to go away on a hunting trip. He then proceeded to murder his wife and her lover in their bed.

Gesualdo is said to have stabbed his wife repeatedly, shouting 'She's not dead yet!' After the deed the mutilated bodies were dumped outside the palace in public view, with the Duke of Andria dressed in Donna Maria's nightgown.

Despite this sad and grisly episode, the composer subsequently remarried. This time, as Cecil Gray and Philip Heseltine noted in their book, *Carlo Gesualdo, Musician and Murderer* (1926), the second wife 'seems to have been a very virtuous lady... for there is no record of his having killed her'.

Gesualdo suffered increasingly from acute depression, from which he found relief only in having himself beaten three times daily by his servants.

As if that wasn't all, he also apparently kept a special valet whose duty it was to flog the composer before he went to the toilet.

Perhaps unsurprisingly, Gesualdo's music is as strange as his life – his six books of madrigals and religious music employ an intensely expressive style whose extreme chromaticism would not be matched until the works of Richard Wagner 250 years later.

QUOTE UNQUOTE

It's gonna be a really tough project. You're gonna have to use your head, your brain and your mind too.

Dewey Finn (Jack Black) introduces his fake rock band project to the class in *The School of Rock*

TEN UNFORTUNATE ENDS

Went deaf: Beethoven, Fauré, Smetana
Went blind: Handel, Bach, Delius, Rodrigo
Went mad: Schumann, Wolf, Donizetti, Smetana

NOTABLE NAMES

One doesn't usually think of JS Bach as a great egomaniac but he did have a particular weakness for leaving his own musical signature scattered freely about his oeuvre.

This signature (a music cipher of his name – B, A, C, H, where B = B♭ and H = B natural) appears in some of his works, most notably the *Art of Fugue*, and was subsequently picked up by many other composers.

In fact, a comprehensive study published in 1985 to accompany a Stuttgart exhibition marking 300 years of Bach, lists no fewer than 409 works by 330 composers from the 17th to the 20th century that use the BACH motif.

Famous examples include Liszt's *Fantasia and Fugue on B-A-C-H*, Rimsky-Korsakov's *Variations on BACH*, Francis Poulenc's *Valse-improvisation sur le nom Bach* for piano, and Arvo Pärt's *Collage over B-A-C-H*.

This craze for musical cryptology didn't start or end there. Ravel composed a *Menuet sur le nom de Haydn*, while Schumann's *Carnaval* is largely based on an A-S-C-H motif. This contains musical notes found both in Schumann's name and the home town of his then-beloved, who hailed from a place called Asch.

The Bachian tradition of 'signing' one's own works also found a particularly enthusiastic follower in the shape of Russian composer Dmitri Shostakovich. He introduced a four-note cipher of his name, D-S-C-H (where S=E♭) into several of his compositions, most notably the *Tenth Symphony* and *String Quartet no 8*.

For thoroughgoing cryptological obsessiveness, however, none can match the Austrian Alban Berg whose works featured Mahler's romanticism and Schoenberg's 12-tone technique. His *Chamber Concerto*, for example, is based almost entirely on musical ciphers of his own name, plus those of Schoenberg and Anton Webern, another 12-note devotee.

For good measure his *Lyric Suite* for string quartet is similarly dominated by two motifs, linking his own name (A-B) with that of Hanna Fuchs-Robettin (H–F), for whom apparently he entertained burgeoning illicit feelings.

His wife Helene, luckily for him, seems to have been none the wiser.

DON'T CONFUSE THESE MUSIC GREATS...

- **Domenico Scarlatti** (1685-1757), celebrated composer of 555 keyboard sonatas – his father, Alessandro Scarlatti (1660-1725), wrote opera and for the church.

- **Franz Josef Haydn** (1732-1809) – his brother, Michael (1737-1806), was also a composer.

- **Franz Schubert** (1797-1828), not to be confused with Johann Schobert (c1735-1767), a leading composer and harpsichordist whose music influenced the young Mozart and who died in Paris, along with his wife and one of his children, after eating poisonous mushrooms.

- **George Frideric Handel** (1685-1759), not to be confused with Slovenian musician Jacob Handl (1550-1591), a leading composer of religious music including three passions and 445 motets.

- **Carl Maria Weber** (1786-1826), not to be confused with Anton Webern (1883-1945): pioneering early romantic, and pioneering early 12-note composer respectively.

- **François Couperin** (1668-1733), not to be confused with great French claveciniste, and his uncle, Louis Couperin (1626-1661), another of the era's leading composers and keyboard players.

- **Robert Schumann** (1810-1856), not to be confused with American William Schuman (1910-1992), a notable composer in his day, though he lacked Robert's genius, as well as his second n.

- French composer **Florent Schmitt** (1870-1958), not to be confused with his near contemporary, Austrian composer Franz Schmidt (1874-1939). Both wrote prolifically in a broadly post-romantic idiom.

- **JS Bach** with JC Bach, JCF Bach, WF Bach and CPE Bach (who are his sons).

EVERY GOOD BOY

Music at school started simply. First things first, you had to learn the notes. So, we learned that each stave has five lines and four spaces and that the notes of the treble clef's five lines are E-G-B-D-F, popularly mnenomicised to 'Every Good Boy Deserves Favour' (although 'Every Good Burger Deserves Fries' has recently become more popular), while the notes in the four spaces spell F-A-C-E, which is slightly easier to remember; particularly if you were a fan of *The A-Team*.

NOW THAT'S WHAT I CALL MUSIC...

'There's music, and there's music,' as the famously eclectic Italian composer Luciano Berio once put it, which pretty much sums up the music curricula in school. For while the subject we studied at school was, of course, called 'music', it was only a very certain kind of music – that's to say Western classical music, and a small part even of that. In fact, the works that most adults studied, and attempted to perform, at school were written between c1720 and c1910 by (male) Austrian or German composers. And, as far as the school syllabus was concerned, there was no such thing as a living composer; indeed, there was precious little 20th-century music full stop, apart from the occasional work by user-friendly conservatives like Britten or Copland. There was no reference to popular music, no coverage of the great non-European musical traditions of places like India or Indonesia, and there was absolutely nothing about the great wealth of music which is nowadays called World Music, but which then had no name, probably because, as far as the Musical Establishment was concerned, it didn't even exist.

The tendency of the classical fraternity to ignore all music that was not Western, classical and written by dead German (or Austrian) men was formerly an inescapable fact of scholastic life. The 1994 edition of the *Grove*

Concise Dictionary of Music, for example, has an entry on John Lenton (English composer and violinist in the King's Private Musick, d London c1719), but absolutely nothing on John Lennon. It has entries on binary form (AB), and ternary form (ABA), but makes no mention of ABBA. There are a few tokenistic references to non-Western and non-classical music (Elvis, for instance, gets 10 lines – the same as American publisher and musical philanthropist Theodore Presser, d1925).

Things have changed a lot since then. Today's music students are more likely to learn digital sampling or how to run a recording studio, than how to harmonise a Bach chorale. And there has been a healthy pushing back of the boundaries in terms of the music that is considered worth studying. Of course there have also been losses along the way. One is far less likely nowadays to meet someone who can improvise a three-part fugue, or read a 15th-century vocal score from its original soprano, mezzo-soprano and alto clefs, and one can't help feeling that there has been a gradual erosion of traditional technique and musical fundamentals. Old-school musicians are wont, with some reason, to regret such changes, although schools can at least say that the name of music itself, nowadays, is far less likely to be taken in vain.

MUSICAL SCALES

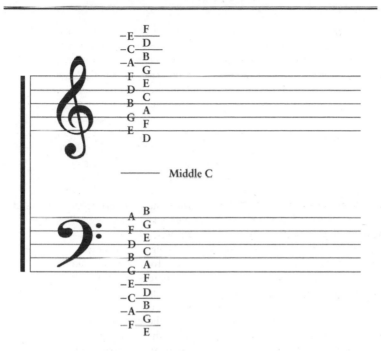

Diagram showing where notes are positioned on the bass and treble clefs.

ESSENTIAL REPERTOIRE: 18TH CENTURY

1. Corelli, *Christmas Concerto*
2. Biber, *Mystery Sonatas*
3. Bach, *The Well-tempered Clavier*
4. Handel, *Messiah*
5. Couperin, *Ordre 8ème de Clavecin*
6. Vivaldi, *L'Estro Armonico*
7. Rameau, *Suites from Les Indes Galantes*
8. Domenico Scarlatti, *Keyboard sonatas*
9. Haydn, *String Quartets op 33*
10. Mozart, *Piano Concerto in C minor K 491*

PASS NOTES: MUSICAL NATIONALISM

1. Nationalism in music is a 19th-century phenomenon, essentially a Europe-wide reaction against the dominance of German music and musicians across the continent, and as a political result of movements for independence occurring after 1848.

2. Nationalist music typically uses indigenous musical material – real or invented folksongs, characteristic folk rhythms and dances – as well as the use of local subjects and vernacular language in songs, operas and symphonic poems. Nationalist works also generally show considerable freedom in their treatment of traditional musical forms and harmonies.

3. Chopin can be counted as one of the first proto-nationalist composers, thanks to his use of Polish dance rhythms and forms such as the *mazurka*. Despite his musical celebrations of his homeland, however, he actually lived most of his life in France.

4. The oldest and perhaps most important school of musical nationalism is that of Russia, which produced arguably the first truly nationalist composer, Mikhail Glinka (1804-1857). Glinka was succeeded by 'The Five': Mussorgsky, Rimsky-Korsakov, Borodin, Balakirev and Cui.

5. Czechoslovakia was another important centre of nationalist music, through the work of Smetana, Dvořák and Janácek. There is also a strong strain of nationalism in Liszt's 'Hungarian' works.

6. Although generally thought of as an impressionist rather than a nationalist, Claude Debussy signed himself *Musicien française* in conscious reaction to Germanic musical domination.

7. Other important nationalist composers include Jean Sibelius (Finland), Edvard Grieg (Norway) and Isaac Albéniz and Enrique Granados (Spain).

8. Nationalism also played an important role in 20th-century British music, particularly in the outlook of composers such as Vaughan Williams and Holst, and also crossed the Atlantic into the music of Ives, Copland and many other American composers.

9. Nationalism continued to be of great significance well into the 20th century, playing an important role in the work of composers such as Sibelius, Nielsen, Bartok and Kodaly.

10. Famous nationalist works include Glinka's opera *A Life for the Tsar*, Mussorgsky's opera *Boris Godunov*, Smetana's *Má Vlast*, and Sibelius's tone poem *Finlandia*.

1. Beethoven, *String Quartet in C♯ minor, op 131*
2. Schubert, *Symphony no 9*
3. Berlioz, *Symphonie Fantastique*
4. Liszt, *Sonata in B minor*
5. Schumann, *Fantasie, op 17*
6. Chopin, *Ballades*
7. Brahms, *Symphony no 4*
8. Bruckner, *Symphony no 4*
9. Tchaikovsky, *Symphony no 6*
10. Debussy, *Prelude à l'après-midi d'un faune*

MUSICAL MONSTERPIECES

Der Ring des Nibelungen, Richard Wagner. Four operas designed to be performed over consecutive evenings, and lasting a total of some 15 hours; ideally performed in a specially built opera house in Bayreuth, at enormous expense.

Der Homerische Welt ('The Homeric World'), August Bungert. Two linked cycles of four operas apiece, based on episodes from Homer by quasi-Wagnerian 19th-century composer Bungert. Perhaps mercifully, only the second cycle was completed, though it still received over 100 performances before being consigned to oblivion.

Symphony no 8, Gustav Mahler. Popularly know as the 'Symphony of a Thousand', on account of the number of performers it is said to require: the first performance employed an orchestra of 171, accompanied by a 850-strong choir.

Opus Clavicembalisticum, Kaikhosru Sorabji. Written for solo piano, and widely regarded as the most difficult piece of music ever written for a single instrument, its performance lasts at least four hours.

Licht ('Light'), Karlheinz Stockhausen. Goes one (in fact, three) better than Wagner's Ring cycle, by consisting of seven operas, one for each day of the week, lasting a combined total of around 30 hours.

ASLAP (As Slow As Possible), John Cage. The performance of *ASLAP*, for organ, began in a church in Halberstadt, Germany, in 2001 and is scheduled to last 639 years.

MYTHBUSTERS: THE DEATH OF TCHAIKOVSKY

Myth: Tchaikovsky committed suicide by drinking a glass of water contaminated with cholera, after being convicted by a 'court of honour', consisting of fellow alumni of the St Petersburg School of Jurisprudence, incensed by the composer's homosexual advances to a nephew of a certain Duke Stenbock-Fermor.

Tchaikovsky's sudden demise has remained a mystery up to the present day, despite the best efforts of several generations of musicians and medical experts. It seems probable that the composer did indeed die of cholera, although the possibility of arsenic poisoning, whose symptoms roughly mimic those of cholera, has also been proposed. As have the theories that Tchaikovsky's suicide was ordered, not by the court of honour, but by Tsar Alexander III himself; that Tchaikovsky did indeed commit suicide by drinking contaminated water, but that he did so for entirely personal reasons, consequent upon a deep personal depression; and that he died of cholera contracted while having sex with a male prostitute, and that the story of the unboiled water was a later fabrication designed to protect his posthumous reputation. The truth, however, is unlikely ever to be discovered, even if, as some have urged, the composer's corpse is exhumed for forensic testing.

ONCE MORE, WITH FEELING

In the end, it's all about the emotion...

If the beauty or sublimity of music depended solely upon the nature of its composition, and was independent of the qualities of which it is expressive, it would necessarily happen, that the same composition must always be beautiful or sublime, which once were so; and that in every situation they must produce the same emotion, in the same manner as every other object of sense uniformly produces its correspondent sensation. The truth is, however, that no such thing takes place, and that, on the contrary, music is then only beautiful or sublime when it is accommodated to the emotion of which it is intended to express.
From *Essays on the Nature and Principles of Taste*, by Archibald Alison (1757-1839)

WORK IT OUT

What is the name of the fourth degree of a scale?
- Submediant
- Supertonic
- Subdominant
- Supermediant

Answer on page 312

GREAT FRENCH ECCENTRICS:
CHARLES-VALENTIN ALKAN

Charles-Valentin Alkan (1813-1888) is perhaps the 19th-century's greatest forgotten virtuoso composer. One of the most skilled pianists of his time, Alkan was an intimate friend of Liszt, George Sand and Victor Hugo, and was Chopin's next-door neighbour. His compositions, almost exclusively for the piano, include some of the most difficult music ever written for the instrument, notably the two sets of etudes Op 35 and Op 39, which are often claimed to exceed even Liszt's ferociously taxing *Transcendental Etudes* in scale and difficulty. The Op 39 collection includes both a *Symphony for Solo Piano* and a *Concerto for Solo Piano*, and takes over two hours to perform. Alkan also composed many programmatic pieces, such as *Le chemin de fer* ('The Railroad', Op 27), thought to be the first representation of a steam train in music, as well as works such as the piano prelude *The Song of the Mad Woman on the Sea Shore* and the notorious *Marcia funèbre, sulla morte d'un Pappagallo* ('Funeral march on the death of a parrot').

Alkan largely withdrew from concert life after 1848 and appears to have immersed himself in studying the Bible and Talmud – he is believed to have translated both the Old and New Testaments from Hebrew into French (though the translations have been lost), and also harboured desires to set the entire Bible to music.

According to popular legend, Alkan is believed to have died after being crushed by a falling bookcase when reaching up for a volume of the Talmud. The legend also says that he was commemorated with an obituary in *Le Ménéstrel* which began: 'Alkan is dead. He had to die in order to prove his existence.' Neither story, sadly, is completely true. The offending item of furniture was in fact a heavy coat-rack, and the obituary was never published.

1. Elgar, *Cello Concerto*
2. Stravinsky, *The Rite of Spring*
3. Ravel, *La Valse*
4. Mahler, *Das Lied von der Erde*
5. Schoenberg, *Pierrot Lunaire*
6. Sibelius, *Symphony no 7*
7. Bartók, *String Quartet no 4*
8. Berg, *Violin Concerto*
9. Messiaen, *Turangalîla Symphony*
10. Ligeti, *Etudes for piano*

IT'S WHO YOU KNOW...

Like most areas of life, classical music is nothing if not nepotistic. Consider the following, unlikely, family tree, beginning with JS Bach.

JS Bach fathers numerous composer sons, including JC Bach, who travelled to London, where he met and encouraged the young Mozart.

Mozart later married Constanze Weber, a cousin (slightly removed) of the great early romantic composer Carl Maria von Weber.

Carl Maria Weber studied with Michael Haydn, younger brother of Franz Josef Haydn, who in turn numbered the young Beethoven among his various pupils.

Late in life, the young prodigy **Franz Liszt** played for Beethoven, and was rewarded with a celebrated kiss, the legendary *Weihekuss*, or 'kiss of consecration', for his performance.

Liszt's daughter, **Cosima**, married Richard Wagner after leaving her first husband, the famous conductor Hans von Bülow.

Von Bülow later championed the work of the young Richard Strauss, whose friends included Gustav Mahler.

Mahler married Alma Schindler, a former pupil of composer Alexander Zemlinsky, while Zemlinsky's sister, Mathilde, married Arnold Schoenberg, whose pupils included Anton Webern, Alban Berg and, oddly enough, the American avant-garde maverick John Cage.

I don't know anything about music – in my line you don't have to.
Elvis Presley

THE CURSE OF THE NINTH

Arguably the greatest symphonist of them all, Beethoven wrote nine symphonies. As did, whether they liked it or not, many of his successors: Dvořák wrote nine symphonies, as did Vaughan Williams. Schubert claimed to have written nine symphonies – his final symphony is entitled 'number 9', although he never actually seems to have written a seventh symphony. Bruckner's last symphony was also his ninth (and in the same key as Beethoven's ninth), although he also wrote a youthful symphony now known as 'no 0', so his number 9 is, strictly speaking, number 10.

The superstitious Mahler was particularly worried that he would not survive writing a ninth symphony, so he gave his ninth symphony the completely non-symphonic title of *Das Lied von der Erde*. He then wrote a ninth symphony (thus, actually his 10th), and then began a 10th. Unfortunately, he died before finishing it, meaning that his last numbered symphony was... *natürlich*, his ninth. Writing about Mahler, Schoenberg speculated: 'It seems that the ninth is a limit. He who wants to go beyond it must pass away. It seems as if something might be imparted to us in the 10th which we ought not yet to know, for which we are not ready. Those who have written a ninth stood too close to the hereafter.'

Not that all composers succumbed to the curse, however. Among other leading symphonists, Sibelius wrote seven, Tchaikovsky six, Brahms and Schumann four, and Elgar just two, while Shostakovich, the last great symphonist, in defiance of Schoenberg's apocalyptic prediction, managed a magnificent 15 before entering symphonic Valhalla. Even this, however, pales in comparison with Finnish composer Leif Segerstam (b1944), who currently holds the world record, with over 200 symphonies to his credit, and more being added on a regular basis.

PASS NOTES: 12-NOTE MUSIC

1. Twelve-note music is a compositional system devised by Austrian composer Arnold Schoenberg.

2. The technique was first used by Schoenberg in various works of the early 1920s, such as the *Five Pieces for Piano* op 23 and the *Serenade* op 24.

3. Twelve-note music is known by a confusing variety of names: '12-tone technique', 'serialism' and 'dodecaphony' are all widely used. Schoenberg himself described the method (with characteristic Germanic concision) as a 'Method of Composing with 12 Tones Which are Related Only with One Another'.

4. In its purest form, each 12-note composition is based upon a single 'row', consisting of the 12 chromatic notes in a fixed and unvarying sequence. This basic row may appear in its original form, inverted (upside down), retrograde (backwards), or retrograde inversion. All of these forms may also be freely transposed.

5. The essential aim of 12-note composition is to ensure that all 12 pitches are equally represented, without any one being given undue prominence, thus avoiding any reference to the keys of traditional tonality. In practice, however, this is rarely the case.

6. Twelve-note music is not to be confused with 'free atonality' – music not in any particular key – the style developed by Schoenberg (and other composers) during the early decades of the 20th century.

7. Schoenberg himself claimed, with characteristic reticence, that the 12-tone technique would 'ensure the supremacy of German music for the next hundred years'. History, so far at least, has failed to agree with him.

8. The greatest early serial composers, apart from Schoenberg himself, were his two pupils: Alban Berg, who employed the technique with notable romantic freedom; and Anton Webern, who used it with extraordinary strictness.

9. Schoenberg's 12-note music, or serialism, later evolved into 'total serialism', in which the ordering principle is extended to include all musical elements – rhythm, dynamics and tessitura. The technique was first suggested by Messiaen, but is particularly associated with the music written by Pierre Boulez and Karlheinz Stockhausen in the early 1950s.

10. Many leading 20th-century composers used elements of the 12-note technique, including Luigi Nono, Luigi Dallapicolla and Roberto Gerhard, although the most famous later 12-note works are those by Stravinsky, Schoenberg's great musical adversary, who converted to the technique after his rival's death in 1951.

FIVE FAMOUS WRITERS WHO
WERE ALSO COMPOSERS

Jean-Jacques Rousseau
Friedrich Nietzche
Anthony Burgess
Milan Kundera
Theodore Adorno

MUSIC AS A FOREIGN LANGUAGE

As musicians are forever wont to point out, music is its own language, with its own rules and symbols. But music is also a surprisingly good way of learning other languages; particularly, Italian, French and German. In the heyday of classical music, for example, a simple *andante*, *adagio*, *allegretto* or *allegro* usually sufficed. Mozart, for instance, rarely gave more than a single-word tempo indication (except for one famous directive in his *Flute Quartet in A K 298*, marked: *Allegretto grazioso, ma non troppo presto, però non troppo adagio. Così, così, con molto garbo e espressione* [roughly translated as 'Graceful and fairly fast, but not too fast, but not too slow either. So, so, with lots of elegance and expression']).

As usual, it was Beethoven who pushed the boundaries of acceptance. As his career went on, the directions with which he plastered his scores became increasingly long-winded. The third movement of his great *Piano Sonata* op 110, for example, takes almost as long to read as to play, opening up with *Adagio ma non troppo (una corda)... Recitativo... più adagio... andante (cresc)... adagio (sempre tenuto)... tutte le corde... ritardando (dim)... cantabile (una corda)... meno adagio (cresc)... adagio (dim Smorzando)...* and this is before the movement even properly gets going.

Later composers followed Beethoven's cue, with ever-more elaborate verbal directions. Satie was a particular master of the outlandish performing directive, penning instructions such as 'from the top of your back teeth', 'like a nightingale with toothache', or, simply, 'do your best'. The logical outcome of this literary endeavour was Karlheinz Stockhausen's *Aus den sieben Tagen*, which has no notes whatsoever, but whose 'score' consists entirely of a set of poems, which the performers are invited to musically interpret as they see fit.

IX

MATHEMATICS

As far as the laws of mathematics refer to reality, they are not certain; and as far as they are certain, they do not refer to reality.

Albert Einstein

THE LANGUAGE OF NUMBERS

Counting number	A real number above zero	{1, 2, 3, . . .}
Natural number	A real number above zero that includes zero	{0, 1, 2, 3,. . .}
Integer	A real, whole number above and below zero	{..., -3, -2, -1, 0, 1, 2, 3, ...}
Rational number	Where the exact value of the number can be written down as the ratio of two whole numbers	eg 3, 2½ , 5.72, 3¼
Irrational number	Where the exact value of the number cannot be written down	eg π, √2, √3, √5
Prime number	A real number divisible only by itself	2, 3, 5, 7, 11, 13 ...
Multiple	How a real number multiplies itself up via whole numbers	The multiples of 12 are 12, 24, 36, 48 ...
Factor	How a real number divides itself down via whole numbers	The factors of 12 are 1, 2, 3, 4, 6 and 12
Ratio	A fraction; a comparison between two numbers, always given as simply as possible	The ratio of 400m to 2km: $\frac{400m}{2000m} = \frac{1}{5}$ = 1:5
Denominator	The lower number in a fraction, where the top number is the numerator	Denominator 14: $\frac{4}{14}$
LCD or LCM	Lowest Common Denominator or Lowest Common Multiple shared by two numbers	LCD of 7 and 3 is 21
Percentage	Fraction whose denominator is 100	$\frac{62}{100}$ = 62%
A squared number	A number multiplied by itself; where the number represents measurements of a square, the square's area would be revealed	$2 \times 2 = 4$ $2^2 = 4$
Square root	The inverse of the 'square' operation	√4 = 2
Standard form	Using powers to write out large numbers	In standard form, $0.004 = 4 \times \frac{1}{1000} = 4 \times 10^{-3}$

It has now become the generic cry of exultant discovery and we probably (mis)remember that it involved someone jumping out of their bath and running down the street stark naked, but what was the story behind 'Eureka!'?

The runner and shouter was Archimedes (287-212BC), a very great Greek mathematician who, when he wasn't designing luxury ships and war machines for the king of Syracuse, kept himself busy working out the density of a fancily wrought golden crown.

The story we know is one that was told by Vetruvius 150 years after the actual event occurred. Realising that the level of the bath water rose as he got in for a wash one day, Archimedes was led to work out that a solid will displace an amount of water equal to its own volume. So, by dividing the weight of the crown by the volume of water it displaced, its density could be calculated – no matter how irregular and unmeasurable its shape.

Archimedes master King Hieron must have been a demanding monarch because where the rest of us would have stayed soaking, congratulating ourselves on our own brilliance, Archimedes, so excited that he forgot to dress, took to the streets, crying: 'Eureka! – I have found it!'

What he also found, and what *he* considered to be his greatest achievement, of course, was the proof that where a sphere and a cylinder have the same height and diameter, the sphere has two thirds the volume and surface area of the cylinder. It was a sphere and circumscribing cylinder that was eventually placed on the tomb of Archimedes, apparently at his request.

HOW TO REMEMBER...

SOHCAHTOA
Some officers have curly auburn hair to offer attraction

Sine = opposite side over hypotenuse
Cosine = adjacent side over hypotenuse
Tangent = opposite side over adjacent

Some of the building blocks of maths at school were sets and the algebra of sets. Suddenly a set wasn't something that you were trying to get into at school, but the first faltering steps into a world beyond times tables and long division. The idea was that if you understood the rules of sets, then you would start to understand the application of algebra to solve real life problems. The trouble was that sets came accompanied by a lot of rules...

● A set is a collection of elements: elements are **members** of that set, using curly brackets { } to denote them. So, S = {2,4,6} is a set with three members 2, 4, 6. {2, 4, 6, . . . } would indicate that the pattern continues; S = {even numbers} is an alternative.

● A set can also be described with algebra: S = {x:0<x<6 an integer) which reads 'the set of members x is such that x is an integer greater than 0 and less than 6'.

● **Equal sets** have the same number of members – so if X = {1, 2, 3) and Y = {a, b, c} then n(X) = n(Y) = 3.

● **Empty sets** are usually denoted by ∅ or { }.

● **Proper subsets** (ie not the set itself or the set when it is empty) are sets that fit into another set: if set S = {a, b} and set T = {a, b, c} then S is a subset of T, written S ⊂ T.

● **The universal set** is the set which contains all possible members, usually denoted by [ξ].

● **The complement of a set**, denoted with an apostrophe, is the set of members of [ξ] which do not belong to it – ie if [ξ] = {2, 4, 6, 8} and S = {2, 6} then S' = {4, 8}.

● The **union** of two sets is when two sets are combined, written A ∪ B – so if A = {1, 2} and B = {2, 3, 4} then A ∪ B = {1, 2, 3, 4}.

● The **intersection** of two sets is where they share members, written A ∩ B – so on the above example A ∩ B = {2}.

● The **symmetric difference** of two sets, written A Δ B, is another set whose members belong to the union but not the intersection – ie the members they don't share – so on the same example A Δ B = {1, 3, 4}.

● A **power set** of, eg, {a, b, c} includes those elements, its four subsets and (by convention) the empty set ∅ and so = {a, b, c, abc, ab, ac, bc, ∅} with eight elements or 2^3 - and if the original set has N elements the power set now has 2^N.

From here it was but a hop and a skip into the comfortingly pie-charty world of Venn diagrams...
(See 'Work It Out' opposite)

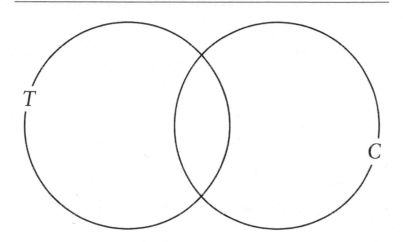

At a disco attended by 30 kids, 17 can sing along to *Tainted Love* (T) and 19 can sing along to *Come on Eileen* (C) and two can't sing at all– how many can sing along to both?

Answer on page 312

TO INFINITY AND BEYOND

Buzz Lightyear has a lot to answer for. When we were at school we had it easy: infinity was a comforting riddle; limited by the very tyranny of its limitlessness. After all, if there is nothing greater than infinity (however limitless it may be), then there must be a point at which numbers stop and infinity takes over – and then continues on infinitely. But then along came *Toy Story* with its dumb astronaut and his catchy tagline, thereby confusing the next two or three generations into thinking that there can be something 'beyond' beyond infinity.

For the rest of us, however, it was only when we mixed infinity with numbers that the trouble started; for nothing can be added or subtracted from infinity, because infinity is not a number but a concept. So 17 plus infinity is like saying 17 plus misery, clearly nonsense. Yet divide a number by zero and paradoxically you do get a mathematical answer: the answer is infinity. Huh?

IS MATHS MORE DANGEROUS THAN THE NAVY?

This excerpt from a life of 18th century Swiss mathematician, Leonard Euler, shows that the stress of attacking problems can – in rare cases – make the Navy look like peanuts. Our story picks up in the late 1720s...

Having reached St Petersburg... Euler resolved to enter into the Russian Navy, and had actually received the promise of a lieutenancy, and rapid promotion, from Admiral Sievers; but fortunately for geometry, a change took place in the aspect of public affairs in 1730, and Euler obtained the situation of Professor of Natural Philosophy. In 1733 he succeeded Daniel Bernoulli, when that illustrious mathematician retired into the country; and in the same year he married Madamoiselle Gsell, a Swiss lady, and the daughter of a painter whom Peter the Great had carried into Russia upon his return from his first tour. In 1735, a very intricate problem having been proposed by the Academy of St Petersburg, Euler completed the solution of it in three days; but the exertion of his mind had been so violent, that it threw him into a fever which endangered his life, and deprived him of the use of one of his eyes.

From *Letters of Euler on Different Subjects in Natural Philosophy*, Addressed to a German Princess, by David Brewster, LLD, 1833

PYTHAGORAS – MORE THAN THE SUM OF HIS PARTS

We all (should) know that we owe it to Pythagoras for our understanding of triangles, and the general proof that in a right-angle triangle the squares of the two sides of the triangle are equal to the square of the hypotenuse (ie $a^2 + b^2 = c^2$). But few know that Pythagoras's theorem is much more than just a neat way of working out the properties of a triangle; for Pythagoras's discovery marked the moment when mankind truly believed in a divine relationship between numbers and nature. In fact, Pythagoreans believed that numbers held the answer to everything. For example, they found that most music could be rationalised, and that most simple, beautiful harmonies could be explained by simple ratios of length. We are still making such discoveries today – apply a mathematical operation on a scenario and, with a bit of blood, sweat and inspired toil, it may be that we can explain that scenario, from the way a flower bends to the sunlight to the Hawkingesque brilliance of analysing Black Holes in space.

A Glossary of mathematical symbols

=, ≠	Equals, doesn't equal	$2 + 2 = 4, 2 + 2 \neq 5$
±	Plus or minus	The distance was 25 ± 5 miles – ie the distance was between 20-30 miles
>	More than	$5 > 2$
<	Less than	$2 < 5$
∞	Infinity	
π	The magical pi	$\pi - 3.1415926$ and counting
Σ	The sum of	$\Sigma \{2, 3, 4, 5\} = 14$
√	Square root of	$\sqrt{4} = 2$ ie $2 \times 2 = 4$ or $2^2 = 4$
⊂	Is a subset of	if A $\{1, 2\}$ and B $\{1, 2, 3, 4\}$, $A \subset B$
∪	Union	if A $\{1, 2\}$ and B $\{2, 3, 4, 5\}$, $A \cup B = \{1, 2, 3, 4, 5\}$
∩	Intersection	if A $\{1, 2\}$ and B $\{2, 3, 4, 5\}$, $A \cap B = \{2\}$
∅	Empty set	
ξ	Universal set – includes all members mentioned	
∈	Is a member of	If A $\{1, 2, 3\}$ then $2 \in A$
{ }	Curly brackets to denote a set or collection of elements	A $\{1, 2, 3\}$ = the set of A contains the members 1, 2, 3
n(A)	The number of elements in set A	If A $\{1, 2, 3\}$ then $n(A) = 3$
°	Degrees of an angle	A right angle is 45°
^	Denotes angle – Â is the angle denoted by the point A of a triangle.	Â = 45°
'	1) Minutes – but often used in context of degrees 2) In the context of sets, the complement of a set	1) Â = 45°17' 2) ξ = S + S'
∴	Therefore	$x - 2 = 4 \therefore x = 6$

Arithmetic is being able to count to 20 without taking your shoes off.

Mickey Mouse

IT'S ALL IN THE WORDING

When you think back at the algebra you learned at school, there are immediate grounds for panic; but often the panic is caused, not by the numbers, but by the vocabulary used. 'Calculate', we are still familiar with – perhaps erroneously – but, what about 'evaluate', 'express' and 'simplify'? Did they mean then, what we take them to mean now?

- **Express:** to 'set out, showing your workings'.

- **Evaluate:** to 'find the value of', so the question 'Evaluate (10+4)' is the same as 'What is 10+4?' The fine tuning comes in the need to pay attention to the order of operations – so evaluating 3–(2-3(2-7)) means having to look closely at the bracketing, starting on the inside and working your way out, so 3–(2-3(2-7)) = 3–(2-3(-5)) = 3–(2 + (3x5)) = 3 – (2+15) = 3–17 = -14.

- **Simplify:** to make more simple (obviously), but in a maths context, this means boiling things down to the baldest possible number, equation, fraction and so on, thereby making it easier to solve, understand and operate on. The equation $-3x(7-(3x-5))$ is impossible to solve because no value is given for x but it can be simplified, reducing the number of symbols and elements while still retaining the sense and balance of the 'expression'. So first off with $-3x(7-(3x-5))$ we distribute the innermost minus sign: taking it out of the bracket cancels it out:
$= -3x(7-3x+5)$ then put the numbers 7 and 5 together
$= -3x(12-3x)$ then multiply out of the remaining brackets
$= -36x + 9x^2$ then we always try to internalise the minus sign
$= 9x^2 - 36x$ which is probably the 'simplest' form, though perhaps a more meaningful, elegant way would be $9x(x-4)$.
It's short, it's sweet, it's that simple. Right.

THE TRIANGLE FAMILY

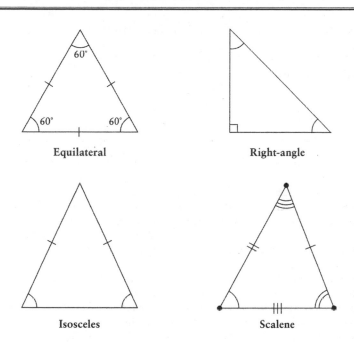

Equilateral

Right-angle

Isosceles

Scalene

Equilateral triangle – the sane elder brother, where all three sides are of equal length and all angles are 60°; area = $a^2\sqrt{3}/4$.

Right-angle triangle – the right-on quirky one – a triangle with one right angle (ie a 'corner' of 90°). Enter Pythagorean theory, stage right... where the angle C is a right angle, $c^2 = a^2 + b^2$; and the area is a positively simple = $ab/2$.

Isosceles triangle – the flared-trouser-wearing one, where two sides are equal length, with the 'bottom' angles (ie where the same length sides connect with the third side) being the same.

Scalene – the white-trash trailer dweller of the triangle family, where no sides or angles are the same and where the formula for working out the area obviously required a special calibre of geometry genius since it is known sometimes as Hero's Formula.

WORK IT OUT

In 1202, Leonardo of Pisa – aka Fibonacci – set this problem about how quickly rabbits could breed in ideal circumstances:

Suppose a pair of newborn rabbits – one male, one female – are put in a field. Rabbits are able to mate at the age of one month, so at the end of their second month, the female can produce another pair of rabbits. Suppose that our rabbits never die and that the female always produces one new pair (one male, one female) every month from the second month onwards. How many pairs will there be in one year?

Answer on page 312

MONEY, MONEY, MONEY

A basic understanding of percentages finally gave us a life skill with which we could handle talk of profit and loss, simple and compound interest – next stop the Governorship of the Bank of England. Profit, for example, is usually expressed as a percentage of the cost price:

$$\text{Percentage profit} = \frac{\text{selling price - cost price (profit)}}{\text{cost price}} \times 100\%$$

WORKED EXAMPLE

A ticket tout for that David Bowie concert you so desperately want to go to wishes to make a whopping 80% profit when he sells you a ticket which cost him £30. What must his selling price be?

Percentage proft = 80, cost price = 30, so if s is the selling price:

$$80 = \frac{s - 30}{30} \times 100$$

$$\frac{80}{100} = \frac{s - 30}{30}$$

$$0.8 \times 30 = s - 30$$
$$24 + 30 = s$$
$$54 = s$$

So the selling price is £54. Meaning you're going to have to wash up several weeks' worth of china just to be David's China Girl...

At school, everyone is fond of overstatement: telling someone that your new drainpipe jeans were a gazillion times better than theirs was nothing unusual, but the hard business of large numbers was enough to silence even the most boastful. Asking schoolchildren to contextualise, say, a billion, usually invited the teacher to come up with illustrative examples, like the fact that she was born a billion seconds ago (since all teachers seemed unimaginably old, this was impressive) or that a billion days ago, the species of man had only just evolved. With billions being part of everyday national debt, however, they were the last large number to get into the real world: after that it was megatron and quintillion which seemed like *kapow* and *kerrang* words straight out of the comic books.

Writing down such large numbers obviously presents its own problems – which is where 'powers' or exponentiation enters the fray. Raising a number to a power means multiplying it by itself as many times as the little number hanging on to its right ear suggested. Hence, $3^3 = 3 \times 3 \times 3 = 27$. Writing out a billion $100,000,000$ starts to tire the hand – how much easier to think of a billion in terms of $10 \times 10 \times 10 \times 10 \times 10 \times 10 \times 10 \times 10 \times 10$ or 10^9? Suddenly even numbers like the unimaginable googol are a puny 10^{100}. As any comic reader knows, powers can also bail out the little people too – in this case, infinitisemal fractions. By simply placing a minus sign in front of the power we can rationalise down to the nano level – so 10^{-1} is a $1/10$ or a tenth, while 10^{-6} is $1/1,000,000$ or a millionth.

HOW TO REMEMBER...

Multiplication tricks:
Minus times minus is plus,
The reason for this we need not discuss.

Easy checkout:
Even times even is even
Even times odd is even
But odd times odd is always odd.

If you're talking big or zeroing in on the unimaginably small, you're going to need the vocabulary to match... The following are the globally agreed System Internationale (SI) terms for both toptastic and tiny.

Multiplier	Symbol	Name	Mnemonic
10^{12}	T	Tiera	To
10^{9}	G	Giga	Give
10^{6}	M	Mega	Me
10^{3}	K	Kilo	Kicks
10^{-3}	M	Milli	My
10^{-6}	µ (mu)	Micro	MUsicians
10^{-9}	N	Nano	Now
10^{-12}	P	Pico	Play
10^{-15}	F	Femto	For
10^{-18}	A	Acto	Ages

PERCENTAGES

Percentages were those rare beasts in our maths studies that spoke to us of the future; we could see how they would be useful in real life and we were right; hardly a day goes by that doesn't have some sort of percentage in it, whether it's 40% of trains being delayed, or the Tories gaining on Labour with 53% of the vote, or interest rates being cut by a basis point of a percent. Their most basic definition is that they are a fraction whose denominator is 100 – so 65% is 65/100.

Changing fractions to percentages involves getting the fraction's denominator up to 100, then multiplying the numerator on top by the same factor – so 4/5 in percentage terms goes through the following process: 4 x 20 / 5 x 20 = 80/100 = 80%. Expressing one number as a percentage of another is another way of looking at the same basic equation: so 7 as a percentage of 20 = 7/20 x 100% = 700/20 = 70/2 = 35%. Then we can also increase or decrease quantities by a given percentage – so if we increase £30 by 7%, we take the £30 to be 100%, 1% of £30 = 1 x 30/100, then 107% of £30 = 107 x £30/100 - £321/10 = £32.10.

A HERO NOT JUST A ZERO

We take the humble zero for granted, but it has a different background to other numbers – more arriviste and definitely nouveau riche, really only coming along in about AD6 when the Chinese realised that they had a gap in their place-value notation and were having to write numbers like 101 as 1-1. The full implications of the zero were then developed by the Hindus of India as part of their full-blown speculations in the The Void, which shared elements of the Buddhist concept of nirvana – achieving nothingness, attaining salvation by merging into the formless void of eternity.

Soon it became clear that the zero had its own code of behaviour. If a zero were a person, our mothers would not have let us play with it in the playground. Multiplying anything by zero then makes zero – something we just take on board – but taken further, it becomes clear that the zero can then create some mischievous paradoxes: if 2 x 0 = 4 x 0, and then you cancel the zero, then 2 = 4: at which point the brain starts to hurt.

Adding and subtracting is easier because nothing is affected, but dividing a number by zero is another trick question: the answer is infinity. Muslim mathematician Ibn Yahya al-Samawal, who wrote his treatise, *The Dazzling,* in AD1135, when he was only 19 years old, came up with the evocative phrase: 'The Power of Zero', whereby anything raised to the power of zero is one – $x°$ = 1 – because if you multiply a number by itself no times at all, you just get the unit.

Q. What did the zero say to the eight?
A. Oooh, I like your belt!

A GROOVY THING TO KNOW ABOUT A TRIANGLE

If there is an external angle – ie if one of the sides of the triangle extends, creating a line along which the total 'angle' must add up to 180°, then we know that the interior angle and the exterior angle therefore add up to 180° – and from that we can work out that the exterior angle of a triangle is equal to the sum of the two interior opposite angles... think of it like sudoku: everything is in balance, so if you know one angle, then you can work out the value of its opposite angle.

QUADRILATERAL SHAPES

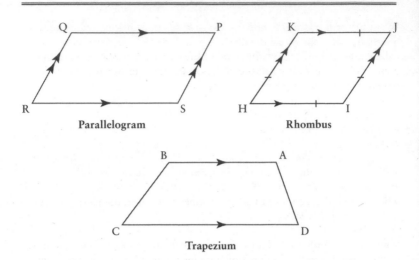

Parallelogram

Rhombus

Trapezium

THE EVOLUTION OF BRITISH MATHS TEACHING

1970: A logger sells a truckload of lumber for £100. His cost of production is 4/5 of the price. What is his profit?

1980: A logger sells a truckload of lumber for £100. His cost of production is 4/5 of the price, or £80. What is his profit?

1990: A logger sells a truckload of lumber for £100. His cost of production is £80. Did he make a profit?

2000: A logger sells a truckload of lumber for £100. His cost of production is £80 and his profit is £20. Your assignment: Underline the number 20.

2007: A logger cuts down a beautiful forest because he is selfish and inconsiderate and cares nothing for the habitat of animals or the preservation of our woodlands. He does this so he can make a profit of £20. What do you think of this way of making a living? Topic for class participation after answering the question: How did the birds and squirrels feel as the logger cut down their homes? (There are no wrong answers.)

INDICES AND LOGARITHMS

When we write a x a as a^2 or b x b x b as b^3 we are using power or index notation, where the a or b is called the base and the little tiny ^{2} and ^{3} are called indices. This is basically to make life easier when dealing with huge numbers because we can use the indices to do our sums for us, where the base a or b or x are the same:

- To multiply, add the indices – eg a^3 x $a^3 = a^6$
- To divide, subtract the indices – eg $a^4 / a^2 = a^2$
- Sometimes you will then get negative indices – e,g, $-x^2 / x^3 = x^{-1}$ but this is also $= 1/x$
- To raise a base and index to a power, multiply the indices – eg $(x^2)^3 = x^6$
- Or to find the n-th root of a base number and index, divide the index by n – eg little $\sqrt[3]{x^6} = x^{6/3} = x^2$

Logarithms (another word for index or power) are simply the extension of this, usually used in conjunction with log tables when we wander over from algebra to the field of arithmetic. They are supposedly helpful in working out big number sums (eg 128 x 16 is 'instantly' worked out using 2 as the base = 2 to the power of 7 x 2 to the power of 4, add the bases and hey presto, 2 to the power of 11 or 2048) but we are unconvinced: you need to have your log tables handy at all times and what's so handy about suddenly having to work out what 2 to the power of 11 is?

HAPPY NUMBERS

Proof, if proof were needed, that mathematicians are easily pleased with their lot, they call 'happy numbers' those numbers where, if you square the digits and add them, the number eventually boils down to the number 1.

Take the number 23:
$$2^2 + 3^2 = 13$$
$$1^2 + 3^2 = 10$$
$$1^2 + 0^2 = 1$$

Another happy number that plays into the hands of those who worship its significance throughout life, the Bible, the natural world and now maths – is, of course, 7.

WORK IT OUT

A man was in love with a young lady whose Christian name was Hannah.
When he asked her to be his wife she wrote down the letters of her name
in this manner...

```
H  H  H  H  H  H
H  A  A  A  A  H
H  A  N  N  A  H
H  A  N  N  A  H
H  A  A  A  A  H
H  H  H  H  H  H
```

...and promised that she would be his if he could tell her correctly in how
many different ways it was possible to spell out her name, always passing
from one letter to another that was adjacent. Diagonal steps are here
allowed. Whether she did this merely to tease him or to test his cleverness
is not recorded, but it is satisfactory to know that he succeeded. Would
you have been equally successful?

**Take your pencil and try. You may start from any of the H's and
go backwards or forwards and in any direction, so long as all
the letters in a spelling are adjoining one another. How many
ways are there, no two exactly alike?**

Answer on page 312

DID YOU KNOW?

What does calculation mean? In mathematical terms, it means the process
whereby we manipulate all manner of numbers to get an answer, but the
origin of the term lies not in the process, but in the way that calculation
was interpreted. *Calculus* is Latin for pebble and the ancient Greeks
used pebbles to count and perform simple calculations, hence the use
of calculate and calculation. However, given that the pebbles were then
strung onto wires in 10 strings of 10 (an abacus) we could just as easily
have forsaken the word calculation in favour of abacation, and that would
have been good news for students everywhere, as that would mean a swap
of something hard for something that is child's play...

Mnemonic for a circle's circumference and area:

Fiddlededum, fiddlededee,
A ring round the moon is π times d
If a hole in your sock you want repaired
You use the formula π r squared

INTERESTING, MR BOND

The money you borrow from a bank or spend on a credit card will be charged interest calculated on a percentage (more usually called a rate) of the sum you have borrowed (the principal). If this interest is paid each year – ie, the principal remains the same, the interest is called simple interest (SI) and is calculated as follows, based on the principal (£P), the time of the loan (T years) and the interest rate (R%), as being SI = P x T x R/100.

But life is inevitably more complicated than this and it is more usual, on a deposit account for example, for the interest gained during a year to be added to the amount originally invested, thereby producing a larger principal for the next year – with the process repeated each year with the accumulating principal described as compound interest (CI).

WORKED EXAMPLE
Find the compound interest on £3000 at 6% for three years:

Principal at start of 1st year P^1 = £3000
Interest for the 1st year, I^1 = 6/100 x £3000 - £180
Principal at start of 2nd year P^2 = £3000 + £180 = £3180
Interest for the 2nd year, I^2 = 6/100 x £3180 = £190.80
Principal at start of 3rd year P^3 = £3180 = £190.80 = £3370.80
Interest for third year, I^3 = 6/100 x £3370.80 = £202.25 (rounded up to nearest penny)
Total (compound) interest = $I^1 + I^2 + I^3$ = £573.05

Babylonians (c2000BC)
Squires of the sexagesimal system
Laid down a counting system based on 60 and its multiples that survives to this day – circles have 360 degrees, hours have 60 minutes, minutes have 60 seconds.

Chinese (c1400-1100BC onwards – peaked in early AD1400s)
Brilliance in isolation
Unbeknownst to the rest of the world, Chinese used a base 10 system of numbers centuries before anyone else – with symbols for one to 10, a hundred, a thousand and ten thousand. In AD5, a father and son team Tsu Chung Chi and Tsu Keng Chi obtained a value of π to 7 decimal places: a figure not reached in the West until the 1700s.

Pythagoras (569-500BC)
Ancient Greek grand-daddy of mathematics
Laid the foundations of geometry and algebra (and set out the relationship between them). The first to prove what became known as the Pythagoras Theorem on right angle triangles. Also a civic leader of a mysterious brotherhood that practised ascetic exercises, abstinences and a vow of secrecy about numbers that, luckily, did not outlive them.

Euclid (323-285BC)
Father of demonstrative geometry
His work, *The Elements*, provided a system of geometrical proofs, defining terms such as 'point' and 'line', measuring quantity, proving properties of constructions using instruments like a ruler and compass without resorting to either construction itself or merely numerical, theoretical proofs. His common notions included staples such as two things equal to a third are equal to each other and all right angles are equal; not to mention two lines which cross a third line with interior angles whose sum is less than two right angles will eventually meet.

Archimedes (287-212BC)
The guru of the curved shape
Devised ways to measure both surface areas and volumes of a number of curved figures and solids like spheres and cylinders. While he was at it, he worked out an approximate value of π. Oh, and he invented the 'Archimedes screw' without which we'd all be in the dark.... Since it forms the crucial part of the drill used to extract oil and gas.

Indians (four periods of greatness spanning 2500BC-AD1500)
Combined religious ecstasy with the hunt for mathematical proofs
Ritual geometry, large numbers, irrational numbers, powers, the Zero and mathematical riddles set to music: the Indians seemed to have genuine fun with numbers.

Islam (long dominance in European Dark Ages AD500-1600)
Imams of modern algebra and trigonometry
By cleverly fusing the algebraic and arithmetic traditions of Babylonia and India with the geometric laws of Greece, what the Arabs called 'scientific art' came to rule the world of maths for over a thousand years. From al-Khuwarazmi (dAD850) who coined the term algebra (al-jabr was the process of transferring terms across the = sign to eliminate negative quantities) to al-Kashi (d1429) who introduced methodical ways of dealing with decimal fractions and did π to 16 decimal places.

Rene Descartes (1596-1650)
Arch algebraicist and philospher
A restless philosopher and soldier, whose discovery of 'cartesian' geometry came to him in a dream before the battle of Prague. In liberating algebra from words and providing a standardisation for describing algebraic relations, Descartes laid the foundations then improved upon by German philosopher and mathematician Leibniz – to unleash calculus, differentiation and integration onto an unsuspecting world

Pascal and Fermat (1623-1662) and (1601-1665)
Staked it all on the throw of a dice
Not only did Blaise Pascal invent the first adding machine in 1642 but he also worked with fellow Frenchman

Fermat on probability after entering into correspondence with a gambler who wanted to know why he lost at dice. Showed that absolute certainty is not necessary in maths or science.

Charles Babbage (1792-1871)
Mr Computer
Having built a small adding machine in 1822, 10 years later he came up with his 'Difference Engine', a precursor of the digital computer. Ambitious 1834 plans for a bigger, better version were not realised until the Science Museum built part of it in 1991 – meanwhile his pioneering methods were ignored and even the computer builders of the 1930s worked largely in ignorance of Babbage's trailblazing.

George Cantor (1845-1918)
Tamed the infinite
He proved, where others had only speculated, that the set of 'real numbers' cannot be enumerated and then came up with a method for generating higher orders of infinity: power sets, exponentially denumerable and denoted by the old Hebrew letter Aleph.

Andrew Wiles (b1953)
Solver of Fermat's Last Theorem
For 350 years previously mathematicians had sweated blood to solve Fermat's 'unproveable' Last Theorem: the equation (x to the power n + y to the power n = z to the power) has no whole number solution for n greater than 2. Now based in US, at Princeton.

For a quick recap – a circle is a set of points the same distance from a fixed point (the centre) and that distance from centre to any point on the circle is called the radius. Straight lines crossing a circle from one point to another are called chords. A chord which goes through the centre is called a diameter. Chords that do not go through the centre separate the circle into segments, major and minor, with the parts of circumference described by that segment also being classified as major and minor arcs – if the chord is a diameter the segments are clearly semi-circles. A straight line outside the circle which just touches one point on the circle is called a tangent. There are 360 degrees (°) in a circle.

- To work out the diameter, double the radius: $d = 2r$

- To work out the circumference, bring in magical Mr Pi: $C = 2\pi r$ or πd

- To work out the area (K), square the radius and multiply by pi: $K = \pi r^2$

- To work out the length of an arc (AB) , use the angle formed by the straight sides of the arc coming from points A and B on the circumference to the centre – often referred to as θ (theta)°: AB = θ °/360 x circumference.

- To work out the area of a segment involves judicious use of sin and a formula imported from the triangle family: that the area of a triangle is ½ ab sine c (little letters meaning the length of triangle sides) and substituting a and b with the radius: segment area = θ°/360 x πr^2 - ½ r^2 sine θ° – which I think we can all agree just trips off the tongue.

- For working out angles of chords within a circle, there are no less than 12 theorems – at which point we have strayed into the realms of Information on a Need To Know basis only...

QUOTE UNQUOTE

Some of you may have met mathematicians and wondered how they got that way.
Tom Lehrer, US singer-songwriter, satirist, pianist, and mathematician

BUCKLE UP

Before we've even started the algebra car, there are some basic operational laws that must be obeyed if the engine is going to run smoothly – the Mirror-Signal-Manoeuvre of the equation world:

- always do the operation inside the brackets first.
- a negative number multiplied by a negative number gives a positive number.
- you can 'multiply out', so: $a(b - c)$ can also be treated as $a \times b - a \times c$ and written as $ab - ac$; $-1(b + c)$ becomes $-b - c$; and $-1(b - c)$ cancels out the minuses to give $-b + c$, or more elegantly, $c - b$.

DID YOU KNOW?

The earliest standardised units of measurement were the breadth of the palm of the hand, the length of the foot (aka the length of the inside arm from the elbow to the wristbone) known as the 'cubitt'. This was better when everyone was equally small and of the same race but when the giants of Upper Cowford started comparing measurements with the notorious midgets of Lower Cowmouth, the weaknesses of the body scale were obvious.

Now our measurements are more scientific. Different standards still abound but the most common is the Systeme Internationale, derived from 10 metric system introduced during the French Revolution, based on the unit of 10. An exception was time, where the French iconoclasts attempted to derail the Babylonian second, minute, hour, day system, dividing a lunar month into three 'decades' of 10 days each, with each day broken down into 10 hours of a hundred minutes each: not a popular move and soon dropped.

The basic metre was originally conceived by the tricoleurs as one 40/millionth of the world's circumference; or 1/10,000,000th of the distance from the Equator to the North Pole through Paris. As recently as 1983, after a short time when it was calculated to do with the distance travelled by an orange-red wavelength in a radiation vacuum, it was set by the distance travelled by light in an absolute spectrum in 1/299792458ths of a second (which is certainly a snappy number to remember).

- A common or vulgar fraction is what normal mortals call a fraction (top number is called the numerator, the bottom number is called the denominator).

- A proper fraction is one where the numerator is less than the denominator – eg $^2/_5$ – and all is as it should be.

- An improper fraction is one in which the numerator is bigger than the denominator, eg $^{11}/_5$

- A mixed number (hmmm…) is the sum of an integer and a fraction, eg $3 + ^1/_2$, usually written as $3^1/_2$

- An improper fraction can be changed to a mixed number because it is always larger than 1 – so $^{11}/_5$ can be written as $2^1/_5$

- The Lowest Common Denominator is the smallest possible integer that is a multiple of all the denominators in a group of fractions – thereby easing the comparison of the size of fractions.

- The LCD (sometimes also called the LCM – Lowest Common Multiple) is also crucial for the addition and subtraction of fractions:

eg $\dfrac{1}{2} - \dfrac{1}{4} = \dfrac{4}{8} - \dfrac{2}{8} = \dfrac{2}{8} = \dfrac{1}{4}$

- For multiplication, multiply both numerators and denominators to get your answer:

eg $\dfrac{3}{4} \times \dfrac{3}{5} = \dfrac{3 \times 3}{4 \times 5} = \dfrac{9}{20}$

- To divide by a fraction, multiply by its inverse: the opposite or yin to the original fraction's yang: if a mixed number is involved, change it into an improper fraction:

eg $\dfrac{2}{5} \div \dfrac{3}{4} = \dfrac{2}{5} \times \dfrac{4}{3}$ (ie the inverse of $\dfrac{3}{4}$) $= \dfrac{8}{15}$

WORK IT OUT

A painting job can be completed by eight painters in 48 days. If 32 more painters join the team eight days after starting work on the job, then how many more days are required to complete the job?

Answer on page 312

228 *The Universal Crammer*

PROPERTIES OF SOLID SHAPES

Shape	Properties	Picture
Cube	Volume = a^3 Surface area = $6a^2$	
Prism (Solid with uniform cross-section)	Volume = area of end section x length Surface area = (2 x area of end section) + (perimeter of end section x length)	
Cuboid (rectangular block)	Volume = abc Surface area = $2ab + 2bc + 2ac$	
Cylinder (special prism)	Volume = πr^2 x height Surface area = (area of two ends) + (area of curved surface)	
Sphere	Volume = $\dfrac{4}{3} \pi r^3$ Surface area = $4 \pi r^2$	
Pyramid	Volume = $\dfrac{1}{3}$ x base area x height Surface area = (area of base) + (area of triangular faces)	
Cone (right circular)	Volume = $\dfrac{1}{3} \pi r^2$ x height Surface area = $\pi r^2 + (\pi r$ x length)	

I have hardly ever known a mathematician who was capable of reasoning.

Plato

BY THE RIVERS OF BABYLON

Trigonometry is where the pencils started to get a little blunter. Suddenly we'd left the tinkly triangle far behind and there were ancient Greeks littering the frame, bandying terms around like hypotenuses and theorems and what have you. Yes, you, Pythagoras: step forward as charged. His theorem states: 'in a right-angled triangle, the square on the hypotenuse equals the sum of the squares on the other two sides', the hypotenuse being the side opposite the right angle'. This was something which had been known to the ancient Babylonians, over 4,000 years ago, who had knotted ropes corresponding to the side lengths of 3, 4, 5 to mark out right angled triangles (thereby working the theorem backwards) but Pythagoras was the first man to prove that there was a steady state relationship between a right-angled triangle and the length of its sides – triangles in the ratio of 3, 4, 5 or 5, 12, 13 just happen to be very common manifestations of the relationship.

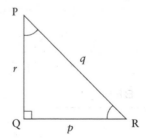

So, in the triangle above, PR is the hypotenuse so $PR^2 = PQ^2 + RQ^2$ or if you follow the convention of assigning a little letter to the sides of the triangle $q^2 = r^2 + p^2$.

Once we know this formula, and you know the length of two sides of the triangle plus the fact that the triangle is a right angled one, then you can work out the third side (and then hang out the bunting).

A **transformation** is a movement of a plane shape (triangle, quadrilateral etc rather than Boeing 747) from one position to another in its plane – think of it as a mixture of *Alice in Wonderland* and air traffic control – you are sending the shape to another part of the graph on which it is plotted (ie map) and it may well shrink or enlarge along the way, according to its instructions. Isometries – translation, rotation and reflection – are all transformations in which the original and transformed shapes have not drunk any of Alice's potions and are still congruent – ie, the same shape and size. Just moved.

Translations are determined by a displacement vector in the form of a forward shooting arrow written over the new position; with **rotations**, where the shape is not moved entirely but merely turned through an angle either clockwise or anti-clockwise, it's all about finding the fixed centre of rotation. The method looks complicated when drawn but is surprisingly simple: connect up two corresponding points – eg, corner A with the rotated corner A(i), corner B with the rotated corner B(i). Draw in the perpendicular bisector of each line – ie, the line that cuts our A-A(i) line in half at 90° and do the same for B-B(i) – and where those two new lines cross is the fixed centre of rotation. Piece of cake.

Finally, to determine a **reflection**, the position of the mirror line must be known. Because, say, corner A is equidistant from new reflected corner A(i), and because the mirror line bisects the angle between them, all you have to do is draw a line between A and A(i) and, what do you know, the perpendicular bisector of that line *is* the mirror line.

HOW TO REMEMBER...

Simpson's Rule
For the area under a curve
Add first to last, and to this add
Twice even, four times odd.
By one sixth n then multiply,
The area is found, by God!

X

BIOLOGY

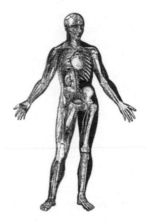

*The capacity to blunder slightly is
the real marvel of DNA. Without this
special attribute, we would still be
anaerobic bacteria.*

Lewis Thomas, US nature writer

Chromosomes are important single pieces of DNA within cells; the structures that make us who we are. The word 'chroma' means colour in Greek and 'soma' is body. Chromosomes are different in every living creature, and some cells house more than one type of chromosome as part of the DNA contained in their nucleus. A single DNA molecule can either be a single or double strand which is in a line or circular. Eukaryotic cells with nuclei have linear chromosomes and prokaryotic cells without nuclei have circular chromosomes. Every human cell has 23 pairs of linear chromosomes. These chromosomes can be either duplicated or unduplicated in the DNA. If they're duplicated, bunched up together and squished side by side they have an 'X' shape. It has been debated whether this shape is linked to the X and Y name of sex-determining chromosomes, as Y just happened to be the next letter in the alphabet after the X chromosome was found, but Y chromosomes do tend to be shorter and look more like the letter 'Y' so we were taught at school that X and Y chromosomes got their name from their shapes. Humans have two chromosomes out of the 46 that decide what sex we will be. Males have XY chromosomes and females have XX chromosomes.

THUMBING A LIFT – INSIDE YOU

Being a parasite isn't a pleasant job. But then, as we all know, there were plenty of different kinds of parasites at school. We learned about parasites by discovering they were one species living off another host species, usually inside that host. The parasite either coexists or damages the host in some way, by feeding on its nutrients, eating its eggs or simply growing to a size that kills the host. But, of course, not all parasites are bad. Whale sharks have Remora suckerfish that swim with them and, although often seen as parasites hitching a ride, they actually assist the host in a positive way (a process called commensalism) by eating bacteria off the shark's skin. The most well-known human parasite is the tapeworm, which lives in our guts feeding off what we eat. The disturbing thing about tapeworms is they often cause no symptoms or illness and can live inside people, sucking up nutrients to their heart's content, without the host even noticing.

WORK IT OUT

What is the closest relation that your father's sister's sister-in-law could be to you?

Answer on page 312

WHO TURNED OUT THE LIGHTS?
ENDANGERED TO EXTINCT

The top 10 reasons animals first become endangered and then extinct

1. Humans – we've destroyed more species than any creature in history, we are officially bad for the environment.

2. Pollution – oil spills, acid rain and water contamination, all caused by humans.

3. Destruction of habitat – urban growth that fills up swamps, dams up rivers, reclaims land and cuts down trees to build homes, gives nature nowhere to go.

4. Over-hunting and fishing – species are literally hunted to the very last animal or fish.

5. Natural evolutionary process – where a species adapts over time to its environment, meaning its ancestors die out and a 'new' form of itself takes over.

6. Loss of food – by killing one species, humans and other hunters take away a food source from another species. Humans also do this by destroying areas of wilderness.

7. Ice ages – natural phenomena, such as long periods of bad weather and cooling Earth temperatures can wipe out species almost over night.

8. Fire – raging flames can often cause whole forests to disappear along with plant species.

9. Disease – part of natural selection, the sick don't survive when a particular strain of virus takes hold of one individual species and attempts to kill them all, eg: the human plague known as the Black Death.

10. Volcanic eruptions – nature's über-dramatic way of destroying some species unlucky enough to be living on an island that's blowing its lava load that decade.

Charles Darwin seemed to get everywhere during our school years – we couldn't get away from his bearded old face. For someone constantly prone to illness, he managed to get a lot done in his life, and if you couldn't shake him off in double History or single Chemistry, then you'd definitely hear from him in Biology – thanks to his theory of natural selection. This was his way of describing the constant evolution over the generations of an organism's existence. In that, any useful phenotypes – strong physical, biological or emotional traits – are kept and stored in the continuing development of an organism's DNA, and that any weak or pointless genetic characteristics are jettisoned. In other words, any trait apparently irrelevant to a species' survival was dropped from that species' biological equation. These were replaced with stronger traits that sometimes meant the complete discontinuation (extinction) of that species in certain forms, to be replaced by a spanking new, shinier species. Darwin explained his theory on the 'survival of the fittest' in his 1859 book *The Origin of the Species*.

WELCOME TO AN EMPTY JURASSIC PARK

When we combine biology with history, it's clear that the dinosaurs played a huge part in our lives. They were the exciting part of archaeology – the creatures that adventurers in brown hats and whips went to find out about in remote deserts. But the biggest question of them all, that still hasn't been *thoroughly* answered (and may never be), is: why did all the dinosaurs suddenly die out at the end of the Cretaceous Period 65 million years ago? The most recognised theory given to us back in the days of schoolbook biology was that a huge comet or meteorite crashed into the Earth, spitting up billions of tons of dust into the atmosphere that cut off sunlight and poisoned the air, killing all animals almost overnight. Other theories included mass disease, lack of food, a drop in temperature, volcanic eruptions and naturally polluting gases, rising sea-levels and even changes in the Earth's magnetic field from alterations in the planet's orbit around the sun. These were all very well, but later studies showed that dinosaurs seemed to die out pretty quickly so the answer is likely to be a combination of all of the above, with the comet providing the main nail in the dinosaurs' coffins.

BREAK IT DOWN: WHAT'S INSIDE A CELL?

Creatures are made up of many different types of cells, but the most highly developed animals and plants have eukaryotic cells that contain the same basic ingredients of life – called organelles. They are:

● **A nucleus** – the brain of a cell. This contains DNA passed down through generations kept separate from the rest of the cell by its own nuclear membrane. The nucleus tells the cell how to work and how to divide itself.

● **Golgi apparatus** – kind of shelf-stacking membranes inside the cell, which contain enzymes that sort, package-up and alter any proteins and lipids – natural fat molecules with binding qualities – for transportation to parts of the cell and a creature's body. The Golgi apparatus gets these proteins from the...

● **Rough Endoplasmic Reticulum** – this is a set of tubes that takes proteins and lipids to parts of the cell and its external membrane. Inside these bumpy networks are Ribosomes – little factories that make the proteins the cell needs to grow.

● **Smooth endoplasmic reticulum** – the main transportation system of the cell, its tubes do specialist tasks such as lipid synthesis.

● **Cell membrane** – made up of a double layer of lipid molecules. It protects the cell from the external environment, giving it insulation but it also has pores to let in food.

● **Cytoplasm** – is the gel-like fluid called cytosol inside the whole cell, apart from the nucleus, that houses all the cell's other parts in a protective cushion.

● **Mitochondria** – the cell's power stations, generating energy by consuming sugar molecules with the help of oxygen we breathe. This gives off carbon dioxide created by the mitochondria which we exhale.

● **Lysosome** – little sacks of enzymes dotted all over the cell that eat old DNA molecules, protein and lipids to make them into new and re-usable molecules.

SIZE ISN'T EVERYTHING: MICROBIOLOGY

Organisms come in all shapes and sizes, and scientists used micro- and nanometres to measure the world of microbiological life forms. Micrometres are one millionth of a metre and nanometres are one billionth the size of a metric metre. The smallest known micro-organism is thought to be a nanobe, which lives in rocks, and is just 20 nanometres in size, smaller than any bacteria.

The noses of women, we cannot help noting, are often at the same level as the armpits of men.

Carl Sagan, US author

THE EARTH TAKES A DEEP BREATH: PHOTOSYNTHESIS

Ask anyone you know from your school days what is the one topic they always remember from Biology, and without fail – apart from sex education – it's photosynthesis. It's probably the weirdly cool-sounding name, *photosynthesis*, that helped. But then ask the same school friends what it actually means...

If they tell you it's the chemical enzyme-driven process that organisms such as plants use to convert carbon dioxide and the energy in light into carbohydrate food sources like sugar, glucose and starch, which results in the by-product oxygen, then they'd be right. Top of the class.

Photosynthesis occurs in the leaves of plants, with enzymes using the light energy to power the making of *triose phosphates.* This is a three-carbon sugar made as the plant splits up oxygen and carbon dioxide (a process we would have learned was called the Calvin-Benson Cycle). The oxygen is released into the atmosphere for us to breathe and the carbon dioxide is changed into energy-rich nutrients the plant uses to grow.

This was expressed in the scientific equation:

$$6\ CO_{2(g)} + 12\ H_2O_{(l)} + \text{photons} \rightarrow C_6H_{12}O_{6(aq)} + 6\ O_{2(g)} + 6\ H_2O_{(l)}$$

$$\text{carbon dioxide} + \text{water} + \text{light energy} \rightarrow \text{glucose} + \text{oxygen} + \text{water}$$

Photons are the particle carriers of electromagnetic radiation (which includes sunlight, eg ultra-violet light) and these provide the plant with the energy for the photosynthesis that takes place in the *thykaloid* membrane system of a plant's cells called *chloroplasts*. But, of course, you'll remember that it isn't just plants that photosynthesise; algae and bacteria also help breathe life into the Earth.

A FOOD CHEMIST'S BEDTIME STORY

Vitamin A
Keeps the cold germs away
And tends to make meek people nervy.
B's what you need
When you're going to seed
And C is specific in scurvy.
Vitamin D makes the bones in your knee
Tough and hard for the service on Sunday.
While E makes hen scratch
And increases the hatch
And brings in more profits on Monday.
Vitamin F never bothers the chef
For this vitamin never existed.
G puts the fight in the old appetite
And you eat all the foods that are listed.
So now when you dine, remember these lines;
If long on this globe you will tarry
Just try to be good and pick out more food
From the orchard, the garden and dairy.

ANIMAL, VEGETABLE, MINERAL... OR OTHER?

One of the key phrases we learned in Biology was how to distinguish between different organism types by asking the question: is it animal, vegetable, mineral or other? It was a simple shorthand to help us recall information – an animal is a living creature that moves around, eats and reproduces; a vegetable is a plant that grows in soil or elsewhere and can often be eaten; a mineral is a collective mixture of inorganic chemical compositions that can be transformed into metal and salt by geological occurrences such as volcanic eruptions, but what, pray, was the other? The animal, vegetable and mineral game of 20 Questions was a classic learning method in Biology class. So, if what you were trying to work out wasn't part of the animal kingdom, a plant or something born of geology, then it was 'other', ie anything else – aliens, your weird Uncle Freddie, your Nan's fake teeth... that sort of thing.

Remember when you giggled behind your hand in biology at that bad, soft-focus video of the boy and girl growing up? How their 'bits' became longer, wider and grew more hair? And, how, with the worst acting in history, the boy's voice descended from a high-pitched screech to a deep growl?

Embarrassing memories like these were part of our Biology lessons on sexual reproduction, which covered topics from plant procreation to human sexual intercourse. The main things we learned were the physical differences between girls and boys (as if we didn't already know) and how, at a later stage (the teachers hoped it was later), sexual intercourse occurred and babies were created. They told us:

A young man, who has been through the changes of puberty, has a fully developed penis and testes. These two testicles – hard oval-like balls carried inside a scrotum sac of dangly, hairy flesh – make and carry sperm as well as the male hormone testosterone. Sperm is kept at a lower temperature than normal body heat to ensure the spermatozoa works properly, hence why boys' scrotums hang away from the body – one 'ball' usually lower than other. The penis is made up of three different tissues and the foreskin over its end, as well as the hole urine is ejected from – the meatus – and the tube through its middle connected to the testicles, through which sperm is ejaculated during sex.

A young woman, who has been through the changes of puberty, has two ovaries that contain eggs released into the fallopian tubes once a month (causing the menstrual blood unless the eggs are fertilised). To enable these eggs to become a baby, the young woman also has a vagina – an elastic-like muscular canal that can stretch during sex – that is connected from the uterus or womb inside to the outside of the body between her legs to allow the penis to be inserted during intercourse. The vagina's external area, the vulva, includes a sensitive clitoris and reddish-pink skin. The hymen is a protective membrane over the vagina broken after having sex for the first time or after 'losing your virginity'.

The two different male and female reproductive organs come together during sexual intercourse. A woman's vagina becomes lubricated by glands at the front of the vaginal wall when aroused. This enables a man's now-erect penis – which has expanded in width and length and 'stands to attention' at a roughly 45-degree angle from a rush of blood inside the penis tissue – to slide in and out of the vaginal opening (also at a 45-degree angle) until orgasm. This orgasm triggers the release of millions of sperm from the end of the man's penis into the woman's cervix to swim up the uterus and attempt to fertilise an ovarian egg in the fallopian tubes. This fertilisation creates a zygote cell which will attach itself to the womb and eventually become a foetus and baby.

Our teachers encouraged us to have 'safe sex', which seemed to involve rolling a stretchy balloon called a condom over a cucumber. Or, indeed, different magic pills girls could take before or after having sex to ensure they didn't get pregnant. Condoms were especially important because, as well as preventing unwanted pregnancies, they also helped stop us catching Sexually Transmitted Diseases (STDs), also known as Sexually Transmitted Infections (STIs), which involved a painfully revealing trip to your hospital's Genitourinary (GU) Medicine clinic or, even worse, your local GP (who knew your mum really well). These diseases include:

● **Chlamydia** – a common bacteria (*chlamydia trachomatis*) that causes infertility and is caught through unprotected oral or vaginal sex.
● **Genital herpes** – has two strands and neither have a cure: type 1 causes cold sores around the mouth and can infect eyes and genitals with sores; type 2 causes itchy blisters around your genitals and anus.
● **Genital warts** – unlikely to spread to other parts of the body, genital warts are caused by the Human Papilloma Virus

● **Gonorrhoea** – known as 'the clap' back then, gonorrhoea is a strong infection brought to you by *gonococcus* bacteria that can cause infertility in men and women.
● Hepatitis B and C – Hep B causes inflammation of the liver and symptoms like weight loss, flu and aching muscles are common after coming into contact with infected blood, needles, semen or vaginal fluids; Hep C causes similar illnesses but is more serious and long-term.
● **HIV and AIDs** – the Human Immuno-Deficiency Virus (HIV) attacks the blood's white cells that fight off infection. HIV kills these vital immune system cells – called t-helpers – until Acquired Immune-Deficiency Syndrome (AIDs) develops and the body is no longer able to guard against any diseases.
● **Pubic lice (crabs) and scabies** – the highly contagious full-stop sized parasites love the sweaty warmth of genitals, laying their eggs on pubic hair and causing itchiness. Scabies are mites that burrow under the skin of your penis, vagina, bottom or breasts after sexual contact.
● **Syphilis** – this age-old complicated infection comes from the *treponema pallidum* bacteria. Caught through contact with ulcers on the mouth or genitals, syphilis causes tiny ulcers on whichever part of the body the bacteria is passed on to. These later develop into warts and brownish infectious sores all over the body, headaches, fever and sore throats. If left untreated, syphilis can cause blindness, heart disease and death.

Many years ago, a wealthy lord died and left a fortune to his only child – a son – who couldn't be traced. Several young men came forward claiming to be the heir. They all fit the description of the true heir. Then an old friend of the deceased suggested a test. All the candidates went through with it but one. Those who did were impostors and the one who refused was the rightful heir. What was the test and why would the rightful heir refuse?

Answer on page 312

'OOH, HASN'T SHE GOT YOUR EYES AND HIS NOSE!'

Deoxyribonucleic acid (DNA) is the blueprint of who we – and all living organisms – are, stored in 'information molecules' inside the nucleus of cells. This molecular information is called genes – a combination of physical, emotional and behavioural evolutionary traits handed down by parents that construct a specific species. DNA's purpose is to hold the key to telling cells how to grow, divide and create important components such as proteins and Ribonucleic acid (RNA molecules). Unlike RNA, which is a nucleic acid that has a single helix combination of genes made of a long chain of nucleotides (these contain critical building blocks or the 'amino acids' phosphate, ribose and a nitrogenous base that pairs up genetic information) handed down through generations, DNA molecules have a double strand of genes. These two nanometre long repeating polymers (like strings of information) of nucleotides entwine into what's called a double helix. This repeating information contains the 'glue' of the molecule, holding the long chain together, and also a 'base' that works alongside the other half of the chain. A base can be connected to a sugar – a nucleoside – or linked to a phosphate and called a nucleotide (DNA nucleotides contain the same amino acids as RNA except they have deoxyribose sugar). Sugar in DNA is an important element along with carbon atoms. All of this is bound together by phosphate (yes, similar to that phosphorous stuff that glows white when it's exposed to oxygen) that creates a bond between atoms.

HOW TO DISSECT A COW'S EYE

To help us learn how our eyes work, we were given a cow or bull's eye to dissect as part of Biology lessons, something that is now banned in the UK. So for all those that missed out:

Side view of eye

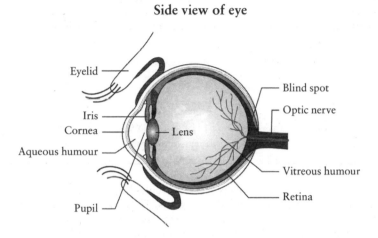

- **Vitreous humour** – the jelly in the eyeball that gives it shape.
- **Lens** – a clear and flexible part (flexible so it can focus) that makes an image on the retina.
- **Retina** – light-sensitive cells lining the back of the eye that detect images from the lens and send messages to the brain to interpret.
- **Optic nerve** – the tiny nerve fibres attached to the retina at the back of the eye that takes image information to the brain.
- **Iris** – the muscle that controls how much light enters the eye, like in a camera, and is usually brown in a cow's eye and green, blue, brown and grey in humans.
- **Cornea** – a tough shield protecting the iris and inner eye, this layer bends light coming into the eye and is the first step to creating an image along with the lens.
- **Pupil** – the dark circle in the middle of the iris that expands and contracts to let in light; a cow's is oval-shaped but ours are round.
- **Aqueous humour** – clear fluid that keeps the cornea's protective shape.
- **Blind spot** – the part at the back of the eye where the retina meets the optic nerve and where there are no light-sensitive cells.
- **Tapetum** – the shiny layer behind the retina that assists with night vision and reflects light back through the retina.

DARWIN'S MAIN MAN

James Hutton has often been credited as a direct influence on Charles Darwin's theory of evolution by natural selection. This passage shows why:

'We know little of the earth's internal parts, or of the materials which compose it at any considerable depth below the surface. But upon the surface of this globe, the more inert matter is replenished with plants, and with animal and intellectual beings.

Where so many living creatures are to ply their respective powers, in pursuing the end for which they were intended, we are not to look for nature in a quiescent state; matter itself must be in motion, and the scenes of life a continued or repeated series of agitations and events.

This globe of the earth is a habitable world; and on its fitness for this purpose, our sense of wisdom in its formation must depend. To judge of this point, we must keep in view, not only the end, but the means also by which that end is obtained. These are, the form of the whole, the materials of which it is composed, and the several powers which concur, counteract, or balance one another, in procuring the general result.'

From *Theory of the Earth*, by James Hutton (1726-1797)

IT'S ALL GREEK TO ME

To help us grasp the historical context of biology at school we ploughed through subjects we thought were more suited to double History, such as learning about ancient Greek theory – especially Aristotle's early beliefs about biology. Aristotle developed his theories around 350BC, including one directly linked to the most important part of biology, reproduction. More through logical objectivity than any scientific dissection, he stated that women helped provide the essence of life for a child through their monthly menstrual blood. He also concluded that men provided everything else a baby needed to grow, all the base materials of life, from semen. He said that the woman provided the 'soil' and the man the more important 'seed' which held all the essential ingredients to kick start a child's life. This idea was, of course, based on the ancient Greek belief that women weren't as well developed physically and mentally as men. Many of Aristotle's theories still hold true over 2,000 years later, except the one that suggested men's sperm housed a miniature already-developed version of a baby in it that merely grew inside women.

Those crafty teachers played all kinds of tricks on our minds to get us to remember biological facts, statistics and scientific jargon. One of them was turning the red blood cell's haemoglobin – the oxygen transportation protein – into the evil Hema Goblins. Because, let's face it, everyone remembers ugly goblins from their childhood. But how much do you actually remember about what haemoglobin does? Haemoglobin is a metalloprotein – a protein that has an organic compound containing metal. In haemoglobin's case it is iron, which has the sole purpose of getting oxygen from the lungs or gills of creatures, via red blood cells, to other cells around the body. In particular, cells making up muscles would die without haemoglobin.

QUOTE UNQUOTE

The interaction of genetic and external influences makes my behaviour unpredictable, but not undetermined. In the gap between those words lies freedom.
Matt Ridley, UK author and expert on behaviour and human genetics

IT'S A CELL-UVA THEORY

Although common knowledge now, the idea that all living things were made up of tiny cells that structured the physical make-up of organisms was first suggested in the 17th century. The underpinning theory that all biology is based on cells was first thought up by Robert Hooke in 1665 because of technological advances in microscopes. Hooke thought cells looked like the tiny rooms monks lived in at the time, called *cellula*. Hence the name, cells. Although Hooke didn't find the cells' nuclei and DNA, he did help formulate the theory that all organisms had cells to give them structure and that all cells came from other divided cells.

THE THEORY OF EVOLUTION: A SUMMARY

In a nutshell (one that has evolved and grown spikes over the years), this is what Charles Darwin's theory was back in November 1859 when *The Origin of the Species* was first published:

Variation: there is variation in every population.
Competition: organisms compete for limited resources.
Offspring: organisms produce more offspring than can survive.
Genetics: organisms pass genetic traits on to their offspring.
Natural Selection: organisms with the most beneficial traits are more likely to survive and reproduce.

'MY VOICE IS GETTING DEEPER' – SIGNS OF PUBERTY

The overload of hormones into your body when you were younger was the start of what made you into the person you are today. But do you remember what the top 10 signs of puberty were?

1. Hair growing around the pubic area and underarms.
2. The larynx or voice box grows bigger in boys and girls, but becomes very large in boys causing thicker vocal chords and a deeper voice. Sometimes boys experience the embarrassing wobble of high-pitched screeches and deeper octaves during the change.
3. Boys testicles get bigger so they can make sperm.
4. Girls breasts become a lump and eventually develop into a firm swell to carry milk.
5. The surface of the vagina becomes a darker pink colour and the ovaries grow.
6. The menarche – or first menstruation bleeding – begins with monthly ovulation (periods).
7. A boy's whole body shape changes with increased bone mass and develops more muscles than girls.
8. Girls thighs and hips widen ready for being able to give birth.
9. Body odour (BO) can get smellier, with fatty acids overworking to create excess perspiration during puberty changes.
10. Acne is a result of the overworking fatty acids and is the worst sign of puberty with spots, black heads, pus and greasy-looking skin plaguing millions every year.

Dissection in Biology was usually approached with some trepidation. There was the undeniable fact that the thing – frog, bull's eye, pig's trotter, fish – in front of us on the scratched science worktop had been alive not so long ago. Although some claim this to be an urban myth, many school curricula did actually enact Luigi Galvani's 1783 discovery of getting a frog's legs to twitch in order to demonstrate how muscles worked – or were 'animated' – via pulses of electricity.

Here's how they did it:

- Put on gloves and goggles
- Take hold of scalpel (this is sharp, be careful).
- Slice off frog's back legs (although this was often done for you).
- Make sure some muscle strands and nerve endings are visible on severed part of leg.
- Move an Ever Ready box battery close and connect a wire with a metal crocodile clip to the positive terminal.
- Connect the other end of the wire and its metal crocodile clip to the nerve of the frog's leg.
- Electrical current from the battery travels through the wire and is transported by the nerves to the muscles, making the frog's legs go stiff or twitch.

Although Galvani enacted this 'galvanism', as he called it, by accident, it was Alessandro Volta who later showed these twitching legs weren't, as Galvani believed, the animal's electricity reignited back to life but was actually just the cells carrying external electricity to help the muscles work. Volta later went on to invent the battery.

THE FUNCTIONS OF BLOOD MNEMONIC

Old Charlie Foster hates women having dull clothes

Oxygen (transport), Carbon dioxide (transport), food, heat, waste, hormones, disease, clotting

Depending on whether you count the sternum as one bone or three, the human skeleton is made up of either 206 or 208 bones. Here are all of them. Come on, sing-a-long: 'The thigh bone's connected to the...'

● **Skull cranial bones:** frontal bone, parietal bone (2), temporal bone (2), occipital bone, sphenoid bone, ethmoid bone.

● **Skull facial bones:** mandible, maxilla (2), palatine bone (2), zygomatic bone (2), nasal bone (2), lacrimal bone (2), vomer bone, inferior nasal conchae (2).

● **Middle ears:** malleus (2), incus (2), stapes (2).

● **Throat:** hyoid bone.

● **Shoulder girdle:** scapula or shoulder blade (2), clavicle or collarbone (2).

● **Thorax:** sternum (if considered three bones, it's made up of the manubrium, body of sternum (gladiolus) and xiphoid process), ribs (2 x 12).

● **Vertebral column:** cervical vertebrae (7), thoracic vertebrae (12), lumbar vertebrae (5).

● **Arms:** humerus (2).

● **Forearms:** radius (2), ulna (2).

● **Hands:** Carpal (wrist) bones: scaphoid bone (2), lunate bone (2), triquetral bone (2), pisiform bone (2), trapezium (2), trapezoid bone (2), capitate bone (2), hamate bone (2).

● **Metacarpus (palm) bones:** metacarpal bones (5 × 2).

● **Digits of the hand (finger bones or phalanges):** proximal phalanges (5 × 2), intermediate phalanges (4 × 2), distal phalanges (5 × 2).

● **Pelvis:** coccyx, sacrum, hip bone (innominate bone or coxal bone) (2).

● **Thighs:** femur (2).

● **Legs:** patella (2), tibia (2), fibula (2).

● **Feet (52):** Tarsal (ankle) bones: calcaneus (heel bone) (2), talus (2), navicular bone (2), medial cuneiform bone (2), intermediate cuneiform bone (2), lateral cuneiform bone (2), cuboid bone (2).

● **Metatarsus bones:** metatarsal bone (5 × 2).

● **Digits of the foot (toe bones or phalanges):** proximal phalanges (5 × 2), intermediate phalanges (4 × 2), distal phalanges (5 × 2).

THE HUMAN SKELETON

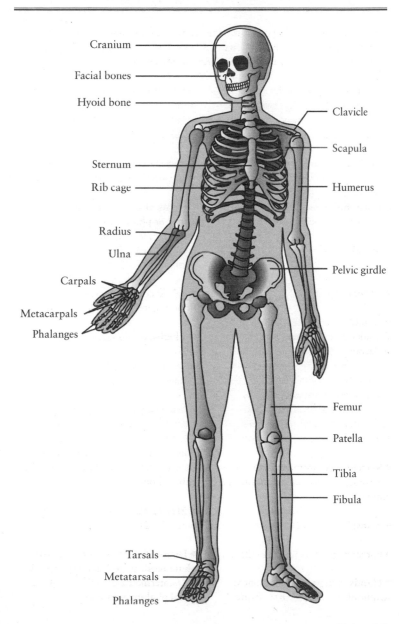

Cranium

Facial bones

Hyoid bone

Clavicle

Scapula

Sternum

Rib cage

Humerus

Radius

Ulna

Pelvic girdle

Carpals

Metacarpals

Phalanges

Femur

Patella

Tibia

Fibula

Tarsals

Metatarsals

Phalanges

I, ROBOT: ARTIFICIAL LIFE

Back in school the coolest forms of artificial life was that robot with the big head on *Lost in Space*, or *Robocop*. But we did learn about artificial life, or 'Alife' as the boffins call it, because it was a modern branch of Biology. The study and research into creating Alife uses the logic of natural living organisms and how they interact in artificial environments. The three different forms of Alife we would have explored:

1. Soft Alife – the use of software on computers to act in a manner that suggests it is 'alive', thinking for itself and adapting within its environment.
2. Hard Alife – the use of hardware, in whatever form, to build a machine existing on its own.
3. Wet Alife – the use and manipulation of biochemistry to create whole organisms, or part machine and part chemical/biological, creatures or 'cyborgs' that grow, learn and appear to have a mind of their own.

NOW WE'RE GETTING PERSONAL: BIOLOGICAL HOMEOSTASIS

Homeostasis was the rather complicated-sounding term our science teachers used to mean: keeping everything the same. Admittedly, this is a simplistic explanation of what actually is a living organism's internal, constantly-adjusting system that ensures it remains functioning appropriately within its environment. But it's still correct, because homeostasis is nature's way of ensuring the status quo prevails until which time evolution or, indeed, old age and death means homeostasis ends within individual creatures. The best way to remember homeostasis is to think about someone you know well. Imagine they're getting right up close in your face to the extent you get annoyed and push them away. You've just made homeostasis happen because you've adjusted your environment with the push to ensure your internal stress levels remain normal. This concept was invented in 1865 by Claude Bernard who said that any organism has parameters which it uses to keep itself separate and functioning within an environment. And these parameters are constantly changing to keep the organism's internal condition stable by using dynamic equilibrium – opposing chemical forces – and regulation mechanisms, such as pushing people out of your face.

How is it possible for a boy and girl to be born on the same day, in the same year and to the same parents, but not be twins?

Answer on page 312

CARNIVORES GO 'GRRR!' AND VEGETARIANS GO 'DON'T BUILD THAT RUNWAY!'

The main difference between animals, we learned at school, was the food they ate. And what they ate classified them in Biology as carnivores, herbivores or omnivores:

Carnivores

(*Carne* in Latin means 'flesh' and *vorare* means 'to eat'.) Consume mostly meat from animals they have hunted as prey. But carnivores are not just lions and tigers, they are also spiders, whales, snakes, birds of prey and frogs, as well as plants and fungi that eat insects.

Herbivores

Eat mostly plants, algae and bacteria that provide energy from their nutrients. Herbivores come in all shapes and sizes, from rhinoceros to deer, and insects to elephants – all of them daily grass-chompers.

Omnivores

Animals that eat both meat and plants, their digestive systems not specifically developed to focus on one or the other. Many scavengers, such as crows, are omnivores, but so are pigs and humans (most of the time).

A vegetarian is an anomaly, as it is a human who has specifically chosen not to eat meat even though meat is considered an important part of a human's mixed diet. They are an environmental anomaly, not only because they use moralistic reasoning to make their decision, but because they are one of just two creatures on the planet that have made such a positive, discriminatory choice about their diet. The other is a panda, a species whose digestive tract evolved to eat meat, but it decided it liked bamboo more and has only eaten that ever since.

All those extinct animals we remember from excursions to the Natural History Museum and bad textbook illustrations. But do you remember when they kicked the evolutionary bucket?

1. Dodo – in 1681 the last flightless bird of Mauritius was being gobbled up by Portuguese sailors at the same time as their imported pigs and monkeys were eating its eggs; the poor bird was doomed.

2. Sabre-tooth tiger – living in the European and North American wilderness, the big-toothed tiger started life 20 million years ago and ended its cumbersome too-heavy-for-its-own-good reign 10,000 years ago.

3. Woolly mammoth – a close relative to its Asian cousin the hairy mammoth, the woolly variety lived in the Arctic regions of Europe. Standing 3m/11ft tall, it became extinct because of early stone age hunters around 10,000 years ago.

4. Tyrannosaurus rex – this 7,000kg/7-tonne carnivore with the huge jaws, known as the tyrant lizard, was the 'king' of dinosaurs (*rex* means 'king' in Latin) and he became extinct 65 million years ago, as if Steven Spielberg hadn't told you enough times.

5. Archelon – measuring 5m/15ft in diameter, this giant turtle was a slow swimmer of the ancient seas, living on jellyfish, but died out 65 million years ago.

6. Pterodactyls – often mistaken for dinosaurs, this winged vertebrate was actually a classification of 29 different types of beasts soaring, with 6m/20ft wingspans, over Africa, Europe, Asia and North America, before becoming extinct at the end of the Jurassic period.

7. Tasmanian tiger – known as thylacine, or its Australian name the kangaroo wolf, it was wiped out as recently as 1936 by farmers defending their livestock.

8. Zeuglodon – this lizard of the sea, known as the basilosaurus, grew between 18m/60ft and 46m/150ft long and lived until about 34 million years ago although, some say, the gigantic sea serpent still pays a visit to Loch Ness every now and then.

9. Quagga – this unique half-horse half-zebra lived in Africa and was hunted to extinction for its hide and meat, the last of its kind dying in 1883 in captivity. DNA tests revealed that it was part of the zebra family.

10. Steller's sea cow – this 3,000kg/3-tonne defenceless fatty of the Bering Sea was discovered by naturalist George Steller in 1741. Growing up to 8m/26ft, it took just 27 years for hunters to wipe it out.

On old Olympia's towering top a Finn and German vault and hop

The sequence of cranial nerves: olfactory, optic, oculomotor, trochlear, trigeminal, abducens, facial, auditory, glossopharyngeal, vagus, accessory, hypoglossal

MAKING A BEELINE FOR THE MATING HONEYPOT

Back then it wasn't just us thinking about sex. That's because other creatures were doing it too. In fact, they were all at it in their own ways, including plants. And bees. But the old saying – when your mum sat you on the edge of the bed to talk about the 'birds and the bees' – is incorrect. It should actually be the 'birds and the plants' or 'plants and the bees' because of how they all work together to reproduce.

For any plant to survive it needs to reproduce its seeds by spreading pollen grains around via pollination (like sowing its oats). Think of the pollen as sperm, which it is, and think of the plant's carpel (little feeler-like parts inside flowers) as its vagina and ovaries. The pollen must get from one plant to another for them to mate. For this kind of sex to work, the pollen must be literally inserted into the carpel for all but 10% of the world's plants. And without the help of pollinators, normally insects like bees, virtually all plants on Earth would die out.

Bees are the Earth's saviours. The planet simply could not survive without them because they ensure plants reproduce (even if it is by accident, as they collect pollen seeds on their hind legs while gathering nectar for their colonies), and those plants, in turn, change carbon dioxide into oxygen for every creature to breathe or use.

But bees are not the only pollinators that assist plants in their reproduction cycle. There are, in fact, 200,000 different types of insect pollinators. Pollination by insects is called entomophily and when it's done by other animals, like humming birds or fruit bats, it's zoophily.

Of course, some plants just rely on the wind to spread their seeds, called anemophily, and even by water, which is hydrophily. But, predominantly, it was the bees we learned about at school. They are the planet's accidental matchmakers. So, next time you see a bee, give it the love it deserves.

The strongest organisms living on the planet today

● **Gonorrhoea bacteria** – this sexually-transmitted disease can pull 100,000 times its own weight, equivalent to humans pulling 10 million kilos... phew! That's a lot of pain for some pleasure.

● **Escherichia coli (E coli)** – no ordinary food-poisoning bug, this bacteria is found in virtually everyone's lower intestine and is usually harmless. But it can survive outside the body and cause gastroenteritis, diarrhoea and death.

● **Malaria** – like so many infectious diseases this one adapts to beat drugs, infecting up to 500 million people each year and killing one million. The crafty malaria switches back and forth between human host and mosquito to survive bad weather and new drugs thrown at it by doctors.

● **Necrotising fasciitis** – known as the flesh-eating bug, this bacteria doesn't really eat human flesh, but destroys it by releasing destructive toxins, such as streptococcal pyogenic exotoxins, that make skin cells create too many protein-based cytokines which, in turn, tells your own immune system to destroy your body tissue and its cells.

● **Botulism** – the *Clostridium botulinum* is the organism that creates the world's deadliest toxin. A so-called 'Superbug', this horror doesn't mix with humans for a long period because it kills them and then uses the decaying body as new food. Just 2kg of this stuff is enough to kill everyone on the planet.

CAN YOU CATCH IT FROM THE TOILET?

There was much debate about school playground myths when we were younger and one of these had to do with knowledge of the AIDS epidemic. Biology lessons included 'useful' information for under-prepared young people about using a condom or just not having sex, but also tried to dispense wrongly-held beliefs like you could get diseases from the dirty toilet seat in the loos next to the drama studio. So, to remind you, you cannot catch HIV or AIDS – or even most types of diseases – from a toilet seat, even if 50 HIV sufferers have sat on it before you. It is possible you could catch some minor viruses from bacteria on a toilet seat, but to do that you'd have to seriously rub your bits all over the infected area. And why would you do that to a toilet?

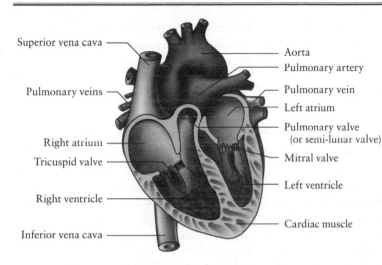

Superior vena cava

Pulmonary veins

Right atrium

Tricuspid valve

Right ventricle

Inferior vena cava

Aorta

Pulmonary artery

Pulmonary vein

Left atrium

Pulmonary valve
(or semi-lunar valve)

Mitral valve

Left ventricle

Cardiac muscle

The human heart beats about two and a half billion times in an average lifetime, pumping red blood cells around the body to keep our organs and muscles growing and living. When the heart stops, we stop.

You will remember from the plastic models scattered around the science room, that the heart is a complex and powerful organ; a constantly-working muscle made up of different open sections, called atria and ventricles, that blood flows through. The two atria sit above the two ventricles on either side of the heart's pear-shape. The mitral valve connects the left atria to the left ventricle below and the tricuspid valve connects the right atria to the right ventricle.

The body's main artery, the aorta, is connected to the top of the heart and this carries blood full of nutrients to different parts of the body. The pulmonary artery connects the heart to the lungs, forming part of the body's important pulmonary circulation system. This provides de-oxygenated blood, collected in the heart's right side, with oxygen that then goes into the heart's right atria and is pumped out to the body via the right ventricle.

The heart feels as if it is in the left side of our chests, but it isn't. It is actually in the middle, behind the thorax, but because the strongest parts of this muscle, the ventricles, are usually offset to the left within the heart's protective pericardium cushion, then we feel the pumping on the left side of our bodies.

10 things the great 19th-century evolutionist Charles Darwin said about science, natural selection and biology

1. 'The fact of evolution is the backbone of biology, and biology is thus in the peculiar position of being a science founded on an improved theory, is it then a science or faith?'

2. 'Probably all organic beings which have ever lived on this Earth have descended from some one primordial form... There is grandeur in this view of life that, whilst this planet has gone cycling on according to the fixed law of gravity, from so simple a beginning endless forms most beautiful and most wonderful have been, and are being evolved.'

3. 'I have called this principle, by which each slight variation, if useful, is preserved, by the term natural selection...'

4. 'It is those who know little, and not those who know much, who so positively assert that this or that problem will never be solved by science.'

5. 'In the struggle for survival, the fittest win out at the expense of their rivals because they succeed in adapting themselves best to their environment.'

6. 'I am turned into a sort of machine for observing facts and grinding out conclusions.'

7. 'I cannot persuade myself that a beneficent and omnipotent God would have designedly created parasitic wasps with the express intention of their feeding within the living bodies of caterpillars.'

8. 'False facts are highly injurious to the progress of science, for they often endure long; but false views, if supported by some evidence, do little harm, for everyone takes a salutary pleasure in proving their falseness; and when this is done, one path toward errors is closed and the road to truth is often at the same time opened.'

9. 'I am aware that the assumed instinctive belief in God has been used by many persons as an argument for his existence. The idea of a universal and beneficent Creator does not seem to arise in the mind of man, until he has been elevated by long-continued culture.'

10. 'Man with all his noble qualities, with sympathy which feels for the most debased, with benevolence which extends not only to other men but to the humblest living creature, with his god-like intellect which has penetrated into the movements and constitution of the solar system... still bears in his bodily frame the indelible stamp of his lowly origin.'

DESTROYING THE EARTH'S LUNGS

Even back then our science teachers were banging on about the destruction of the rainforests. Although there has been debate in the past few years about how much the world's six billion hectares of forests actually contributes to the slowing of climate change, there was no doubt in our science teachers' minds back at school: the rainforests are the Earth's lungs. But, as well as absorbing massive amounts of atmosphere-destroying carbon dioxide, and turning it into oxygen, the planet's forests also do many other jobs:

- They prevent erosion and keep soil healthy.
- They provide fruit for creatures to eat.
- They provide shelter for tree-dwelling creatures.
- They manage the flow of water.
- They cool air.
- They provide cures for diseases.
- They house millions of different species.

If all the forests in the world were to be cut down – and almost half have been since 1950 – then the only mass-oxygen-making system left on the planet would be plankton, and many organisms would begin to die.

BOTANY: AN INEXACT SCIENCE

A beautiful treatise on natural diversity from one of history's greatest biologists.
...mathematical accuracy must not be expected. The forms and appearances assumed by plants and their parts are infinite. Names cannot be invented for all; those even that have been proposed are too numerous for ordinary memories. Many are derived from supposed resemblances to well-known forms or objects. These resemblances are differently appreciated by different persons, and the same term is not only differently applied by two different botanists, but it frequently happens that the same writer is led on different occasions to give somewhat different meanings to the same word. The botanist's endeavours should always be, on the one hand, to make as near an approach to precision as circumstances will allow, and on the other hand to avoid that proxility of detail and overloading with technical terms which tends rather to confusion than clearness. In this he will be more or less successful.
From *Flora Hongkongensis: a description of the flowering plants and ferns of the island of Hong Kong* (1861), by George Bentham

If all mankind were to disappear, the world would regenerate back to the rich state of equilibrium that existed ten thousand years ago. If insects were to vanish, the environment would collapse into chaos.

Edward O Wilson, US biologist and naturalist

YO HO HO ME HEARTIES: WALKING THE PLANKTON

One of those topics that never exactly lit up the imagination, many of us nonetheless recall that learning about plankton was an important part of both biology and the wider ecological process of how the planet runs itself.

This was because plankton, its name derived from the ancient Greek word *planktos* meaning 'wanderer', is one of the most essential food sources in the world. But, despite what we might assume, plankton is actually made up of many different types of organisms and so the name plankton is given to any plant, animal, algae (which isn't a plant, OK) and bacteria that live in what's termed by marine biologists as the 'pelagic zone' of the oceans – any bit of the sea that isn't near the bottom. Which is, let's face it, most of it.

As well as food, plankton has the biogeochemical role of fixing the sea's carbon levels because plankton photosynthesises to create energy to live. It is the surface-dwelling algae phytoplankton that does this, whereas zooplankton is baby crustaceans and other animals that eat other plankton, and the bacterioplankton, made up of bacteria, helps to alter organic molecules in the ocean into essential minerals such as nitrogen.

Most plankton is susceptible to the ocean's currents as it's too small to swim against them. This makes plankton easy food; the ocean's equivalent of a 24-hour Chinese takeaway. Fish larvae and larger animals such as blue whales feed on plankton, travelling the world's seas with the currents to stay where the plankton is nearby. Just like living next door to the takeaway.

'YOU CANNOT HARM ME – MY WINGS ARE LIKE A SHIELD OF STEEL!'

Our immune system is a bit like a radar station keeping an eye out for enemy invaders; it has spies scattered throughout our body, watching for signs of alien life forms or foreigners that don't belong in these 'ere parts.

The immune system within all organisms, no matter how small, is a mechanism in which living things protect themselves from disease. It helps organisms identify cells that are bad – like pathogens (germs to you and me) and tumour cells – and then finds ways to attack and destroy these cells to save the organism. The immune system battles viruses but needs to understand that the cells it's killing off are not part of the organism's healthy tissue. This is done with antimicrobial peptide defence cells called defensins and phagocytosis – which is when defence cells form a solid barrier around the invading virus particle to physically halt its progress and 'quarantine' it from the healthy body.

Over time, germs and bacteria have adapted to this detection and can often pretend to be healthy cells; secret double agents, if you like. The buggers. And creatures like fish, reptiles, plants and insects succumb to this problem all the time. But these evil double agents are usually no match for the well-developed immune system of vertebrates like humans.

Our immune system is made up of complicated proteins, organs and cells all working together in a coordinated fashion, waiting to strike if viruses attack. What's more, our intelligence-led operation remembers the faces – or rather genetic structure – of these attackers and learns how to fight them off with stronger tactics the next time they try it on. This process is called 'immunological memories' and is how vaccines force our bodies to remember to recognise and destroy potential germs.

One of the first visible signs of the immune system working (if the foreigners have got past our skin, got past the protective bacteria on it and got past the innate non-specific and adaptive parts of our immune system) is inflammation of an infected area. People are often scared when parts of their body swell up, but the swelling means their body is working hard to make them better. Go inflammation!

XI

CHEMISTRY

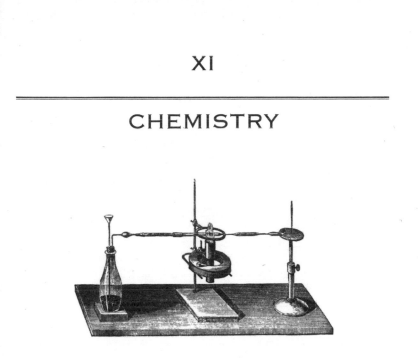

Nothing in life is to be feared.
It is only to be understood.

Marie Curie

WHAT IS CHEMISTRY?

Chemistry deals with substances: their properties, their structure, how they change and why, how they interact with other substances and what they emit or absorb when they change. It is the chemical structure of a substance which gives it form and colour, or lack thereof, and which determines whether it is soluble, corrosive, explosive, radioactive or any of the other myriad states and qualities that matter can have in our universe. Chemical structure is dependent on the kind of atoms formed by the smallest particles of matter: protons, electrons and neutrons. Of course, as is often the case in life (and school), the story is even more complicated than this: there are other particles, and in some circumstances the particles are not actually considered particles... But leaving the subatomic domain to one side: atoms are the smallest units of any particular substance, and substances are what chemistry is mainly concerned with.

It's been said that biology is applied chemistry, while chemistry is applied physics, and physics is applied mathematics. Which begs the question: What's on the upper layers of this intellectual pyramid?

DNA EXPLAINED

Chemical formulae describe what makes up a substance. But for very complicated structures, a 3D representation is necessary to really understand what's going on. One of the most beautiful and complicated is the double-helix model of deoxyribonucleic acid – DNA – unveiled by James Watson and Francis Crick in 1953. They won the Nobel Prize for it.

DNA is a polymer like polythene, but a very, very complicated one. Crick and Watson's discovery of the structure of DNA was a landmark in genetics, and has formed the basis of a host of technologies, such as DNA fingerprinting. The sequencing of DNA in an individual is so idiosyncratic that this testing is virtually 100% accurate.

In 2000 the Human Genome Project finished sequencing, or determining the order of, the genetic information in the 'average' human being, and is now working on identifying what gene does what. This could have – and, indeed, is having – radical implications for medical science, but ethical questions are popping up too...

WORK IT OUT

Solve the following periodic puzzlers:
- You may go there to see a show
- I'm on another planet
- I could be a great Roman element
- $E=MC^2$

Answers on page 312

GETTING YOUR EQUIPMENT IN ORDER

Chemistry lessons just wouldn't have been the same without all the paraphernalia that went with the practical 'experiment' lessons. Experiments were the closest school ever got to Hogwarts: frothy liquids, flashes and bangs, and the odd peculiar smell (that's hydrogen sulphide, that rotten egg whiff). And the contraptions that went with them were just as weird...

Bunsen burners – invented by a man called Mr Bunsen, they were designed as a way to produce a controlled flame for the many experiments requiring it. If you didn't have enough air going in with the gas the flame would be yellow, producing little heat and lots of soot. Not very useful for experiments, but very useful for making things go black, like your neighbour's pencil case.

Safety pipettes – like Bunsen burners, safety pipettes had a duel purpose. One was to measure, collect and transfer liquids in the course of an experiment – particularly ones which you didn't want to get on your hands, like acids or alkalis. The other was to squirt water on the back of the person in front of you. Before safety pipettes were invented, chemists used open-ended pipettes, where you collected the liquid by sucking the end, stopping before it reached your lips.

Goggles – yes, they were necessary. Yes, you felt safer wearing them when doing an experiment where something might fizz up and hit you in the face. But, didn't they make you look an idiot?

Heat sheets – again, a fine multipurpose instrument. Something to do experiments on, and something to put over the bin when you'd accidentally set fire to it.

BREAKING DOWN THE ELEMENTS

Elements are the simplest substances in existence. That's because they cannot be broken down into another substance, but they do bind together in certain fixed ways to form chemical compounds.

There are 92 naturally-occurring elements – plus 16 more that have been manufactured – but there are around eight million natural or manufactured compounds. Of those elements, the most in number are metals, but the most common are largely non-metals, such as nitrogen and oxygen.

Elements get their characteristics from something even simpler: their molecular structure, and this in turn depends on atomic structure. The building blocks of nature itself, atoms, are made up of the same thing, whether you're talking about a fish or a piece of iron: protons, neutrons and electrons.

When it comes to the periodic table, elements were always easy enough to identify: they have symbols of one or two letters, such as oxygen, O, and iron, Fe.

CHEMISTRY IN SPACE: STAR TREK

Science fiction has always been a great way to imagine the science of the future, but sometimes the old tricks are the best ones. Take the 1967 episode of *Star Trek* in which Captain Kirk is trapped on a planet by an alien race, called the Metrons, who force him to fight another alien, called the Gorn, in a gladiatorial-style contest. Initially it looks bad for Kirk, who is disadvantaged against the Gorn, being just a man up against an enormous bipedal lizard. But then – and that's why he's Captain of the *Enterprise* – Kirk discovers chemicals which he thinks might be useful. Carbon, sulphur and saltpetre, ie potassium nitrate, which together make… gunpowder! Kirk finds a hollow reed and some naturally-occurring diamonds (don't say it) and makes a gun to defeat the Gorn. When Kirk wins, he magnanimously pleads with the Metrons not to kill the Gorn, and everyone warp-travels home happy.

I remember watching a repeat of this on TV once and being incredibly impressed with the special effects… but then, I was only six.

Carbon dioxide gas – turns limewater milky.

Chlorine gas – turns moist blue litmus paper red then white (bleaches it).

Acids – turns blue litmus paper red (but doesn't then bleach it).

Alkalis – turn red litmus paper blue.

Ammonia gas – turns moist red litmus paper blue.

Hydrogen gas – extinguishes a lighted splint with a popping sound.

Oxygen gas – relights a glowing splint.

Acids, alkalis and bases – turn universal indicator paper the colours of the rainbow, from red for highly acidic to indigo for highly alkaline.

Sodium ions – turn a flame yellow (even in weak concentrations of one part per billion of sodium).

Lithium ions – turn a flame red (lithium chloride is used in fireworks).

Ascorbic acid – titration with the dye 2,6-dichlorophenolindophenol, or DCPIP.

THE SHAPE OF THINGS TO COME?

Alkenes are hydrocarbons like alkanes, but they have a slightly different chemical composition. The molecules of alkenes, such as ethene (otherwise called ethylene), can also be joined together to make chain-like large molecules called polymers. Polyethene, or polythene, and other polymers such as polyvinyl chloride (PVC) have many industrial and commercial uses. New, specialised polymers – or plastics – are being developed, including 'smart' materials which remember shape. Polyisobutene, or Kevlar, is five times as strong as steel and is used in body armour and tyres. The downside is that many plastics are not biodegradable, and if they are burnt they can release toxic chemicals, causing disposal problems.

Mrs B: ... we shall go on to the next simple substance, HYDROGEN, which we cannot, any more than oxygen, obtain in a visible or palpable form. We are acquainted with it only in its gaseous state as we are with oxygen and nitrogen.

Caroline: But in its gaseous state it cannot be called a simple substance, since it is combined with heat and electricity?

Mrs B: True, my dear; but as we do not know in nature of any substance which is not more or less combined with caloric and electricity, we are apt to say that a substance is in its pure state when combined with those agents only. Hydrogen was formerly called inflammable air, as it is extremely combustible and burns with a great flame. Since the invention of the new nomenclature, it has obtained the name of hydrogen, which is derived from two Greek words, the meaning of which is to produce water.

Emily: And how does hydrogen produce water?

Mrs B: By its combustion. Water is composed of 89 parts, by weight of oxygen, combined with 11 parts of hydrogen; or two parts, by bulk, of hydrogen gas, to one part of oxygen gas.

Caroline: Really! Is it possible that water should be a combination of two gases, and that one of these should be inflammable air! Hydrogen must be a most extraordinary gas that will produce both fire and water.

Emily: But I thought you said that combustion could take place in no gas but oxygen?

Mrs B: Do you recollect what the process of combustion consists in?

Emily: In the combination of a body with oxygen, with disengagement of light and heat.

Mrs B: Therefore, when I say that hydrogen is combustible, I mean that it has an affinity for oxygen; but, like all other combustible substances, it cannot burn unless supplied with oxygen, and also heated to a proper temperature.

Conversations on Chemistry, **by Jane Marcet, John Lee Comstock, John Lauris Blake**

HOW TO REMEMBER... THE RARE GASES

Heaven never asked Kriegspiel's extra rent

Helium, neon, argon, krypton, xenon, radon

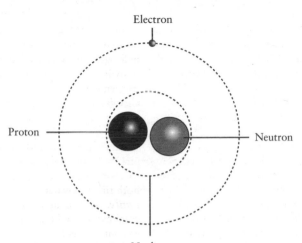

Electron

Proton

Neutron

Nucleus

Atoms are the smallest unit of an element retaining its chemical properties. As we duly learned in school, the sub-atomic particles, which make up an atom are protons, neutrons and electrons. The numbers of particles in atoms of different elements are different. Protons (p) have a positive charge of +1 and an atomic mass of 1. Electrons (e) have a negative charge of -1 and an atomic mass of $^1/_{1840}$ – much smaller than a proton. Neutrons (n) have no charge, but the same mass as a proton. Protons and neutrons (nucleons) together form the nucleus of the atom, while electrons orbit the nucleus at a relatively big distance: if an atom was the size of a football pitch, the nucleus would be roughly the size of a football in the middle. This means that all matter is mostly made of empty space. The number of protons in an atom is its atomic number (z) while the sum of the protons and nucleons, the nucleon number, is the atomic mass (a). The number of protons, neutrons and electrons give an element its chemical and physical properties. Atoms with the same number of protons are the same element, but if they have differing numbers of neutrons they are isotopes. Isotopes have different physical, but not chemical, properties. The relative atomic mass of an element is its mass compared with that of a carbon atom. Atoms are weighed in moles, where a mole of atoms is equal to Avogadro's constant, or 6×10^{23}.

THE CHEMISTRY OF SEMI-PRECIOUS STONES

Diamond – carbon, C

Ruby – aluminium oxide (red corundum), Al_2O_3

Emerald – beryl, $Be_3Al_2(SiO_3)_6$

Sapphire – aluminium oxide (blue or other non-red corundum), Al_2O_3

Opal – hydrated silica, $SiO_2 \cdot nH_2O$

Pearl – crystalline calcium carbonate, $CaCO_3$ (not strictly a gemstone)

Amethyst – form of quartz, silicon dioxide, SiO_2 (sand is also made of silicon dioxide)

WHAT'S SO IMPORTANT ABOUT ETHANOL?

The alcohols are a group of chemicals containing carbon, hydrogen and a hydroxyl functional group (-OH). They are derived from hydrocarbons – compounds containing only hydrogen and carbon – and they have various industrial uses. Ethyl alcohol, or ethanol (CH_3CH_2OH) is the pure form of the alcohol you may drink if you are over 18, and is also used industrially.

The liver has to work hard to metabolise ethanol, and when people speak of 'killing brain cells', they are speaking literally (though we have an awful lot of brain cells, so it's not too much of a problem in moderate amounts). Drinking pure ethanol would be fatal. Until recently, the strongest legal liquor on sale was 55% proof: now, in some places, it's possible to buy liquor which is much stronger. Even at these percentages, ethanol is dangerous: absinthe and potcheen, the strongest spirits, were notorious in their heyday for causing physical and psychological damage to drinkers. It was allegedly the green absinthe fairy who drove the painter Van Gogh to cut his ear off.

Currently, technologies to produce ethanol from corn and grass to replace petrol as a fuel are in development, though there are social and political issues to face, as well as chemical ones concerning the use of a foodstuff to make fuel.

GOING AROUND THE BENDS

Every time we take a breath, more than three quarters of what we breathe in is nitrogen. And every time we do, a very small amount of that nitrogen dissolves into our bloodstream. At normal pressures, and if the pressure remains normal, the effect is negligible. But under high pressure – for example, in deep-sea diving – more nitrogen dissolves. And if pressure on the body reduces too quickly, nitrogen bubbles coming out of solution in the bloodstream can have a very dangerous effect. This is decompression sickness, or 'the bends', and it can be fatal. To avoid it, deep-sea divers must surface gradually; aviators can also suffer from the condition if they travel too high too quickly. Depending on how quickly it is caught and its severity, it can be treated in a decompression chamber.

QUOTE UNQUOTE

No, this trick won't work... How on earth are you ever going to explain in terms of chemistry and physics so important a biological phenomenon as first love?

Albert Einstein

WHAT'S SO IMPORTANT ABOUT HYDROGEN?

Hydrogen is a fascinating element because it has some, but not all, of the properties of a metal. It is in Group 1 with the alkali metals such as sodium, and its oxide – hydrogen hydroxide, otherwise known as H_2O or water – can in some circumstances act as a base in the same way as metal oxides do.

Highly-compressed hydrogen (compressed roughly to the pressure of the Earth's core) becomes opaque and conducts electricity. Indeed, metallic hydrogen, as it is called, does more than just conduct electricity; it is a superconductor, and there are hopes that it could prove to be the much sought-after room-temperature superconductor. Metallic hydrogen could also be used as a fuel to replace the hydrogen/oxygen mix that is currently used in space shuttles.

COMPOUNDING CONFUSION

Chemical compounds are made up of elements, brought together by chemical bonding processes. Some elements are more reactive than others, and only certain elements will bind together. For example, iron and copper will not react together to form a compound, although a mix of the two metals, its alloy, takes on useful new properties – the combination of iron and copper to form bronze ushered in a new technological era for our distant ancestors.

Forty years ago we knew of about half a million different naturally-occurring or synthetic chemical elements or compounds. Now there are more than eight million. And each one of this great multiplicity exists because of the ways atoms can bond with other atoms. There are three kinds of bonding: ionic, covalent and metallic.

SOME FACTS ABOUT FOOD

• Humans are one of a limited number of animals who cannot synthesise ascorbic acid, or **vitamin C**, and must ingest it in food. Another is the guinea pig.

• **Aspirin** is made from salicylic acid, the active ingredient in the traditional headache remedy willow bark tea.

• The molecules which make **asparagus** taste good are soluble in water, so it is better to cook it in butter.

• **Cassava roots and leaves** cannot be eaten raw because they contain cyanogenic glucosides – compounds which break down into cyanide in the presence of the enzyme linamarase, which also, unluckily enough, is present in cassava. Different types of cassava need different degrees of preparation.

• The artificial sweetener **aspartame** was discovered by accident by James Schlatter in 1965. He heated aspartylphenylalanine methyl ester and spilt some on his hand. Later, when he happened to lick his fingers, he realised it was sweet.

• **Bad eggs** smell bad because of a sulphur-based gas – hydrogen sulphide (H_2S). Sulphur compounds are probably also responsible for the 'asparagus pee' phenomenon – the smell that some people can detect in their urine after eating asparagus. Why some people can smell it and some can't is still a matter of debate...

MARIE CURIE: THE LEADING LADY OF SCIENCE

Marie Curie, a Polish scientist who lived from 1867 to 1934, is famous for three things. Firstly, she won not one but two Nobel Prizes: the first for Physics in 1903 with her husband Pierre and French scientist Becquerel; the second for Chemistry in 1911. Secondly, her research led to the development of medical X-ray technology. Thirdly, she effectively died for it.

Pierre, tragically, had already been knocked down and killed in a carriage accident in 1906. But Marie continued the couple's work and devoted herself increasingly to the practical application of her research, helping to install X-ray equipment in ambulances in World War I.

Marie is also famous, of course, because she was a woman: she is probably the most famous female scientist of all, and she had to put up with opposition because of it from her contemporaries. She soldiered on, but by the 1920s her constant work with radioactive material began to take its toll. In 1934, at the age of 66, she died of leukaemia caused by exposure to high-energy radiation. But her work lives on, as does that of Pierre and their daughter Irene, who also won the Nobel Prize for Chemistry.

HOW IT WORKS: COMBUSTION AND OXIDATION

When you burn something, like a match or a bit of your chemistry textbook, what actually happens? How, in fact, does combustion work?

Combustion is an oxidation reaction. When carbon burns in oxygen, carbon dioxide and energy are produced. If there is not enough oxygen, the combustion process can produce carbon monoxide (CO) instead of carbon dioxide (CO_2). This is dangerous if inhaled in large quantities because it combines with the haemoglobin in red blood cells, 'tricking' them into thinking it is oxygen. The body is then deprived of oxygen. Soot, such as that produced by a Bunsen burner on the wrong setting, is carbon produced by incomplete combustion.

Sometimes the process of oxidation is slower than combustion. Iron oxide, a combination of the relatively inert metal iron and oxygen, happens naturally in a process which is gradual and almost unnoticeable. Until you spot it on your car bodywork, then it's rust.

THE ETYMOLOGY OF ELEMENTS

Halogen – from Greek for 'salt maker' (group of elements including chlorine and fluorine)

Oxygen – from Greek for 'acid maker'

Hydrogen – from Greek for 'water maker'

Cobalt – from *kobald*, Old German for 'goblin'

Unonoctium – 118th element, artificially made in 2006, from Latin for 'one one eight'

Iron – Anglo-Saxon *iren*; but symbol, Fe, is from Latin for iron – *ferrum*

Iridium – named after Iris, Greek goddess of rainbows (which also gives us 'iridescent')

Fermium – named after Enrico Fermi, a nuclear physicist

Helium – from Greek *helios*, meaning 'sun'

Nickel – from German *kupfernickel*, the 'Devil's copper' (or 'St Nicholas' copper')

Sulphur – from *sulvere*, Sanskrit for 'sulphur', or Latin *sulphurium*

Tin – *tin*, Anglo-Saxon

Lutetium – *Lutetia*, the Latin name for 'Paris'

IONIC BONDING

Ions are charged particles made when an atom or group of atoms loses or gains electrons. Ionic, or electrovalent, bonds are held together by electrostatic attraction between positive and negative ions.

When metals react with non-metals they form ionic compounds. Salts, such as common salt (sodium chloride) and metal carbonates and nitrates (containing carbon and oxygen, or nitrogen and oxygen) are all examples of this kind of bonding. Ionic compounds generally have a high melting point and conduct electricity when in solution or liquid (molten) form.

The electrons in the ions in this kind of compound are configured in the same way as the noble gases such as neon, argon and krypton. The outermost shell of these gases has eight electrons, making it stable and unreactive (helium is also a noble gas, but has two electrons in its outer shell).

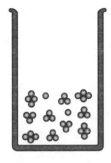

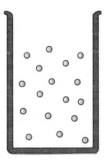

Solid	**Liquid**	**Gas**
• Has a high density	• Has a high density	• Has a low density
• Is hard to expand or compress	• Expands or compresses to take the shape of a container	• Is easy to expand or compress to fill a container
• Has a rigid, fixed shape		

WHEN SYNTHETIC CHEMICALS GO WRONG

Compounds manufactured by human hand in a laboratory are synthetic. As the technical expertise and range of experiments by chemists has increased with the years, more and more complicated synthetic compounds have been produced – sometimes by accident. But there are some complications.

Firstly, complex as they have become, it can be very challenging to reproduce organic compounds, the highly diverse and highly useful set of compounds which occur naturally. Secondly – and this is a problem with technological innovation generally – designed chemicals can sometimes have

unexpected properties. In the realm of pharmaceuticals, one of the most important applications of synthetic chemistry, this is a matter of life or death, quite literally, which is one of the reasons for clinical trials of new drugs. In the 1990s, the unexpected properties of a very useful set of chemicals used in aerosols and refrigerators also turned out to be a matter of life and death – chlorofluorocarbons (CFCs) have been banned throughout most of the world because of the damaging effect they have had on the ozone layer, but they are still used in some countries.

THE ART OF CHEMISTRY: CERAMICS

Ceramics are, chemically speaking, inorganic non-metallic solids, for example metal oxides. Though ceramics are a much more diverse group than is suggested by the lay use of the word, there are some similarities between ceramics as a group of substances and your casserole pot: they are hard and can be heated to high temperatures without burning or melting, but they are usually brittle. However, ceramics are being made now that are much more durable, and could be used as turbines in jet engines, and in the place of metals in other situations. In 1987 a ceramic was discovered that was a superconductor at 100K (-173.1°C or -279.7°F). Before the discovery of ceramic superconductors, chemists had worked with metals and alloys, and the highest recorded temperature for a metallic superconductor was 22.3K (-250°C or -417.64°F). This first ceramic superconductor contained yttrium, barium, copper and oxygen: $YBa_2Cu_3O_7$.

CHEMISTRY IN SPACE: MARS DOESN'T ATTACK

The study of organic chemistry also plays a big part in the search for life on other planets. Recently, we (as in the human race – the big 'we') have been sending probes to Mars, to investigate evidence that there was once water… and, organic chemistry tells us, where there was once water there may once have been life. The *Phoenix* probe that was launched in 2008 has a chemistry lab in it, where soil samples could be analysed. If there was life on Mars, it's more likely to have been bacteria than little green men, but exciting nonetheless.

One day we will have the technology to take our chemistry labs even further afield, eventually to planets outside the solar system. And then… who knows? Science fiction writers have long speculated that silicon (the main constituent of sand and glass) might also serve as a basis for life. Silicon is in the same group in the periodic table as carbon and shares many of its characteristics; however, it does not have its flexible bonding properties and, unlike carbon, forms a solid when it oxidises, which would cause problems for organic systems. Still, it's fun to speculate that if one day we met little green men, they might not be green, or little, or men, they might just be made of silicon.

Chemistry can be a good and bad thing. Chemistry is good when you make love with it. Chemistry is bad when you make crack with it.

Adam Sandler, US actor

WORK IT OUT

Find the odd one out:
- Sodium
- Lithium
- Osmium
- Potassium
- Francium

Answer on page 312

THE EARTH'S CRUST

The Earth's crust, or outer layer, is about half oxygen, a quarter silicon, and a quarter other elements, including hydrogen and the metals aluminium, iron, calcium, potassium, sodium and magnesium. The silicon and oxygen are mostly present as silicon dioxide, which is sand, quartz and most of sandstone. Calcium is present as marble and limestone – calcium carbonate – while other metals are present as ores. Some are metal oxides, such as bauxite (aluminium) and haematite (iron), while others are sulphides, such as cinnabar (mercury) and zinc blende (zinc), or carbonates like malachite (copper). Common salt, or rock salt, is sodium chloride. Reactive metals are extracted from ores by a process called electrolysis, while less reactive ones like iron can be extracted by reduction with carbon. Because it is less reactive than carbon, the carbon replaces the iron in the iron oxide when they are heated together in a blast furnace, to form iron and carbon dioxide. This process is one of the oldest chemical techniques humans have used.

SUPER-DUPER CONDUCTORS

High-temperature superconductors, discovered in the late 1980s, are an example of how, in science, you never know what's around the corner. Usually, when electricity is passed through a conductive material, the material offers a greater or lesser degree of resistance, which makes it heat up slightly. Superconductors offer no resistance to electricity, making them very useful in present-day and future technology; for example, in computer circuitry and energy storage. An electric current can circulate in a ring-shaped superconductor forever, or until something external stops it. Because of the way electromagnetism works, a magnet can be levitated above a superconductor in a process called diamagnetism, or the Meissner effect after the man who invented it. Chemists and physicists are searching hard for a substance that is a superconductor at room temperature: if it is found, it will revolutionise electronics and energy storage.

WHAT'S SO IMPORTANT ABOUT METHANOL?

Methyl alcohol, or methanol, is the simplest of the alcohols in chemical structure, with a formula of CH_3OH. When added to ethanol, it is sold as 'methylated spirits'. Methylated spirits is tinted with luminous colours so that it's not confused with ethanol and inadvertently drunk… not that you would, but chemical manufacturers are careful people.

Though methanol itself is not directly poisonous, drinking it even in small quantities is extremely harmful to the body. When it is oxidised in the liver by the action of the enzyme dehydrogenase, formaldehyde is produced – a chemical which is used in embalming. When ingested, methanol can destroy the optic nerve. Potcheen, the Irish liquor, is traditionally made from potatoes, but in rural areas there were tragic cases of mass blindness caused by illegal potcheen, or 'moonshine', made from wood. Here is a prime case where knowledge of chemistry is important: distilling alcohol from wood does not produce ethanol, but methanol.

Methane (CH_4), the alkane gas to which methyl alcohol is related, is a potent greenhouse gas. It occurs naturally, for example in decomposing vegetable matter (another name is 'marsh gas') and in cows' digestive tracts. In the latter case, the methane is emitted when the cows breathe, burp and break wind. Amusing as that sounds, livestock are a major source of greenhouse gas emissions.

WHAT THE PHLOGISTON?

'Phlogiston' means 'inflammable' in Greek. It is also a 17th-century theory and great example of how the scientific community can fervently believe and defend something that turns out to be completely wrong (no doubt we still do today about some things). It was proposed by Johann Becher and developed by George Stahl, and postulated that material has three components: phlogiston, impurities and the pure material. Phlogiston has no colour, taste, smell or weight, but when a substance was burnt it was released. So when wood is burnt, for example, the ash that remains is the pure material, minus phlogiston, while the rust that is left when iron oxidises is the pure iron, minus phlogiston.

For a century, there was no criticism that was put to this theory that could not be, sometimes ingeniously, countered by avid phlogistonists. At one point it was even suggested that phlogiston had a negative mass. It was Lavoisier's experiments in the 18th century which finally did for the phlogiston theory, and ushered in the phlogiston-unfriendly principle of drawing conclusions from experiments rather than making theories fit visual observation.

A SOUR TASTE OF CHEMISTRY

Acid. The word acid, synonimous [sic] with sour, is used to express a certain set of bodies, which have a sour taste. They are characterised by the following properties:
1. Applied to the tongue, they impart a sour taste.
2. They change vegetable blues, as litmus, or litmus paper, to red. When certain colours have been previously converted to green, by alkalies, the acids restore them to their original colour.
3. They combine with water in indefinite proportions.
4. They unite with alkalies, earths, and most of the metallic oxydes [sic], and form a class of bodies called slats. Every acid does not possess all these properties. It may be remarked, however, that they have a sufficient number of them to enable us to distinguish them from all other bodies. With respect to the classification of acids, they have been divided, by some, into five classes; as acids, whose bases are united with oxygen and hydrogen; with oxygen only; with hydrogen only; or irregular constitution; and those in which oxygen and hydrogen are present.
James Cutbush, *A Synopsis of Chemistry* **(1821)**

WHAT'S THE DIFFERENCE BETWEEN
A PENCIL AND A DIAMOND?

...a pencil has wood wrapped round it.

It's true – apart from the wood, there is no chemical difference: pencil lead, made of graphite, and diamonds are both forms of carbon.

But, at school, we just weren't convinced. There had to be some sort of difference between graphite and diamond, didn't there? After all, science is not only about what you read in books, but also what you can see with your own eyes, and taste and hear, touch and smell. Diamond is clear and very hard: the hardest substance in nature – so hard that it's used to cut other very hard things. Graphite is dark and soft, easily snapped or sheared off onto a piece of paper to make markings that become writing. A diamond would beat graphite in a fight any day. So how can they both be carbon?

They can be, we learned, because these two chalk-and-cheese alter egos of carbon are allotropes, or different molecular configurations. You see, carbon is a very special element, with very special properties.

Carbon is an enormously important – unique – element because of the huge number of ways its atoms can combine to form molecules and compounds. Its versatility makes it the building block of organic chemistry, the structure of living things. In fact,

even that wood around the pencil is based on carbon, as are we.

Diamond and graphite are not the only allotropes of carbon. Some have also been created in chemistry labs, such as buckminsterfullerene, invented in 1985. The molecules of this form of carbon, C_{60}, consist of 60 carbon atoms bound together in a spherical formation, which reminded the chemists who found it – Richard Smalley, Robert Curl and Harold Kroto – of the structures designed by architect, futurist and philosopher Buckminster Fuller, hence the name.

Molecules of buckminster-fullerene, or 'buckyballs', belong to a group of carbon allotropes called the fullerenes, which also includes nanotubes ('buckytubes') and a nanofabric called graphene. One of their most important current and future uses is in nanotechnology, the science of very small structures (the prefix nano- meaning 'one billionth'). Carbon nanotubes are used to make all sorts of things strong and light, from tennis rackets to car parts and yacht masts... The nanofibres are put into composite materials so that they act a bit like the steel tubes in reinforced concrete, but on a tiny, tiny scale. Recently there have been fears that in some forms nanotubes might pose health risks. It's unlikely to be the case in the things we handle every day, but chemists are working hard to find out for sure.

Unscramble the following chemical terms:
- Itchy tearoom
- Diabolic Peter
- Corn pope cabaret

Answers on page 312

COVALENT BONDING

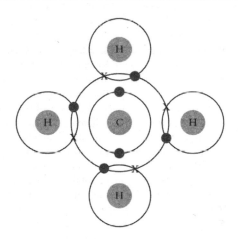

Covalent bonds are made when atoms of the same element, react together in such a way that they end up sharing electron pairs. The resultant grouping is called a molecule. A stable atom needs eight electrons in its outer shell so that it is configured like a noble gas (argon, neon, etc...). The molecules of non-metallic elements like oxygen and chlorine are formed by covalent bonding. A chlorine atom has seven electrons in its outer shell, called valence electrons, so two chlorine atoms bond together to share one electron from each other in a single bond Cl-Cl, to make Cl_2. An oxygen atom has six electrons in its outer shell, so two oxygen atoms combine by sharing two of each other's electrons in a double bond, making O_2.

Covalent compounds work in a similar way: each molecule of water, H_2O, is formed from two hydrogen atoms, which have one valence electron each, and one oxygen atom.

FRACTIONS OF CRUDE OIL

(Obtained by fractional distillation)

Fraction	Boiling temperature	Use
Petroleum gas	below 40°C	fuel – cooking/heating
Petrol	40 to 75°C	fuel – cars
Naphtha	75 to 160°C	plastics and detergents
Paraffin	160 to 250°C	fuel – aircraft
Diesel	250 to 300°C	fuel – cars, trains
Lubricating oil	300 to 350°C	lubricating engines
Heavy fuel oil	350 to 400°C	fuel – ships, power stations
Bitumen	more than 400°C	road surfaces (tar)

WHAT'S SO IMPORTANT ABOUT HYDROCARBONS?

Hydrocarbons, chemicals which consist entirely of carbon and hydrogen, are an extremely useful set of compounds. They form the main components of natural gas and petroleum and can be used as fuels, as well as to make many other substances, including plastics, solvents and explosives.

One type of hydrocarbon is the alkane group. The gases methane, ethane and propane are all alkanes. Another is the olefin group, alkenes, including ethylene and propylene. These are more reactive than the alkanes. Ethylene is used to make polystyrene and – when it links to itself like a chain to form a long molecule called a polymer – polyethylene.

When hydrocarbons are burnt with enough oxygen, they produce water and carbon dioxide (if there is not enough oxygen, carbon monoxide is produced). This is the root of how fuel consumption contributes to the greenhouse effect, though there are other factors, too.

Many hydrocarbons occur naturally. Naphthalene, used in mothballs, is a crystalline hydrocarbon found in coal tar. It is classed as an aromatic hydrocarbon – so called because many give off pleasant (or at least strong, as in the case of naphthalene) smells.

A tidy laboratory means a lazy chemist.
Jöns Jacob Berzelius, Swedish chemist, 1779-1848

THE BIRTH OF CHEMISTRY

Once upon a time, there were men who believed that it was possible to turn ordinary base metal – ie things like iron – into gold. They believed in the existence of an object called the philosopher's stone, which would make this process possible. They were alchemists. If it sounds like they believed in magic... well, they did, but then so did everybody else: before the 18th century there was little difference between magic and science. The Age of Reason had not yet begun. And yet, alchemy was the forefather, or possibly the mad uncle, of chemistry.

Alchemy began in the ancient world – in Greece, Rome and Egypt – and was then taken up by Arabic cultures. From there, it filtered into Europe via Spain after the end of the Crusades, along with mathematics, geometry and much ancient philosophy.

The principles of alchemy are based on the interconnectedness of all things, and the philosopher's stone is not necessarily a substance to literally turn metal into gold. The stone, or the elixir of life, is also metaphorically a search for

truth and value, in line with the interests of the great philosophers like Aristotle.

That science and magic were interrelated in the ancient and medieval mind can be seen in the pursuits of John Dee, one of the most famous figures in 16th-century England. Dee was a mathematician and natural philosopher, but he was also a magician and astrologer. These were far from mutually exclusive pursuits in his time.

Of course, if you put an alchemist in today's world, he or she would probably still believe in magic. Science has advanced to such a degree that inventions and technologies which were completely unimaginable in the time of John Dee are entirely unremarkable today. X-rays, television, mobile phones, computers... the list is endless. As science fiction writer Arthur C Clarke once famously said, any sufficiently advanced technology would be indistinguishable from magic to a person who happened upon it for the first time.

THE PERIODIC TABLE

The periodic table, which lists all the elements which exist, has been many hundreds of years in the making. The chemist most famously associated with it is Dmitri Mendeleev (he is the man with the big beard in school textbooks), but there have been other contributors to this great work of chemical classification: Dobereiner, Newlands and Moseley among them. The table is arranged in order of atomic mass, into groups and periods (see opposite page). Chemists had noticed that there was a pattern in the properties of chemicals depending on their atomic mass, for example that every eighth element had similar properties (sodium is the eighth after lithium, potassium the eighth after sodium), but it was Mendeleev who, in the late 19th century, correctly predicted the properties of yet-to-be discovered elements germanium and gallium.

Periodic classifications
Alkali metals • Alkaline earth metals
Transition metals • Other metals
Other non-metals • Halogens
Noble gases • Rare earth elements
Lanthanide elements • Actinide elements

A LITTLE BIT OF ALCHEMY

- *The Summary of Philosophy*, by Nicholas Flamel (traditionally 14th century)
- *Alchemical Anthology: an essay on alchemy*, by Dr Sigismund Backstrom (late 18th century)
- *Theatrum Chemicum Britannicum. Containing Severall Poetical Pieces of our Famous English Philosophers, who have written the Hermetique Mysteries in their owne Ancient Language. Faithfully Collected into one Volume, with Annotations thereon*, by Elias Ashmole, Esq Qui est Mercuriophilus Anglicus [who is the English lover of mercury] (1652)
- *Hieroglyphic Seal of the Society of Unknown Philosophers* by Sendivogius (17th century)
- *Speculum Sophicum Rhodostauroticum*, by Theophilus Schweighardt (1617)
- *The Hieroglyphic Monad*, by John Dee (1564)
- *The Alchemist*, by Paulo Coelho (1993)

The Periodic Table

1 H Hydrogen																	2 He Helium
7 3 Li Lithium	9 4 Be Beryllium											11 5 B Boron	12 6 C Carbon	14 7 N Nitrogen	16 8 O Oxygen	19 9 F Fluorine	20 10 Ne Neon
23 11 Na Sodium	24 12 Mg Magnesium											27 13 Al Aluminium	28 14 Si Silicon	31 15 P Phosphorus	32 16 S Sulphur	35.5 17 Cl Chlorine	40 18 Ar Argon
39 19 K Potassium	40 20 Ca Calcium	45 21 Sc Scandium	48 22 Ti Titanium	51 23 V Vanadium	52 24 Cr Chromium	55 25 Mn Manganese	56 26 Fe Iron	59 27 Co Cobalt	59 28 Ni Nickel	64 29 Cu Copper	65 30 Zn Zinc	70 31 Ga Gallium	73 32 Ge Germanium	75 33 As Arsenic	79 34 Se Selenium	80 35 Br Bromine	84 36 Kr Krypton
85 37 Rb Rubidium	88 38 Sr Strontium	89 39 Y Yttrium	91 40 Zr Zirconium	93 41 Nb Niobium	96 42 Mo Molybdenum	101 44 Ru Ruthenium	101 44 Ru Ruthenium	103 45 Rh Rhodium	106 46 Pd Palladium	108 47 Ag Silver	112 48 Cd Cadmium	115 49 In Indium	119 50 Sn Tin	122 51 Sb Antimony	128 52 Te Tellurium	127 53 I Iodine	131 54 Xe Xenon
133 55 Cs Caesium	137 56 Ba Barium	139 57 La † Lanthanum	178 72 Hf Hafnium	181 73 Ta Tantalum	184 74 W Tungsten	186 75 Re Rhenium	190 76 Os Osmium	192 77 Ir Iridium	195 78 Pt Platinum	197 79 Au Gold	201 80 Hg Mercury	204 81 Tl Thallium	207 82 Pb Lead	209 83 Bi Bismuth	84 Po Polonium	85 At Astatine	86 Rn Radon
87 Fr Francium	226 88 Ra Radium	227 89 Ac ‡ Actinium	104 Unq Unnilquadium	105 Unp Unnilpentium	106 Unh Unnilhexium	107 Uns Unnilseptium	108 Uno Unniloctium										

140 58 Ce Cerium	141 59 Pr Praseodymium	144 60 Nd Neodymium	61 Pm Promethium	150 62 Sm Samarium	152 63 Eu Europium	157 64 Gd Gadolinium	159 65 Tb Terbium	162 66 Dy Dysprosium	165 67 Ho Holmium	167 68 Er Erbium	169 69 Tm Thulium	173 70 Yb Ytterbium	175 71 Lu Lutetium
232 90 Th Thorium	91 Pa Protactinium	238 92 U Uranium	93 Np Neptunium	94 Pu Plutonium	95 Am Americium	96 Cm Curium	97 Bk Berkelium	98 Cf Californium	99 Es Einsteinium	100 Fm Fermium	101 Md Mendelevium	102 No Nobelium	103 Lr Lawrencium

A X Z
Element

A : Mass Number
Z : Atomic Number

† 58–71 : Lanthanum Series
‡ 90–103 : Actinium Series

Nitrogen is one of the most abundant elements on earth, chemists tell us. It is present on the Earth in the air, in soil, in the sea and in us. Approximately 78% of the atmosphere is nitrogen gas (N_2); in the rocks, soil and sea it's found as the mineral sodium nitrate and as ammonia and ammonium salts; in organisms it is a constituent of organic compounds, including proteins. It can be combined with oxygen to make nitrous oxide, (N_2O), or 'laughing gas', which was used as an anaesthetic in the 18th century. It could not be used for too long, though – prolonged inhalation is fatal.

For some time before nitrogen was discovered in 1772, it was known that there was a part of the air that did not burn. Daniel Rutherford – who was the first to publish, although his discovery was contemporaneous with that of other scientists, including Joseph Priestley – called it 'fixed air'. Some of nitrogen's compounds have been known for even longer: to the alchemists, nitric acid was *aqua fortis*, 'strong water'. One of its compounds, saltpetre, is a constituent of gunpowder.

METALLIC BONDING

In a metal lattice, valence electrons become dislodged from the metal nuclei to form a 'sea' of delocalised electrons in which the positively-charged nuclei float. This structure gives metals particular properties: they are very good conductors of electric charge and heat, and they are malleable, ie can be bent and beaten into different shapes. If a substance conducts electricity when both solid and liquid (molten) it is definitely a metal.

In other respects, metals can be very different from each other: they can be very unreactive, such as gold and platinum, or very reactive, such as caesium, lithium and sodium. They can be very strong, such as iron, or able to be cut with a knife like butter, for example sodium and the other reactive metals mentioned above, which are stored under oil to prevent them oxidising in the air. Some reactive metals, including magnesium, form a protective oxidised surface which prevents the rest of the metal reacting with the air. There is a branch of chemistry devoted to studying surface reactions like this, which also play a part in the action of catalysts, or substances which help other substances to react with each other.

WORK IT OUT

Find the odd one out:
- silver chloride
- silver bromide
- silver iodide
- sodium hydroxide
- lead chloride

Answer on page 312

THE CHEMICAL COMPOSITION OF PERFUMES

Ester*	Odour
Ethyl ethanoate	Pear drops (used for removing nail varnish)
Ethyl methanoate	Raspberry
Ethyl butanoate	Pineapple
3-methylbutyl ethanoate	Banana
Octyl ethanoate	Orange

*Esters are made from alcohols and acids; found naturally in plants and synthetically in laboratories.

CRAFTY CRAM... ACIDS, BASES AND SALTS

Acids dissolve in water to form hydrogen ions (H+), and have a pH of less than 7. They can be organic, such as citric acid or vitamin C – which has a very complex structure – or inorganic. Hydrogen chloride, sulphuric acid and nitric acid are often called mineral acids because they can be made with minerals. Some acids are highly corrosive and/or poisonous, while others, such as citric acid, are necessary to the human body.

Alkalis are soluble metal oxides, or **bases**. They contain hydroxide ions (OH-) and have a pH of more than 7. When acids and alkalis are combined, the hydrogen ions in the acid react with the hydroxide ions in the alkali to form water. The remaining metal and non-metal ions react to form a **salt** – for example sodium hydroxide and hydrochloric acid react together to form sodium chloride and water.

XII

PHYSICS

*We can't solve problems by using
the same kind of thinking we used
when we created them.*

Albert Einstein

There is much interplay between the difference sciences – chemistry, physics, biology and their sub-disciplines – that it can be difficult to see where one science starts and another one ends. But generally speaking, physics is at the foundation of the other sciences. It studies energy, motion and matter – the fundamental structures of reality. 'In science there is only physics; all the rest is stamp collecting,' said Ernest Rutherford, the father of nuclear physics (interestingly, he was awarded the Nobel Prize for chemistry in 1907).

Physics studies the structures of reality from a scientific point of view, and its special language is mathematics. Other disciplines which deal with this are philosophy and theology, and even they sometimes are referenced by physicists, positively and negatively. The development of quantum mechanics and its principle of indeterminacy (see pages 298 and 302) gives grist to the mill of philosophers and physicists – sometimes the same thing – who see in it an escape clause for free will in the hitherto rigorously mechanistic world of Newtonian physics. The sciences of cosmology and astrophysics send the human mind to the furthest reaches of space and time, to the beginning of the universe and its possible end.

It's not just what knowledge you have, but what you do with it that matters. Nuclear physics, for example, was employed in the 20th century both in creating new forms of fuel and in destroying whole cities, the latter of which Rutherford certainly did not publish his theories for. But what a splendid thing physics is, nonetheless – a glimpse into how the universe works.

ABSOLUTE ZERO

Though in other parts of the universe extremely high temperatures can be reached – in the centre of the sun, for example, it's a toasty 15 million degrees or so centigrade – absolute zero is surprisingly 'warm', at only -273.15 degrees Centigrade (-459.67 degrees Fahrenheit or 0 Kelvin). In relative terms that means that the surface of the Earth is cold, and that the band of temperatures which will support life as we understand it is incredibly narrow. One more reason, if you will, that living things are rather special.

SIZE OF SPACE OBJECTS RELATIVE TO EARTH

Asteroid: pebble sized to 1,000km diameter.

The Moon: diameter approximately one quarter of the Earth's.

The Earth: diameter approximately 12,760km.

Jupiter: diameter more than 10 times that of the Earth.

The Sun: diameter more than 100 times that of the Earth.

Solar System: diameter 10,000,000,000km, or about 11 light hours.

Nearest star (Proxima Centauri): 4.2 light years away.

Milky Way approximately 100,000 light years across.

HOW HEAT HAPPENS

Heat, put simply, is caused by the vibration of atoms. The temperature of an object is the average of how hot it is. Heat is spread by conduction, which is the process of vibrating atoms colliding with other atoms, passing kinetic energy to them and setting them vibrating too. Metals conduct heat very well because of their structure – 'free' electrons within them can conduct heat energy, just as they can conduct electrical charge.

If, then, heat energy is basically atoms jiggling about, absolute zero (-273.15°C to -459.67 °F) is the temperature at which nothing jiggles about... ie all matter comes to a complete rest. Nothing can be colder: indeed, absolute zero is itself a theoretical limit which cannot be reproduced experimentally.

It was Lord Kelvin's work on temperature which led to the proposing of absolute zero. Appropriately enough its temperature is 0 on the Kelvin scale – not, however, on the centigrade or Fahrenheit scales, which in different ways both take the freezing and boiling points of water as their more worldly points of reference. Centigrade divides the difference in temperature between the freezing and boiling points of water at sea level into 100 degrees ie 0°C to 100°C. Fahrenheit takes as its starting point the coldest temperature that its inventor, Gabriel Fahrenheit, could produce with ice and salt (sodium chloride) in 1724. There are 180 degrees between the freezing point of water, 32°F, and its boiling point, 212°F.

RADIOACTIVE RAYS

Radiation sounds like a scary thing, and it can be, but it is also something we are exposed to at low levels all the time, naturally. This is called background radiation, and comes from cosmic rays, rocks such as granite, radioactive nuclei in organisms, hospital X-ray machines and other industrial and medical equipment, and occasionally leaks from waste or power stations. The worst leak recorded was at Chernobyl, in Russia, in 1986.

Radioactive nuclei are not stable in the way that the nuclei of ordinary atoms are, and when they decay they emit rays: alpha, beta and gamma rays. The harmful aspect of radiation is to do with its ionising effects. Alpha rays are strongly ionising but stop after a few centimetres and cannot even travel through paper. Beta rays can be stopped by a thin sheet of metal. But gamma rays, though weakly ionising, can travel through many substances and are reduced only by thick lead or very thick concrete.

THE BEHAVIOUR OF LIGHT

Optics is a branch of physics which studies the behaviour of light, the band of electromagnetic frequencies which are visible to the eye (plus ultraviolet and infrared, which are just out of range). Light has different colours because of the different photon energies it possesses – blue light photons have more energy than red, for example. White light is not in fact white, but a mix of all the colours of light. When white light is passed through a prism, it splits up into all its different colours. This is called refraction. Rainbows we see in the sky on a day that's both sunny and rainy are produced by a similar process, tiny droplets of water in the sky acting as prisms. And indeed, the colours of the rainbow show the different frequencies of light.

Water also affects light, bending and reflecting it, which is why underwater things look strange when viewed at an angle above the water surface. This is caused by refraction as well. The reflection produced by mirrors, another related process, has been known about for thousands of years and the making of mirrors is one of the oldest technologies. More recently the study of light has been responsible for the development of the manual camera, medical understanding of how the eye works, the development of lasers, new insights into astronomy and many other things.

10⁻⁴³ seconds: The Planck era – the universe is hot, dense, and all forces are unified.

10⁻³⁵ seconds: Grand Unification era – the 'superforce' starts to divide. Universe expands from smaller than a single particle to bigger than its current volume.

10⁻³² seconds: Matter begins to appear – matter and antimatter annihilate each other, but some matter is left scattered in pockets.

10⁻¹¹ seconds: Electroweak era – the fundamental forces finally become ones we could recognise when a unified force splits into electromagnetism and the strong and weak nuclear forces. With gravity, these constitute the four forces observed in the present universe.

10⁻⁶ seconds: Protons and neutrons form from quarks.

200 seconds: Protons and neutrons start to make atomic nuclei; hydrogen and helium form before the universe cools down too much. Other elements will have to wait millions of years to form.

300,000 years: Recombination era: electrons begin to bind themselves to the nuclei to form a universe that consists of about three parts hydrogen and one part helium. The universe becomes visible.

200 million years: Hydrogen gas clouds collapse into themselves, triggering nuclear fusion and making stars.

0.5 billion to 1 billion years: Stars are pulled by gravity into galaxy formations, which then cluster. One of these groups contains our Milky Way galaxy.

9.1 billion years: In the Milky Way galaxy, gas and dust thrown into space by exploding stars begins to collapse, forming another star with rocks and gas around it. The material in this disc eventually merges to form our solar system. *Source: www.guardian.co.uk/ science/2008/apr/26/universe. physics*

QUOTE UNQUOTE

The microwave oven is the consolation prize in our struggle to understand physics.

Jason Love, US satirist

If you fired a gun straight ahead and there was no obstacle in the way of the bullet, what would happen? Well, if you were on Earth, it would move in a very long curve downwards until it hit the ground (you'd have to be somewhere pretty barren to try it though). This is because of air friction and gravity, using its inevitable powers of attraction to stop a speeding bullet, and probably Superman too, if he tried it. But if you fired the gun in the frictionless vacuum of space, it would be a totally different story. Unless it ran directly into the path of an object or passed close enough to a planet (or a black hole) to be sucked into its gravity field, it would carry on moving... and moving... and moving... at the same speed, forever. This strange fact is described by Newton's first law of motion, the law of inertia. Inertia is not just the thing which made you put off doing your physics homework: it's one of the fundamental principles of the universe. Newton put it thus: 'Every object persists in its state of rest or uniform motion in a right [ie straight] line unless it is compelled to change that state by forces impressed upon it'.

Even more strangely, this law also entails that an object moving in space with uniform motion – ie not accelerating – need not be put into motion by something else. Uniform motion does not need a cause... which faintly echoes the ideas of another great, and much older, thinker whom Newton was certainly familiar with. Long before the birth of Christ, Aristotle spoke of the unmoved mover, the cause of all which has no cause itself... God, perhaps.

'I am now convinced that theoretical physics is actually philosophy,' said the physicist Max Born. He was talking after the development of quantum physics, but the musings started much earlier than that; in fact, it was only relatively recently that the term 'natural philosophy' became no longer synonymous with 'physics'. It's not surprising, therefore, that the study of the physical structures of existence might lead one to think about the meaning of existence too. And that might be why so many physicists have been, shall we say, eccentric.

Speaking of his life's endeavours, Newton said (rather humbly, considering): 'I know not what I appear to the world, but to myself I seem to have been only like a boy playing on the sea shore, and diverting myself in now and then finding a smoother pebble or a prettier shell, whilst the great ocean of truth lay all undiscovered before me'.

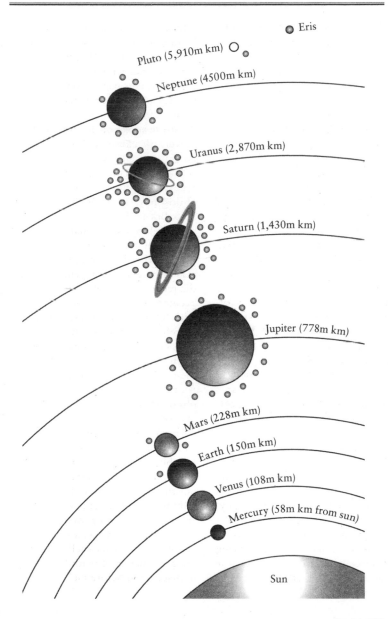

Eris

Pluto (5,910m km)

Neptune (4500m km)

Uranus (2,870m km)

Saturn (1,430m km)

Jupiter (778m km)

Mars (228m km)

Earth (150m km)

Venus (108m km)

Mercury (58m km from sun)

Sun

SPEED OF LIGHT AND SOUND

The fastest it is possible for anything to travel is 299,792,458 metres per second, approximately 670,616,629.4 miles per hour. This is the speed of light, and indeed all other electromagnetic waves. It is Einstein's 'universal constant' (see page 306). The only matter that can get anywhere near that on Earth is particles in supercolliders (see page 308) and supercolliders are very, very, very expensive to make. Sound, which is a wave disturbance of the air, travels much more slowly at approximately 340 metres per second or 760 miles per hour through standard atmosphere. Some specialist vehicles, including planes, can travel faster than the speed of sound. The huge sonic 'boom' which used to accompany Concorde was due to air waves accumulating in front of the plane like water waves at the bow of a ship.

THE CHARACTER OF GENIUS:
STEPHEN HAWKING

Born in 1942, Professor Stephen Hawking is Lucasian Professor of Mathematics at Cambridge University, a position once held by Sir Isaac Newton. He is best known for his work on black holes and the Big Bang, and the best-selling book *A Brief History of Time*, which reached an unusually wide audience.

The widespread success of *A Brief History of Time* – it has sold millions of copies – puts it in the 'pop science' category for some physicists (though it's hardly a Jackie Collins). But Hawking has resolutely beavered away at popularising the most esoteric science, explaining what would happen if you fell into a black hole and what the start of the universe would have been like (extremely strange), and lending it all a strange fascination, even to those who would struggle to remember how to do a quadratic equation.

In the 1960s, while still a student at Cambridge, Hawking learned that he had developed amyotrophic lateral sclerosis, a degenerative disease which gradually took away his motor functions. But it did not affect his mind, and he continues to work, though today almost completely paralysed. It was in fact well after the disease began to manifest itself that Hawking published the theories and books which he has become famous for. 'It matters if you just don't give up,' he once said.

ENERGY AND MOTION: WORK

Work, like weight, mass and momentum, has a specialised meaning in physics: it is what occurs when a force puts something into motion. Work results from transfer of energy, and like energy it is measured in joules. When a body performs work it loses energy and when work is done on it, it gains energy. The work done by a force (in joules) is equal to the force itself (in newtons) multiplied by the distance moved by the force in the direction of the force (in metres). This is relatively simple for forces in straight lines but becomes a lot more complicated with circular or curved motion... but that's another story.

QUOTE UNQUOTE

God does not play dice.
Albert Einstein

Not only does God play dice, but...
he sometimes throws them where they
cannot be seen.
Stephen Hawking

THE VAN DE GRAAF GENERATOR

Remember the glass globe with the lightning in it? The way the lightning would move towards your hand if you put it on the surface? That was the Van de Graaf Generator that was used to demonstrate the effects of static electricity to schoolchildren all over the UK. It would also make your hair stand on end slightly. It wasn't just the spectacle that was memorable though. It was something about how simple it was to create electricity that suggested to us the world might be fizzing with energies and laws which we didn't yet know the first thing about... but soon would, at least before the exams, hopefully.

WORK IT OUT

A professor was in the frozen north studying climate change. He radioed in his research to the nearest base, and reported the temperature as -40°. 'Celsius, or Fahrenheit?' asked his contact. 'I couldn't care less!' replied the professor. Why would he be so casual about this crucial piece of data?

Answer on page 312

COULD DO BETTER

Physics: Coren's grasp of elementary dynamics is truly astonishing. Had he lived in an earlier eon, I have little doubt but that the wheel would now be square and the lever just one more of man's impossibilities.

School report of Alan Coren (1938-2007), journalist and broadcaster; East Barnet Grammar School.
Extracted from *Could do Better*, edited by Catherine Hurley

MASS, WEIGHT AND GRAVITY

It is hard to explain exactly what mass is – easier to illustrate it by explaining what weight is. Weight is the force created by gravity, and gravity is what attracts two bodies of mass to each other. All bodies which have mass (are 'massive' in the physics sense) are attracted to each other. Gravity increases with mass and decreases with distance. But the force is only observable when at least one of the bodies is very big, such as the Earth. The other can be small, such as the apple which apocryphally dropped on Sir Isaac Newton's head, leading him to his theory of gravity. The acceleration of objects in free fall towards the Earth is a constant 9.8m/s^2. It is only air friction that makes a difference to this, which is why a feather and a ball bearing will fall at the same speed in a vacuum. Weight in physics is measured in newtons, after the great man himself, and the strength of the Earth's gravitational field is assumed to be 10N/kg.

PICKING UP MOMENTUM

Momentum is mass multiplied by velocity, and is the reason that a bullet fired from a gun can do more harm to you than a rock thrown by hand. The latter is heavier, but it has a lot less momentum. Momentum, like velocity, is a vector, ie it has direction. Resultant force (in newtons, the same as weight, which is also a force) is mass multiplied by acceleration, but force is also change in momentum divided by the time taken for the change. When this is translated into numbers, it means that a large stopping force, such as that generated by a fast collision, causes a lot of damage. The bodies will share the damage in proportion to how soft or hard they are relative to each other. So an arrow shot into an apple, or a bullet into a body, causes much more harm to the apple or the body (in fact the bullet has so much force that it is often not fully stopped, just slowed down). The principles associated with force and momentum are used to design car parts that minimise the impact of a collision, such as airbags. Crash helmets work in the same way as an airbag.

IT'S A WOMAN'S WORLD, TOO

Henrietta Leavitt – American astronomer who discovered Cepheid variable stars, used to measure distances between galaxies. Her middle name was Swan.

Marie Curie – Polish scientist, mainly known as a chemist but won Nobel Prize for Physics in 1903 with husband Pierre Curie (and then a second one in 1911 for Chemistry). Her daughter Irene also won a Nobel Prize.

Winifred Goldring – American paleontologist and geologist, first woman president of the American Paleontological Society.

France Anne Cordova – American astrophysicist. Before going back to university to study physics she was a writer, working for *Mademoiselle* magazine.

Maria Goeppert Mayer – German-American nuclear physicist and mathematician.

Mary Somerville – 19th-century Scottish science writer; Somerville College, Oxford is named after her.

Chien-Shieng Wu – Shanghai-born physicist who disproved the law of conservation of parity (she died in 1997 at the age of 84).

WHEN IS A PARTICLE NOT A PARTICLE?

The next development in science, the new field of quantum mechanics, was gaining ground in Einstein's lifetime and he contributed to it. Though his revolutionary thinking about how the universe behaves on a grand scale undoubtedly gave confidence to the young innovators peering into the workings of the tiniest structures and events, Einstein himself was not comfortable with some aspects of quantum mechanics. His most famous quote: 'God does not play dice', is about it. 'I like to think there is a moon even if I am not looking at it,' he also said... a little enigmatically, but then quantum mechanics is pretty enigmatic too.

Einstein said these things because of the element of probability which is bound into the theory, and its emphasis on observation.

The quantum world, the world at a sub-atomic level, operates in a very different way to the world we see. For one thing, the conscious observer is an integral part of quantum physics because measurement of a system influences what happens in it. For another, electromagnetic radiation and matter both display properties of particles *and* waves. And finally, it is not possible to determine both the speed and exact position of a particle, only one and a probability of the other.

THEORIES THAT EXPLAIN THE END OF THE UNIVERSE

- Steady State theory – the universe has existed always and will always exist (now generally discounted).

- The expanding universe, which started with a Big Bang, will carry on expanding forever.

- The expanding universe will stop expanding and gravity will start to pull matter back towards itself again, until it contracts into a point of infinite mass.

- Same as above, but this will cause another Big Bang... and again... and again... oscillating for infinity.

- The universe will stop expanding but gravity will not be strong enough to pull it back into itself, so it will stay as it is.

WIRES IN A UK ELECTRIC CABLE/PLUG

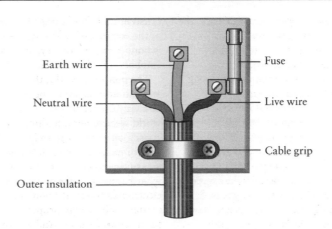

Name	Colour (plastic insulating coating)	Function
Live	Brown	Carries voltage
Neutral	Blue	Completes the circuit
Earth	Green and yellow	Safety wire: 'earths' the appliance to stop a charge passing through it

HOW TO REMEMBER... FLEMING'S RULE

For identifying direction of magnetic field, electrical current, and motion:

Think of Ian Fleming's James Bond, pretending
to shoot with your left hand –
Hold left hand – with thumb, first and second
fingers mutually at right angles
Centre, current
First for field
Then the thumb will motion yield

THE SPEED OF LIGHT AND SPACE TRAVEL

Light is very fast, but it still does have a speed, ie it takes some time to travel over a distance. The fact that light is a universal constant leads to several counter-intuitive phenomena associated with motion. And because it is the upper limit to speed, any signal we would receive from a distant part of the universe would take millions of years to get here. If you had a powerful enough telescope to see planets in another galaxy, what you'd see taking place would have happened millions of years ago. And if aliens living just under 2,000 light years away were to look at the Earth with a telescope now, they would see Mount Vesuvius erupting and covering Pompeii in AD79.

So immutable is the universal constant that if we ever wanted to travel far outside the solar system, we would have to find another way to do it... perhaps using gravity to somehow fold space over like a piece of paper so we could move a much shorter distance between two points. For now, that is very much in the realm of science fiction, but you never know. Sci-fi today often becomes reality tomorrow... or in this case probably the day after.

THE EARTH, THE SOLAR SYSTEM AND THE UNIVERSE

Physics deals not only with things on the tiniest level, but also the biggest. The movement of the planets around the sun, the shape of galaxies, and the birth and death of stars all happen according to known physical laws. There are reaches of space and time, notably the beginning of the universe, where physical laws break down and it begins to get strange. But much of existence on the macro-level (the scale we experience things on, ie not sub-atomic) can be described in terms of a few simple – and beautiful – physical laws. For example the same law which keeps our feet on the ground – gravity – keeps the planets in orbit. Unfortunately, it is also responsible for the orbit near the Earth of large comets and asteroids which could theoretically collide with Earth. Such a collision, though unlikely, could be catastrophic for life. It is proposed as a reason for the extinction of dinosaurs. The orbit of large near Earth objects is monitored carefully, however, and scientists are working on ways to destroy one if it did make its way towards earth.

The whole history of physics proves that a new discovery is quite likely lurking at the next decimal place.

FK Richtmeyer, US scientist and professor

PHYSICS IN THE ARTS

Copenhagen: play by Michael Frayn, based on a real meeting between Neils Bohr and Werner Heisenberg in World War II.

Dirk Gently's Holistic Detective Agency: book by Douglas Adams. Post-*Hitchiker's Guide to the Galaxy* the great polymathic humourist wrote this novel, weaving quantum theory and Samuel Taylor Coleridge into one mindbogglingly seamless plotline.

Doctor Who: BBC1 TV programme (of course). Particular scientific references come in the episode 'School Reunion', where the Doctor poses as a physics teacher and we find out what the formula for time travel is… though that doesn't get rid of the massive paradoxes attached to it conceptually, which is why in another episode, 'Blink', all the Doctor can say about time is that it's 'a big ball of wibbly-wobbly, timey-wimey stuff'.

The Time Traveler's Wife: book by Audrey Niffenegger and a 2008 film starring Rachel McAdams and Eric Bana. Similarly unable to avoid the conceptual snags associated with the central plot device.

Hawking: BBC TV film starring Benedict Cumberbatch about the life of physicist Stephen Hawking (first shown 2004).

Event Horizon: 1997 horror film starring Sam Neill and Joely Richardson. The plot centres around a spaceship that disappears into a black hole and comes back. A group of scientists board the ship to find out what happened… which, as it turns out, is somewhat of a bad choice.

The Planets: seven-movement classical orchestral suite by Gustav Holst. You'll know it if you hear it.

While relativity looks at the grand scale of the universe, quantum physics deals with the behaviour of very small things. As any primary school teacher can attest, when things are very small they can behave unreasonably. In the case of quantum mechanics, this means strange, even startling, phenomena. 'Anyone not shocked by quantum mechanics has not yet understood it,' said Niels Bohr, one of the fathers of the discipline. The world is much, much stranger than we think. One of the ways in which this strangeness manifests itself can be illustrated by a thought experiment invented by Erwin Schrödinger in 1935.

Schrödinger's cat – whom Schrödinger is reputed to have 'wished he'd never met' later in his life, such are the theoretical complications of the experiment – is put in a secure steel box with a vial of hydrocyanic acid. There is also a tiny amount of a radioactive isotope. If just one atom of this radioactive substance decays, it will trigger a mechanism breaking the vial and killing the cat. But... and this is the weird quantum mechanics bit: because of the way the theory works, the cat is neither dead nor alive until the box is opened and the observer discovers what has happened to the cat. This is 'quantum indeterminacy' or the 'observer's paradox' and relates to the way that measurement affects the outcome of an experiment. Quantum mechanics deals with a world, which behaves, in theory, very differently to the scale on which we inhabit the universe. The way in which it plays into the fate of the cat has tricky implications for quantum theory... and indeed for the existence of objective reality.

SPEED AND VELOCITY

Remember those little trolley things that you had to roll down a slope, seemingly endlessly? That was to learn about the forces of motion, and kinetic and potential energy. Speed is basically a measure of how long it takes something to travel over a certain distance. Velocity is a vector, ie it has direction, so it is the measure of the rate of displacement in a given direction rather than distance. The direction is relative to what you are measuring it for, since there is no absolute direction towards something in the universe.

THE CHARACTER OF GENIUS: RICHARD FEYNMAN

Physicists are often thought of by the rest of the world as... well, perhaps not the most well-rounded of individuals. An obsession with experimental particle physics just might be viewed by those who do not share it as a bit geeky. To be sure, it is hardly geeky to have the sort of mind which can understand the splendours of the structure of the universe, but the beards and sandals don't help.

And yet, lots of physicists have been extremely interesting characters, on a personal as well as a professional level. Few people have been more well rounded than Richard Feynman, who was a bongo-playing, Mayan-hieroglyph-translating, living breathing contradiction of the geeky stereotype. He was also a top-league scientist, winning the Nobel Prize in 1965 for his work on quantum electrodynamics. He was described once as 'half genius, half buffoon'. Later, the describer – fellow physicist Freeman Dyson – revised this to 'all genius, all buffoon'.

ELECTRIC CHARGE AND CURRENT

There is an anecdote about a pupil who has failed to do his physics homework on electricity. 'But do you understand what electricity is?' asks the teacher. 'Yes I do,' says the pupil enthusiastically. 'Interesting,' says the teacher. 'That makes two of you – you and God.'

But it is not too tall an order to explain the basics of electricity. The electrons which form one constituent part of atoms carry a negative charge. In certain circumstances, the negative charge carried by electrons can flow towards a positively charged terminal in a circuit. Hence the theories of electricity and magnetism are unified into electromagnetism – metal and magnets attract each other on a related principle and electricity can be induced in a magnetic field.

Different aspects of electricity are measured by different units: charge is measured in coulombs, current in amperes, voltage in volts, power in watts. To understand what each of these are, it's easiest to look at the equations:

power = current x voltage ($P = IV$)
charge = current x time in seconds ($Q = It$)

...and so on.

WHAT'S SO SUPER ABOUT CONDUCTIVITY?

Some substances, at very low temperatures, have no resistance to electricity – they are superconductors. The study of superconductors, which can be metallic or ceramic (in the chemical sense – an inorganic non-metallic compound) constitutes a particular field of scientific study.

In simple conductors, 'free' electrons are able to pass an electric charge through the material, constituting an electric current. Because ordinary conductors have structures and impurities in them which create resistance, some of this electrical current is scattered. But in superconductors, an ordering of the electrons called Cooper pairing means that electrons are not scattered – so there is no resistance. This quality is enormously useful on a practical level.

Though the two disciplines overlap a lot, chemists are generally speaking more interested in finding materials that *are* superconductors – particularly at 'high' temperatures well above absolute zero – while physicists are more interested in finding out how superconductors work at the sub-atomic level.

It took a long time for physicists to work out the principle of superconductors because the energy related to the ordering is so tiny. The publishing of the BCS theory in 1957 forms the basis of how the superconductivity phenomenon is understood. It is named after the three physicists who came up with it – John Bardeen, Leon N Cooper and John Robert Schrieffer, who together won a Nobel Prize in 1972.

A MASS OF GAS

Gases, liquids and solids all have mass and volume. But the atoms in gas are moving with more energy than those in a solid, which means less mass to volume. It also means that a gas will expand to fit the space available, as the excitable gas molecules wander away from each other in search of somewhere more interesting to be. If a gas is compressed, however, more collisions between the gas molecules occur. The collisions which happen against the inside walls of the container result in the pressure of the gas. Reducing the volume of a gas increases the pressure, and vice versa. Heating a gas also increases the pressure, as it imparts energy to the gas molecules, again making them collide more with each other.

TYPES OF ELECTROMAGNETIC RADIATION

Electromagnetic radiation exists as both waves and particles, all travelling at 'the speed of light'. The property of the wave depends on its frequency: at the lower end are radio waves and infra-red, at the higher end gamma and X-rays. Visible light is in the middle of the spectrum, but different colours of light have different frequencies. Photons, or the particles which carry electromagnetic radiation, have different energies which correspond to the frequency of the radiation.

(lowest to highest photon energy)

RADIO WAVES	MICRO-WAVES	INFRA-RED	VISIBLE LIGHT	ULTRA-VIOLET	X-RAYS	GAMMA RAYS

Red   Orange   Yellow   Green   Blue   Indigo   Violet
(continuous spectrum)

SPLITTING AN ATOM

In the early 20th century, physicists discovered that atoms are a bit like the solar system – an atom has a nucleus, which is positively charged, with other negatively charged particles in orbit around it. The nucleus, made up of protons and neutrons, is much more massive than the orbiting particles – protons are 1840 times bigger than electrons. But it is also much, much smaller than the orbit... which means that atoms, and thus every bit of matter in existence, is mostly space. Protons have a positive charge, while neutrons are neutral; the number of protons in the nucleus determines its atomic number, 'Z' (and also its place in the Periodic Table – see page 283).

The number of protons and neutrons in the nucleus constitutes the mass number, or nucleon number, 'A'. Atoms of the same element have the same number of protons, but they can have different numbers of neutrons – this makes them isotopes. Some isotopes are relatively stable, but some are highly unstable and will decay quickly, emitting different sorts of rays and particles as they do so. These are radioactive isotopes.

It's difficult to conceptualise genius when you're at school... it's only as you get older and realise how confusing the world is that it becomes impressive that anyone can make sense of it. We all know that $E=mc^2$ is an important equation, but it takes a genius to work out this equation in the first place. Luckily, that's what Albert Einstein was.

Einstein's gift to the world was twofold. First, there was his theory of special relativity, in 1905; followed by that of general relativity, in 1916. Relativity takes as its starting point the speed of electromagnetic radiation, such as light. Nothing can travel faster than this. Special relativity describes objects moving at a constant speed in a straight line, while general relativity is the theory expanded to non-uniform motion. It is from the latter that Einstein's theory of gravitation ensues.

$E=mc^2$ describes how matter converts to energy. E represents energy, m is mass, and c is the universal constant, the speed of light. If the speed of light is taken as invariable, it leads to some very counter-intuitive properties in the universe. According to the theory of relativity, time moves more slowly for a moving object, though the speeds have to be enormous for the effect to be noticeable. The 'twin paradox' shows the strange repercussions of this theory: one of two identical sisters leaves earth on a spaceship travelling at near-light speed. Because to the Earth-bound sister time moves more slowly for the sister travelling in space than for her, the space sister will be younger than her when she returns. But since to the sister in space it is time on earth that is moving more slowly (another property of the theory to do with relative observation), to her the sister on Earth is ageing more slowly.

In fact, the paradox is resolved by applying the full theory of general relativity, because the spaceship does not move in a uniform straight line – it must turn round to come back to Earth.

What made it possible for Einstein to see the universe in the depth he did, is as great a mystery as the strange truths he saw. Before his theories were published he was an unremarkable patent clerk in Berne; after they were published he was unveiled as one of the greatest minds the world has ever seen. When he was asked how he had come up with theories which unlocked some of the secrets of creation, he is said to have replied simply, that he sat down and thought about it.

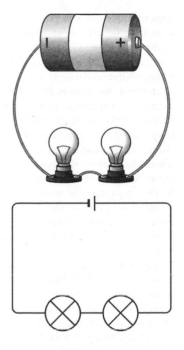

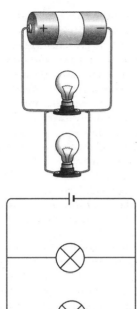

Series circuit

The current goes in one loop only: *battery – light(s) – battery*. If one light is faulty all the others go out too – like old-fashioned Christmas tree lights.

Parallel circuit

The current splits into more than one direction. This means if one light is faulty, the others still stay on.

QUOTE UNQUOTE

Magnetism, as you recall from physics class, is a powerful force that causes certain items to be attracted to refrigerators.

Dave Barry, US satirist

HOW DID WAVES GET SO COMPLICATED?

Waves transmit energy, and sometimes information (if we are there to interpret it), through space or through a medium. Sound waves as we are used to hearing them need air as a medium, which is why space is silent and things sound strange under water. Radio transmitters send radio waves up to satellites, which then reflect it back to Earth where the signals are converted back into to TV programmes, radio transmissions and other forms of communication. Seismic waves cause earthquakes. Light waves can travel in space right across the universe. In fact, nothing travels faster.

Waves can be transverse, or longitudinal, and have different frequencies and wavelengths. They proceed from and stop at a point in space but between these points they vibrate in a region of space, not fixed points. They do not transmit matter, but in strange ways, particles of matter may also be seen as waves and vice versa... this is one of the principles of quantum mechanics.

BLACK HOLES IN SWITZERLAND

...are almost certainly not going to appear. The Large Hadron Collider, unveiled at Cern in Switzerland in June 2008, is designed to find new elementary particles including, just maybe, the Higgs boson, which could lead researchers towards the elusive grand unified theory of gravity and electromagnetism. At its inauguration, physicists told journalists the literal truth – that there was a 'very small chance' that the Collider, instead of finding the Higgs boson, could create tiny black holes. Such a black hole, however tiny, would swallow up not only Switzerland but the entire solar system.

Switzerland wouldn't be so bad, said some (naughty) journalists, but everyone agreed that the whole solar system disappearing into a black hole was something to worry about. Until, that is, you learn that what the physicists mean by 'a very small chance' is one in a number with so many noughts after it that it puts it outside the life span of the universe. A clear lesson, if ever there was one, on the different ways reality is measured in physics and journalism.

USEFUL FORMULAS YOU PROBABLY FORGOT

- Weight = mass x gravitational field strength

- Speed (metres per second, m/s) = $\dfrac{\text{distance (metres)}}{\text{time (seconds)}}$

- Velocity (metres per second, m/s) = $\dfrac{\text{displacement}}{\text{time}}$ *or* $v = \dfrac{s}{t}$

- Momentum (kg m/s or newtons) = mass (kg) x velocity (m/s)

- Force = mass x acceleration *or* F = ma

- Acceleration (m/s²) = $\dfrac{\text{change in velocity (metres)}}{\text{time taken (seconds)}}$ *or* $a = \dfrac{(v - u)}{t}$

  (where a is the acceleration of an object which changes velocity from u to v)

- $E = mc^2$ *(where E is energy, m is mass and c is the universal constant)*

- Electrical energy = voltage x current x time *or* E = V x I x t

- Power = $\dfrac{\text{work done}}{\text{time taken}}$ *or* $P = \dfrac{W}{t}$

ENERGY AND MOTION:
KINETIC AND POTENTIAL ENERGY

This is where trolleys come in. When they are at the top of a slope, they have potential energy stored up; as they roll down the slope they gain kinetic energy, or the energy of moving objects. When they roll off the end of the slope on to your foot because you are talking to someone rather than paying attention to the experiment, the kinetic energy converts into sound, heat and resultant force.

The amount of kinetic energy relates to the mass of the object and the square of the speed. The relations between momentum, work, kinetic and potential energy, speed and velocity, and the rate of transfer of energy, or power, are most easily seen by looking at the mathematical equations, the language of physics (see above).

PUZZLE ANSWERS

I. History

p16 Theodore (Teddy) Roosevelt, the 26th president of the United States, is the person responsible for giving the teddy bear its name

p23 Emmeline Pankhurst

p28 Thomas Newcomen

p33 David Lloyd George, as he is the only non-Conservative prime minister

II. Geography

p40 A River

p49 Cirrostratus, because it is a high level cloud; the rest are low level

p53 Mount Everest

III. English Literature

p63 Thomas Hardy, Emily Bronte, TS Eliot and Edgar Allen Poe

p69
1. 'Snake', DH Lawrence
2. 'Ducle et Decorum Est', Wilfred Owen
3. 'Do Not Go Gentle into That Good Night', Dylan Thomas
4. 'Composed Upon Westminster Bridge', William Wordsworth
5. Sonnet 42: 'How Do I Love Thee? Let Me Count the Ways', Elizabeth Barrett Browning
6. 'Ozymandias of Egypt', Percy Bysshe Shelley
7. 'Macavity: The Mystery Cat', TS Eliot
8. 'A Red, Red, Rose', Robert Burns
9. 'Cargoes', John Masefield
10. 'Ode to Autumn', John Keats
11. 'Elegy Written in a Country Churchyard', Thomas Gray
12. 'The Tyger', William Blake
13. 'Leisure', WH Daview

p72 Oliver Mellors

p79 WB Yeats

IV. English Language

p89 Incorrectly

p94 U after 'g' makes the 'g' hard – to make the sound like 'got'

p104 Engage, Weaker, Occult

V. French

p117 Rumours; A little glass of alcohol in between courses of meals

p121 The Dutch; A kind of cheesy yoghurt

p126 Two boiled eggs and three sausages; Snails and frogs legs

VI. Classics

p139 Theseus

p146 Fenestra, which means window. The rest are body parts

p153 Hyperion

VII. Religious Education

p164 The other name for the 10 Commandments given to Moses is Decalogue

p169 Ruth and Esther

p175 The Magi was the collective name of the Three Wise Men or Three Kings who came from the East and followed the star to Baby Jesus in Jerusalem

p179 The seven pillars of wisdom come from the Book of Proverbs in the Old Testament from The Bible. They are: *Trust, Integrity, Generosity, Diligence, Words, Friendship, Personal Purity*

VIII. Music

p185 Standing on the Shoulder of Giants

p191 Genesis; Dexy's Midnight Runners; Red Hot Chilli Peppers; Britney Spears

p201 Subdominant

IX. Mathematics

p211 Fill in the Venn diagram, starting with the centre, shared part of the diagram – ie who sings both, the unknown figure, so we call it x. The number outside that shared area of intersection has to compensate accordingly – so on the *Tainted Love* (T) side we have 17- x and on the *Come on Eileen* (C) side we have 19 - x

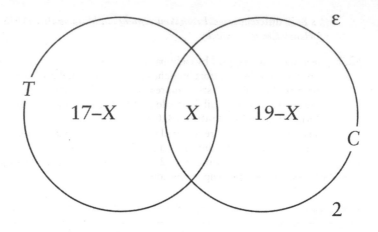

Not forgetting the two outside our pies who can't sing at all, we can then see the following equation:

$(17 - x) + x + (19 - x) + 2 = 30$ (being the total at the disco).

Cancelling out the two balancing plus x and minus x, and adding our numbers, we get:

$38 - x = 30$

$38 - 30 = x$

$x = 8$

So 8 tuneful disco bunnies can sing along to both *Tainted Love* and *Come on Eileen*, leaving 22 people wishing that they would just shut up and dance...

p216 The monthly numbers follow what is known as a *Fibonacci sequence*: 1, 1, 2, 3, 5, 8, 13, 21, 34, 55, 89, 144.

Fibonacci (c.1170 – c.1250) introduced this sequence into Western Europe from Indian maths. It describes a recurrence relation: after two starting values, each new number is a sum of the two preceding it.

p222 Starting from any one of the N's, there are 17 different readings of NAH, or 68 (4 x 17) for the four N's. Therefore there are also 68 ways of spelling HAN. If we were allowed to use the same N twice in a spelling, the answer would be 68 x 68, or 4,624 ways. But the conditions were, 'always passing from one letter to another.' Therefore, for every one of the 17 ways of spelling HAN with a particular N, there would be 51 ways (3 x 17) of completing the NAH, or 867 (17 x 51) ways for the complete word. Hence, as there are four Ns to use in HAN, the correct solution of the puzzle is 3,468

(4 x 867) different ways. *From Amusements in Mathematics (1958), by Henry Ernest Dudeney*

p228 The total effort required by eight painters for 48 days = 8 x 48 = 384 man-days. The initial effort by eight painters for eight days = 8 x 8 = 64 man-days. The job still requires 384 - 64 = 320 man-days, and there are 40 painters available to do it. Additional effort required by 40 painters for 320 man-days = 320 / 40 = 8 days.
Thus, eight more days are required to complete the painting job.
In other words: Eight painters require 48 - 8 = 40 more days to complete the job. Therefore, 8 + 32 = 40 painters will require 40 x 8 / 40 = 8 more days to complete the job

X. Biology

p235 Your mother
p242 A blood test. The true son was known to be a haemophiliac – he refused as he feared he wouldn't stop bleeding
p251 They are two out of three triplets

XI. Chemistry

p263 Palladium; Mercury; Caesium; Einsteinium
p275 Osmium because it is a transition metal and the rest are alkali metals
p279 Atomic theory; Periodic table; Copper carbonate
p285 Sodium hydroxide because it is soluble and the rest are insoluble salts

XII. Physics

p296 At -40° (and only at -40°), the temperature of Celsius and Fahrenheit are exactly the same

BIBLIOGRAPHY

Dream of Rome – Boris Johnson
Mother Tongue – Bill Bryson
Oxford English Dictionary
Why not Catch-21 – Gary Dexter
Shorter Latin Primer – Kennedy
Points to Watch in O Level Latin
Allman Revision Notes – O Level Latin – William G Boyd
Collins Study and Revision Guide Mathematics
Letts Study Aids: Revise Mathematics – Duncan Graham
Letts GCSE Bitesize Revision – Geography
Handy Geography Answer Book – Matthew Rosenberg
O Level Latin Comprehension Practice – Alec Gresty
Letts Passbook Religious Studies – D Stent
Letts English Language Complete Revision – Denys Thompson, Frances
Glendinning – Stephen Tunnicliffe
Letts History Revise 1750-1980 – Peter Lane
Letts French O Level – Gloria Richards
Cambridge English Language Study
Macmillan Master – English Language
Complete Idiot's Guide to Shakespeare – Laurie Rozakis
Letts Keyfacts Geography – R Knowles
Latin for All Occasions – Henry Beard
That Book – Mitchell Symons
This Book – Mitchell Symons
The Book of General Ignorance – Stephen Fry
General Mathematics – Dean Rayner
Transport Machines – Derek Radford
Introduction to Mathematics – Larry Joel Goldstein
Mythology for Dummies – Dr I Blackwell
Introduction To Calculus – Omar Hijab
1966 And All That – Craig Brown

CREDITS

Illustrations courtesy of Diacritech Publishing Services, India
and Clipart.com

ACKNOWLEDGEMENTS

We gratefully acknowledge permission to reproduce extracts of copyright
material in this book from the following authors and, publishers:

Could do Better – Edited by Catherine Hurley © Simon & Schuster UK Ltd

Could do Even Better – Edited by Catherine Hurley
© Simon & Schuster UK Ltd